C0-AWI-935

MEMORANDUM

TO: All Department Heads & Section-Chiefs

FR: Central Administration Executive Board, Offenbach University

RE: The <u>**Major**</u> <u>**Flaws**</u> in **This Year's PERSONNEL EVALUATIONS:**
(The Regrettable Causes; The Ascertained Remedies)

If you become as alarmed as we did when we first perused this year's batch of PERSONNEL EVALUATIONS (attached)—be reassured. *We have recognized* that <u>a major problem exists</u>. We have *discovered its cause.* And we are already *correcting it.*

The **problem**, of course, is that these "EVALUATIONS" present a ***grossly-inaccurate* picture** of the University. Of our *individuals* (faculty, staff, administration). Of our *institution* itself. And because inaccurate, therefore **both unfair and dangerous** as well...

Specifically, these "EVALUATIONS" **seriously misrepresent** far too many of our school's <u>individuals</u>, as presumably both **professionally-incompetent**, and **personally-immature** (some even as fools). Also, these "EVALUATIONS" **contortedly distort** far too many of our <u>programs</u>, as supposedly **bumblingly-inept** (some even as comically-ludicrous).

And, the probable **impact** of this "septic stigmatizing"? Unfair to our colleagues, these skewed, flawed images could possibly *erode our employee-**morale*** internally. Worse, misleading to outsiders, these biassed depictions would probably *damage our **credibility*** in the outside world of parents, employers, legislators, the media, and indeed the general public.

Then, the **cause** of these misshapen depictions? They clearly stem from **flaws within this year's Evaluator.** Too late we found that he brought to his task, **incompetencies of his own...**

Ineptly-selected (alas), this maladjusted Evaluator has tinctured the EVALUATIONS with his own **(1)** <u>**emotional immaturity**</u>. Statements that *might* have become usefully-incisive *correctives*, deteriorate into uselessly-spiteful invective. (Even into "a fussy scolding, picky upbraiding, and preachy nagging," as a Board member so incitefully phrased it.) Now, such **personal animus** is *socially-unproductive*. (It does not even attain to <u>satire</u>, that recreational genre whose "mocking and ridiculing of human vices and follies" could surely have entertained us during the semester's slack times, and even diverted us during the stressful times as well.)

And badly-unsupervised (*eheu*), the unhappy Evaluator also saturated the EVALUATIONS with his **(2)** <u>**suspect ideology**</u>. His <u>criteria</u> for evaluating personnel-&-programs, rely upon *some very dubious yardsticks indeed*. His idiogenic <u>standards</u> of "**INTEGRITY, MORALITY, MATURITY**" [!], & "**DEDICATED EXCELLENCE**" fall short *doubly*. They're **(A) tortuously-idealistic**—far beyond *any* cost-benefit ratio. And they're also **(B) embarrassingly-antiquated**—far behind *any* realistic calibrating of **"the way we instruct, administer, and live in higher education *today*."**

Thus <u>the **EVALUATOR'S**</u> <u>personal peccadillos poisoned,</u> and his <u>ideological intensities inhibited</u>, the <u>"true - positive" image of our University</u> which we <u>surely</u> <u>merit</u>.

And, the **solution** to these "flawed fables"? **Good News:** the EVALUATIONS *shall be redone!* (In fact, implementation of same has commenced apace.) Of course, <u>you might well ask: *why* have we forwarded to you these regrettable reportings?</u> Well, they proffer powerful "grist for the educational mill"; they constitute a "learnable moment" indeed. They offer us a powerful object-lesson about (*inter alia*) **monumental irony.** That is to say, we see how <u>the Evaluator himself, exhibits so-*unmistakeably*, the very same "bad performances" which *he* so-*mistakenly* accused *us* of possessing!</u>.... Two related lessons also emerge (at least, for any personnel elsewhere who still need to learn it.) The <u>danger</u> of employing "moral-normative **criteria**" which are *both idealistic and outmoded, hence unrealistic and counterproductive.* Plus, the <u>risk</u> in selecting "non-standard-ized" **evaluators**, those "egregious maverick outliers" [sik] with which we have *not* securely stamped with *prior institutional pre-approval*...

[handwritten: Chester— Let's SINK this version! Use the new one. O.K.? Fern]

TO: All Department Heads & Section Chiefs

FR: Central Administration Executive Board, Offenbach University

RE: **PERSONNEL-EVALUATIONS** of **Employees** & **Programs**:
Inaccurate, Hence *Unusable*, Hence *Must Be Re-Done*:

      The "BAD NEWS" is that this year's batch of Employee Evaluations (attached) will have to be completely redone, having turned out seriously flawed. The cause is that this year's EVALUATOR (hired via "outsourcing," alas) possessed **psycho-pathologies of immaturity and personal maladjustments** which contaminated and hence vitiated his "work." The resulting set of "*Pejorative Portraits*" is both inaccurate and unfair. Hence quite useless, actually, for measuring performance. And also quite damaging, potentially—both to internal employee morale, and to external public image as well.

      [You'll see how these "*Maculate Manuscripts*" denigrate our victimized co-workers far past simple obfuscation... past satire-&-irony... past slender & liable.... past character-euthanasia itself... and even attained Civil Impropriety! Were they to be released and circulate internally, these "*Poisoned Pennings*" would tincture the "Office Water Troff" with a glissening droplet of **vitroioil**, hence making our morale, miasmic. And were they to escape externally, these "*Skewed Statements*" would taint our image, hence making the public ask, "Well, are our state educational employees really as bad as all this?"]

Well, the "GOOD NEWS" is, of course, "By no means!" Our hardworking colleagues are just, fine! The problem lies only within the **maladjusted psyche** of the immature EVALUATOR himself (as Human Services has already determined in order to exhonorate our true professionals). And H.S. also were able to identify exactly what were the idio-psycho-patho-logical traits of the EVALUATOR [whom some idiot over in Personnel hired unaccountably] which so badly eviperated these evaluations as you'll see:

Psycho-Pathological Traits of Hired EVALUATOR Which Vitiated His Personnel Evaluations:

(1) RIGOROUSLY-INFLEXIBLE **MORAL-ISTIC STANDARDS** for Academic Conduct... At his "small-private-liberal-arts-college" *alum mutter*, the EVALUATOR rigidly absorbed **unrealistically-idealistic imperatives of behavior** which he then could not elastically modiflex and Let Up On later on when evaluating our own "larger, regional, uprising, public comprehensive universities of the today" with our less-uptight, more real-laxed, more "people-paced," realities of communeal life!

(2) AUTOCRATIC EGOTISM In Re Those Very Standards... The EVALUATOR fancies that not only can he set "moral standards" himself (whatever they are), but also can precede to judge his defenseless fellow employees by those very, solipsistic standards! The EVALUATOR thus demonstrates the GRANDIOSITY of **MEGALOMANIA** (as in "I have the power") and its ENTITLEMENT too (as in "I have the right," not to mention even the "duty")!

(3) VINDICTIVE REVENGEFULNESS Upon Colleagues, As Well... This is due to the EVALUATOR'S NARCISSISTIC RAGE due to his PARANOID GRUDGE-HOLDING due in turn to his DELUSIONS of having—somehow!—been **persecuted**, anyhow **"wronged,"** by his innocent co-workers. Such alleged **insults** by others, justifies to him, his "getting back at them" via these "*Diseased Documents*" [akin to the well-known "1,000-injuries-of-Fortunato-syndrome"]!

(4) Further, the EVALUATOR'S **PROJECTION** upon the personnel of his own **immature traits** and **unresolved unconscious conflicts**.....Of course, he unconsciously DEFENDED these miasmic mis-perceptions via RATIONALIZATIONS [such as of the well-known "Tu wrongs don't make moat beam cast-out right Quoque" as "of course we all" well know]!

(5) Topping this psychiatric stew cognitively is the EVALUATOR'S own **OVERLY-ACTIVE IMAGINATIVENESS** [a la the "failed fiction-writer syndrome"]... This quirk torpedoed any chance that these sordid statements about his thus-maligned colleagues could have been objective.

(6) And denigrating this dour data affectively is the EVALUATOR'S **"DOWNER"-STANCE** of being "not a *Booster*, but a *Knocker*".....This quirk poisonously beschmertzed any chance for retaining the so-vital "upbeat" tone in our workplace. It even threatened our so-vaunted "*Collegiality*" {sik}, the so-valued corporate-culture trait of "*Voluntary Complaisance*" whereby "One Supports The Other For All One" as "of course we all" know!

      And so.....vitiated by their **psychopathology** as they indeed are, can these "Evaluations" {sick} serve *any* useful purpose? [Other than a textbook-perfect case of "Failed Auto-Grapho-Catharsis," that is?] The "BAD NEWS" is, of course, "No"; this egregious evidence will have to be re-done. So, *please attend the next scheduled General Meeting with constructive suggestions* on how to evaluate higher-education academic-administrative personnel—our very own colleagues!—in a fashion more realistically *SANGUINE-SALUBRIOUS* and indeed more "*KINDILIER-GENTLER*." *Thank You!* For, the "GOOD NEWS" is indeed that "togehther, we surely

The Emintabloid & Vericracious...

Tablet of Continents...

...of the RePortFolio:

The Pity-Committee

Drumbs Up its Obligatory Boom-Boom in Poetry's Pantoum Room:

Our University, its fame deserves.
Students are "customers," whom we well serve.
And never from bureaucracy we swerve.
(Staff are the peons; and we'll try their nerve.)

Students are customers whom we well serve.
"Learning's" our product, and high grades we can tailor.
(Staff are the peons; and we'll try their nerve.)
(Success where only odd-folks-out say "failure")

Learning's our "product," and high grades we can tailor.
"Excellence-in-Quality": our goal that we seek well,
Success (where only Odd-Folks-Out say "failure")
Measured by surveys? O let us sound a knell.

"Excellance-in-Quanity," our goal that we seek well,
At last a corporate-business enterprise?
Measured by surveys? O let us sound a knell.
(By mavericks only, seen with cold surmise)

At last a corporate-business enterprise!
(Only eccentrics such as I'd reserve)
(By mavericks only, seen with cold surmise)
Our University, It's Fame Deserves...

["**Pantoum**" = a poetic genre, originally from Malaysia, whose specific intricate pattern of repetitions-with-prescribed variations, is, well, illustrated in the example above... No thats all right, You'r'e' Welcome: "No Probe, Have An Ice One, Patch You Latter"...]

"A-Ranking, & [Be-] Rating, With Our PRINCE"

At first glance, doubtless sure, our major gain,
Seemed the Department's hiring of young WILL;
LINGUIST, but more; an EDITOR of fame!
His Journ. Amer. Linguistics filled the bill

To raise Dept's RANK toward first-RATE! *But*,
Behold his pinpoint-focus on the Small:
[Which folks say "bucket," which say "pail"]—Tut-tut,
PHONETICS *only*! Rich vein? ...*Not at all*....

How *could* we RANK such Sandheap-Slag, as Gold?
It lacks SEMANTICS' wealth; STYLISTICS' lore;
AESTHETICS' bloom.... *Our error*, was to hold :
"Well, *any* 'prestigious journal' hikes our Score"

Good "second-RANK" seeks *its* not-perfect *Best*...
But "second-RATE," lauds Image as the Test....

How to be THE TOP ADMINISTRATOR :

To **"ADMINISTER"**: [1] = to <u>**carry out, conduct**</u>, bureaucratically. [2] = to **"Stick It In/sert It In** |03|
Ra-ther" {as in, to "administer a Shot/Dose of the HYPO-DORMIC **NEADLE,** into the Subject's **NODULE"**}.

> **Q**uestion #77. "A faculty member requests a brief appointment. To update you on his/her professional activities (after a successful sick leave). [Projects include: (1) teaching critical **thinking,** (2) work on **"minority and multicultural diversity,"** and (3) a grass-roots project to improve art education and campus aesthetics by **displaying artworks in public campus spaces."**]
> The individual seems <u>committed</u>: shows a <u>genuine and energetic interest</u> in these <u>valid</u> educational goals."

➔ <u>**SERVING SUGGESTION:**</u> <u>Decide</u> which one of the Chancellor's possible three RESPONSES to the interview [below], would be the **best** to achieve the desired **goal** of **personating true "Bureaukratic-Administratif Liedership"**...

Option #1 **"OVERINVOLVEMENT"** You <u>listen</u> carefully; <u>ask</u> questions for clarification; <u>promise</u> available support for the employee's initiatives. [E.g., publicity and promotion....."networking" to identify other faculty interested in these projects.....modest funding if and where possible and necessary.]
--You <u>conduct, and conclude</u>, the interview with *some sincere* **sincerity;** *some genuine* **genuineness;** and *some responsive* **responsiveness** toward the individual.

Option #2 **"CON-STRUCTED"** You pay <u>minimalistic</u> attention to the subject's alleged comments; simply <u>donate</u> a feedback of CONSTRUCTED CONGRATULATIONS and CONCERNED-COMMITMENT which is:
Sincerely-**Simulated.....** *Emotionally*-**Ersatz.....** *Integrally*-**Imitation.....** *Honestly*-**Hawked....**
Faithfully-**Fabricated.....** *Genuinely*-**Gratuitous.....** and *Realistically*-**"Responsive".....**

Option #3 **"DOWN-SIZED, KEEN-&-KLEEN"** Your <u>total</u>, <u>complete</u> response to this whole unnecessary interruption **is, and should be,** <u>these following words and actions</u>, **_and only_** <u>these</u>:

> During the interview, **say _nothing at all_**. At its end <u>say</u> **exactly _and only_** <u>this</u>:
> "VERY GOOD, BRANDON. NICE SEEING YOU AGAIN."
> Then <u>smile</u>... <u>Rise</u>... <u>Shake hands</u> with the individual... <u>Escort</u> him from your office... <u>Close</u> the office door... <u>Discard</u> the note-pad page (upon which you <u>had</u> written *one word*)...
> And <u>return</u> to what must be, instead, your proper duties....

.....**Answer Sheet** for the above?:   [[[[[*"The answer, my fiend, is blowing in the wind....."*]]]]]

Becoming the Acting, Then Permanent, "FIGURE HEAD":

---Greeting the dawn, it was with his *KINDLY BENIGN REGARD* that the **FIGURE HEAD** did confront |04|
his **shoes and cereal**.....

---Next a *THOUGHTFUL, MUSING SMILE* was expressly utilized by the **FIGURE HEAD** in interfacetating with his **morning mail**.....

---And soon it was that into the **important committee meeting,** the **FIGURE HEAD** a *KINDLY BENIGN REGARD,* did in fact infuse.....

---Too, imbued with a *THOUGHTFUL, MUSING SMILE* was the **FIGURE HEAD's** rapport with his **personalized 11:00 coffeecup**.....

---You could subsequently see permeating uponto the **luncheon guests**, the **lunch itself**, and nay the **view from the Dining Room**, from the **FIGURE HEAD** himself, a *SANGUINE, GENTEEL COUNTENANCE*.....

---This did not, however, prevent **the afternoon's major public conference** from being transpired through with a **FIGURE HEAD**-style *MELLOW, SALUBRIOUS PORTRAYMENT*.....

---Upon the **evening's television screed,** and nay the **oak panels of the den** at his home, the **FIGURE HEAD** a *THOUGH-FUL, BENINE ATTITUDE* did inflect.....

---At midnight even into his **"snoring activity-interlude"** seeped indeed the **FIGURE HEAD** a *KINDLY, EVEN A KINGLY, MUSING ASPECT*.....

Well The Storm Troopers Played Beethoven

How surely you shared with me
(that day in your Chancellor's Office)
your *Administrative Acumen* by which
you can (em-)balm sorely-diverse claims
can minimize flareups and Manage....
but first, your *Artistic Appreciation*:

why, you even attended, and praised,
the big *Monet* exhibition in Chicago
and in not only bought the rich catalogue,
but also lent it to me...
...all this when I sought your support
for my modest grass-roots project,
a johnny-appleseed endeavor,
what I called **"PROJECT ART-UP"**:
enthusiastically I proposed to you,

that I'd simply, on the school's bare walls,
mount quality reproductions
of the best visual art and design,
whether *Van Gogh* and *Monet* now-known,
whether *Hockney* and *Hofman* more-new;
simply to educate students beyond Art 101,
simply to embellish grimy surroundings,
simply to refresh all inhabitants
of the "University Community".....

and at scant cost to the institution,
glad to pay pennies from my pocket,
thus to contribute toward Pulchritude--
(could have been Prestige for you too?...)

But you are no weak-willed belletrist;
you showed you could Administer Acutely
a *Coup de* control Oh My *Grace*-ious!

by veritably blindsiding
by dexterously sandbagging
by sedulously shit-canning
by blisteringly blowing-off
my native-naïve *petit*-project!

And here's exactly how you did it.
You said you'd discuss it "in CABINET,"
your weekly 30-person meeting.
Next week you straight-facedly claimed
that they discussed it "for a *half-hour*...."
[They discussed it for *a half hour*?...
a time that I the **PROJECT's** Originator
would have been pressed to fill up!,
not that I'd been invited in
for even **five** clarifying *minutes*...]
....And that "the reaction was lukewarm,"
and that "many" Cabineteers feared
there'd be "major vandalism problems"
[a distortion, as I found out when hearing

a supposedly true version from "RALPH":
one person had merely reported
a few pictures had been drunkenly removed
at some other school some other time—
assuming RALPH'S true version to be true.....]

Well-done!
You extirpated my grass-roots gardening
as if they were mere weeds clogging
your growing of your victory-garden Crop,
your whatever-purposed "Missions"
(I think: *Prestige, Power, & Pocketbook*)...

--you scant realizing that **PROJECT ART-UP**
might have bloomed into a floral
adornment to your lapel after all,
impressing your "bosses in Madison"!
(You could have claimed it some value.)

--A WORKROOM blooming with **"*Flowers & Gardens*—formal and modern..."**

--A STAIRWELL sporting **"*Venice & Paris*—by varied painters..."**

--A CORRIDOR of **"*Women's Portraits*— Van Gogh & Matisse..."**

--An ALCOVE of **"*Japan*: Prints, *and* Postcards past *and* present..."**

--A CONFERENCE ROOM wall illuminated by **"20 *Window-Scenes* by Matisse..."**

And yet you claimed you appreciated
"Those masterpieces of *Monet*."
Well hell, you probably *did*

If before you I knew well Truth #1,
"BETWEEN DEGREE(S) OF HIGHER EDUCATION
AND PERSONAL MATURITY
EXISTS NULL OR NEGATIVE CORRELATION,"

let alone the Truth #2 that will follow,
"HIGHER I.Q. IS JUST AS LIKELY
TO BE MISUSED FOR ILLOGIC, RATIONALIZING,
DEFENSE, ATTACK, AND TRIUMPH
AS MUCH AS FOR BETTER FAIR THINKING,"

then, our "Seminar" taught me Truth #3:
"EVEN THE OPEN INNOCENT NUTRIENT
OF GREAT ART CAN NOURISH
THOSE WHO FROM IT ARE REFRESHED
TO CONTINUE IN THEIR MISCHIEF."

...you refreshed for your Job:
to perform such such adroit balancings
to resolve dissonances, rival claims,
to give to each faction its true due,
to make difficult decisions fairly,
to encourage institutional progress
via cooperation and morale—

Well heck I hear tell *other* **DOERS**
enjoyed their Bach as *they* blasted

"Velvet Glove" but Iron Fi[r]st

and yes **"We"** (=those "uncooperative" FACULTY who defend liberal-learning values)
We sure all *had* been thinking that among all the **ADMINISTRATORS,** it was **you,**
that **you** were the best, well really the one & only ADMINISTRATOR who was
valid, principled, idealistic, dedicated, liberally-reasonable
...**you** the *only* "non-plastic" one of *all* of **Them** up there in the Front Office--

--**you** the *only* "integral" one among **those** "Others," those Mechanistic Movers all dedicated *only* to
  1. avoiding negative media publicity on their watch,
  2. getting the school ranked high in the USNews&WorldReportRatings,
  3. and pleasing their bosses in Even Higher-Up Central Administration...

...for surely on difficult issues, **you** *had* always reinforced among **Us, your** image
as the one single most *reliable principled nuanced sensitive* responder…...

[Oh *certain* Liberal Lounge-Lizards *always* condemned *every* administrator point-blank.
I thought such "knee-jerk" was an ironic *shortfalling* here in our "think-tank"
and I'm glad I {thought-fully} "Reserved Judgment," any bias thus to out-flank—
until "enough hard evidence"... even though soon-enough my torpedoed innocence sank...]

ii.

Well, as was taught in "Publicity & Public Relations" class,
"IF YOU CAN FAKE SINCERITY, YOU'VE GOT IT MADE!"
And indeed **you** *had* "managed impressions," I came to see with a jolt,

You accreted the Capital of *Good Impressions*, a paper profit you banked and then held in reserve
to mask your true allegiance: you are the lackey of the System just like the other **Administrators...**
You willing to spendthrift your bankroll, as I came to see during our Phone Conference that one day,

I had called to protest the glacially-slow non-"progress" of the school's "controversial, risky"
GAY AND LESBIAN TASK FORCE. Which seemingly terrified conservative State senators?
Which anyhow Our **Administrators** had mothballed in bureaucratic abeyances for over a year now...

--And you responded so-reasonably, "Well, the Chancellor has to be convinced that
  a ton of people on the campus really care about this sensitive issue,"

--And I replied so-directly, "He knows; but he's been stonewalling the *completed* reports
  of a *24*-person Task Force on this issue for the last *twelve months!*"

….well then you Knew What To Do, you whannnnnnnged back by launching this
  grapeshot-missive of this bottom-of-the-barrel, Ad Hominem, slandegregation:

  "Why, BRANDON! I'm *scandalized*! You should be _ashamed_ for speaking like that!"

...and I *t*hen *s*uddenly *f*ound *t*hat *I* had "*u*sed *u*p *m*y phone *t*ime" *w*ith **you** *t*hat educational afternoon...

...thus confirming your truer colors. *You the slick suave smart lackey of the Managers,*
     you stupidly *thought* **you** *could* *shame* *an* *activist* !

         But know this: when thus duped,
           I to no forgiveness can stoop;
             from now on in,
               *I **know** & **shall** **tell**,* **your** particular
               [even if sheep-clothinged]
               [all the more because camouflauged]
                 brand of sin

DEMAGOGUELET - IN - TRAINING:

His Self-Study Seminar in Sturm-Drang:

[i.]

Why is it that there has drifted over the
formerly-sunny face of you the Good-Guy-
along-w/-the-Rest-Of-Us (we all just inhabiting
the COMMON GROUNDS of the Deptl Corridor
(tho "lowland", it's PASTORAL-friendly)
...I ask, **why** are your features so umbraged,

a _cloudbank_, now shadowing your visage,

and forecasts, for all of us to preview,

this change in your Personal _Weather_

this blustery coldfronting of your _Climate_,

which sets off your drive to Gain _Altitude_,

your clambering doggedly _uphill_,

toward that _chilled High Ground_ of **Control**?

toward that Tempest-like need to **Direct**?

[ii.]

Why do you clearly lust to Ascend,
to depart OUR LOW FERTILE FIELD-BEDS
(those Collegial Corridors of Community)
to rise to that Eaglesnest of **Power**?
...such a Thin-Air, Chilled Upland indeed...

[iii.]

We all sense this: your _self_-(s)election
to the montane heights of **Administration**!

You champion at the bit restless,
with only a Dept'l Chairpersonship
as Saddle-to-ride for the meantime
before that Higher Perch opens,
So the best you can do now, is Meddle.
You find fodder in everyone's movement:
import _Stormy Weather_ to our GARDENS.
   Even my adjacent Department,
   [not your own yet tho you think so!],
   feels the _backdrafts_ of your Attentions:
   --to our student-evaluation practices,
   --to our workroom-key policies,
   --to our package-delivery procedures,
   --yes, to our microwave-usage, even!

Thus proddding, you tempest our Teapot,
in _Hurricane_-swirling spillover....

[iv.]

But you not only _Peer_, _Note_, and _Poke_;
you _Tamper With_—**&**, _Aggrandize_.
--Initiate untraceable "complaints"
-- Stir "your" Dept like a _duststorm_
(do you lust toward such crop-lashing?),
intently impatient for the **Big Stuff**
which still eludes your grasp.
--And for heavens sake you fight "Space Wars"!
What better training than to **Turf-Grab**,
to capture rooms for "your" Department?
--Plus, you're a minion-mole in the Pipeline.
You sneak all our scuttlebutt to the Bridge,
to our campus' **High Administration**—
that toplofty Heaven you aspire to—
   (that your dark-furrowed visage shows
   you aspire to _Exceed_, to _Surpass_....)

[v.]

But [yet-once-again, & finally]--**why**?
Why seek so to ride an Updraft
toward **Influence**'s gloomy thunderhead?
   Save yourself now! Change your climate!
   Reconfigure your metereopathology!
   Identify your cryptic _Pressure-Systems_!
   What _Cold Fronts_ clash within you?
   What central needs gone unmet,
   thrust you to those lofty-chill Mists
   of **Command**'s crag-faced Summit?
   Did your own "epicenter" come to seem
   an eye-of-the-storm too calm,
   hence too existentially-empty,
   hence to be filled with the vacuum
   of **Administrative Power**,
So is that what's-to-do-here?
You try to ride up a _Storm-Along_
'cause you found your own HOME-LY EARTH
lacked sufficient—Atmosphere?

[vi.]

No; descend, if you can, from that _Thin-Air_
of **High Ground**'s impoverishing power.
Come down from yon **Mountain**-height,
back to OUR MEADOWED LOWLANDS
where, divested of swords and Trappings,
we FREEMEN sanguine democratic
under a Barometer more Steady.....

{[I.]}

WHEREAS **YOU, HENRY,** grabbed the Departmental ChairShip as soon as you could,
thus to launch yourself into the orbit of sheer Power you sought you *savored* you **craved**,
and then retained the Throne for a decade of more-&-more of your Trampling, Strutting, & Shambling;
> [**YOUR** psyche being fingerprint-isormorphic conformable with pathology,
> fitting the DSM-III's clinical description of the "Paranoid" Personality Type]
>> [...to *me* this "ruption" in plain view to learn—but why did our *other* colleagues __not__ then discern...];

And WHEREAS **YOU** demonstrated a tad less than Mature Emotional St-Ability in Deportment:
In fact, **YOUR** "shit-list was chiseled in permanent granite"
[as we naked *Outsiders* had to endure & learn—as the tenure-armored *Insiders* could cheerfully forget, spurn?]

> [...such that when Colleague WHAT-WAS-HIS-NAME made his single mildly-and-naively-critical remark,
> that gaffe was enough to doom him to a departure which YOU, **HENRY,** engineered.....]

> [...such that when I MYSELF felt that YOU, **HENRY** cheerfully "waffled" my asking you about re-hiring
> policies (I still year-to-year insecure)... and so I then simply asked the DEAN as to "What is the
> Department's re-hiring policy?"... that single anxious inquiry was enough to doom *me* to a **HENRY**-
> permanent denigrating...]

In fact, **YOU** showed well your control-freak power-Sadism even then...
--**YOU** saying to me (**still the only non-tenured staff then, re-hired yearly, hence replacably-vulnerable**)
"You're in my power," and this brash & blatant right in front of my tenured colleague-and-friend VICTOR....
And immune from modification: god knows *I* had even earlier spied your hairtrigger-Instability,
tried defusing via politesse and chatting, shop-talk about our mutual interests, but of course all to no avail:
YOUR own Tower-of-Power being so tippy-tottery *needful*, your full-blast Bluster so brutal-brittle *driven*.....

WHEREAS **YOU** abused your entrustment of the Dept'l Chairship: [**clear to *me* then; to *others* __when__?**]
You "demonstrated your remarkable abilities"—to *neglect* duties... to *nonperform* stockpile mandates... to
let unravel important tasks... even to *overload* the Chairship plate with your buying and managing your own
retail business simultaneous with your Chairing!

WHEREAS **YOU** demonstrated a bit *less* than any minimal Professional Manners/Decorum/Civility:
> My gosh, **YOU** referring openly—right in the Deptl meeting—and so sarcastically—to the College's then
> & mild ASSISTANT DEAN, as "one whose highest ambition is simply to be a high school principal".....
>> [**BY GOD ONE DOES _NOT_ GRATUITOUSLY SCORE ONE'S EGO-POINTS PUBLICALLY THUS!**]
>>> [...to critical *me*, your slashing was painfully plain—why did your so-moral *colleagues* see no stain?]

WHEREAS **YOU** demonstrated a touch less than Candid, Open-Book, Disclosing Communication:
--**YOU** mentioning offhand in Deptl meeting "the new faculty transferred from Superior"
[...responsive-responsible peers might have wondered, **BUT HOW HAD SHE BEEN SELECTED?**]
--**YOU** winking to thralled me, "Every meeting I call, I already know the outcome...."
[...incriminating evidence, *I* saw you infected—but why among your *colleagues* not detected?...]

WHEREAS **YOU** demonstrated in your public reign something *less* than Impartial Employee-Treatment:
YOU flushing the Faithless and selecting-protecting your preferentialed Minions-for-advancement...
--**YOUR** depositing into me a kaleidoscope-cornucopia of misinformation—
"We decided this, they selected that, here's what you should do"— only to mislead me onto a primrose path.
--And worse, **YOUR** broadcasting about me, to others & behind my back, a seedbed of outrightly-damaging
lies about me, to try to denigrate my desperate dedication, advance your alternate Acolytes:
"When BRANDON resigned, he burned his bridges here behind him...."
"BUT I NEVER RESIGNED! I ONLY WANTED TO REMAIN HERE!"—
oh how I've had to shout this correction a dozen times over the years, to try to stem your dumped tide of misinformation circulating among **my _Colleagues_ surely so responsible-moral-aware**, before such sludge became
as permanently leached-in to the Community Memory-Bank as other toxic groundwater waste of Slander.....
--And worst of all, the day before the last big decision [=do I or MAC get the one tenure-track slot at last],
YOUR frank electioneering for your Fairhaired-Boy candidate MAC, via your own circulating
to **the voting faculty**, letters-of-reference adulously praising him—you going door-to-door to their offices!
--and **YOUR** masking this unsavory politicking "Well, some people had requested more info about MAC"!

Well I won, made it to Tenure after all and despite you, but barely; you having stallion-trampled things down so daringly...

[...but why were your office-crimes so clear for biassed-insightful *me* to see, all along ...
but not for your <u>so</u>-responsible *colleagues* to perceive & condemn,
despite your machinations being *CLASSIC MORAL WRONGS?*.....]

{[**II.**]}

SO, **HENRY**, FOR YOUR ROSTER OF WRONGS, we surely should censure **YOU**...
But no, wait. What's this now, why it seems that **YOU** are to be SAVED.
"That's right." But saved by no *bell* ... but by "the *hell that's Otherpeople*" ?

{[**III.**]}

BECAUSE <u>MOST OF **YOUR** FINE COLLEAGUES</u>
    [other than *me*—who, being the year-to-year outside-rider, the powerless minority-outsider,
    therefore saw things more clairvoyant, having more to lose via **YOU**-so-violent—]
<u>QUITE ACCEPTED YOU</u>, yes wholesale -&- whole-hog -&- just fine;
neither perceived, nor were perturbed by, your foibles-in-line...

    --Staid **"RACHAEL"** retorting to me, after I told her of my clarion concerns,
    "Well, **HENRY'S** my friend, and I'm not going to say anything against him."]
    (Oh a few years later She Learned, I saw, though never
    any acknowledging amends did she make to me, at all or ever....)

    --[Somber-sober **"AL"** intoning judiciously, just as if he *had* inspected any evidence,
    "Well, **HENRY'S** been doing a Good Job as Chair, and so he should continue"
    (Oh but into his *eleventh* year or so, of his mis-Chairing wobble-orbiting too-&-fro?!)

    --Even collegial **"BRAD,"** **HENRY**'s best friend (maybe the only toward **HENRY**'s *bleary-beery end*),
    to my litany-of-woes, could only say, "Well heck **BRANDON**, you made it aboard over **"MAC,"** so hey...."

"CAN YOU NOT <u>*SEE*</u>," I had wanted to shout, but of course could not yet do so, no doubt.
And, <u>no</u>. <u>For it took over a decade</u> for the **good people** or enough of them
to SEE THRU **HENRY**, & THEN & THUS TO SEE HIM THROUGH and out of the Chairship at last.
    {though of course at the end, when the balloon finally went up and **HENRY** at last stood denuded in rout,
    why *then* naturally to a person all these his *colleagues* to a person had to tout and spout:
    the Onley Treue "Song of Defence": tu-wit, **"Well, *Of Course* We All 'KNEW ABOUT' Bad HENRY In The Past"**}

    (all securely-tenured; hence snugly-encastled from *my own* Panoptic Paranoia—or Perspective?
    —of one who lives encamped iffily Outside the Great Gate),
    they as secure-d Insiders insensitive to such wrongs greater and lesser,
    except when they teach in their classes such misbehaviors as a Theme of Great Literature....
    (Did I seek and envy your security, just so I could be as nonchalant as you?)
    (Do I grouse, a pouting lout, because I was out-on-the-outs—whereas if I had been In like You,
    would I have let no such of HENRY's so-called Injustices cloud my sunny secure view?
    Ah that-there is your ticket to ride, or rather, my view to deride, your serenity to abide!)

WHO WAS IT WHO SAID "All that it takes for the triumph of evil is for good people to do nothing?"
Who-knows-or-cares who the hell said it, but for the word "**good**," I'd snotty substitute "**morally-challenged**".....

SO THEREFORE <u>YOU</u>, **HENRY**, <u>ARE</u> <u>EXCUSED</u>, O pardon **MOI**,
and <u>YOU</u>, dear **COLLEAGUES**, become <u>ACCUSED</u>,
culpable in the keenly-distorted eyes of scared-scarred Myself
the one who TRIED TO TELL AND SHOW YOU—
    you who could "see it," **HENRY**'s Horrors, only when unmistakable at last,
    only when corruption erupted Caligula-like in decadent excrescence.....

Well, it's over now, has been for a decade or more, **HENRY**'s Reign Of Hell.
Past is an interlude of Injustice, a rule of Wrongness, a puncturing of Professionalism
which for **Upholstered You-all** *never even existed*...

No, not even here-and-now, eh?... Even today in afterplay, my knell **you** won't hear-of tell...

    ...Whether because you remained Tenure-armored, hence awareness-numbed, throughout it all—
    or whether because you remain Injustice-insensitive as you always were & would have been withal.....

"NORRIS": BEHEADED IN ACADEME !!

To start with; a smallish HEAD.
Small book of (Modern) Poems way back then,
gave **NORRIS** a HEAD-
start into the *modish, median mean*
of our De-Merited Medio-crisy here.
But soon, some saw **NORRIS** as half-brain-dead....

Then during a Departmental turmoil
the **Administration** deadHEADed
the too-headstrong current HEAD,
and a **Dean** safely selected **NORRIS** as the new "Co-HEAD"
[in tandem with our HEADy **HENRY**]
both *pro tem,* just to keep things stead-
y; easy for **NORRIS** to do as the Figure HEAD
he *had always was become*.
Nay, not even a strong Talking-HEAD--
NORRIS feared the Powers'd have his HEAD,
(felt as overtaxed as if microcephalic).
But, our crown-ambitious **HENRY** HEAD-
ed **NORRIS** off before any atrophy,
dumkopfed him out of the *tete-a-tete*
[a HEAD-and-a-half, worse for **HENRY**'s ambition
than his own one **wrong HEADstrong** HEADing]

So **HENRY** HEADed **NORRIS** off at the Pass,
& back to his (old) Modern Poetry.
More, to Chicago's race track **NORRIS** could now head,
he'd pay *me* $10.00 to give his class
an "exam" {"HEADline the stories we've read"}.
When **NORRIS** retired, few or no HEAD-
lines proclaimed such a gray matter,
and the **Chancellor** wrote instead
a short stately HEADnote
honoring of the pre-dead.
Yeah thus became **NORRIS** beHEAD-
ed; others professing in his stead.

...A Survival-Kit Recipe for this Con-coction:

[I]

It's easy! As easy as **Doing Nothing**:
your goal and achievement already,
which you practiced even Before Tenure....

[II]

If "a group's impression of an individual,"
can be likened to, say, "a slow-cooking food dish,"
why, then, any time your peers' attention
is focussed on you (your "cover-lid" off),
well then you can-&-do "season suggestively."
You'll sweeten your IMAGE, "correct" it
to feed to your Deptl colleagues, it seems.
  (Or at least to the many, whose palates
  seem uneducated? {...or, uncritical?}
  But others, at least me, you **dis-gust**....)

You'll drop into our Group-Soup a deft dollop
of the bottled gravy of your *Good Impression*.
You'll do it even when all are onlooking!
Yes, high-visibility times especially
lie ripe for your tinkering-via-tainting.
  (But I as the Undercover Food-Inspector,
  I-for-one, saw how you "*COOK YOUR BOOKS*")

Yes, even at the CHANCELLOR'S Annual Visit,
you whipped up a pottage for him, and "tableside"!
Your brash signature-dish *so* inventful...
I heard you crow to him *so*-concernedly,
with *so*-modest, *so*-respectable APPEARANCE,
with such "heart-felt" VERSION of Integrity:

  "How hard it is for us to do our jobs well,
  get our research done, do duties fully,
  handle committees and advising, etc.,
  under current working-conditions,
  some of which thus need improvement...."

....and having stirred that in, you settle back,
having tinctured the whole glass of your IMAGE
with that one pale drop of ROSEWATER,
with the *soupcon* of you as(-if) *Valid*,
as *Responsible*-and-*Dedicated* worker.
(You let that grim Gravy, do its binding...)

[III]

....but it's a *false ingredient* ! belied daily
by your "enrichment-free" *True* MENU:
--by your *subminimal-daily-requirement* Syllabi...
--by your "leaner, more modest," Office Hours...
--by your one-less-Paper-than-is-required...
--by your use of class hours for Conferences...
--by your proficient use of the Videotape
  (that pre-packaged, "labor-saving" ingredient)...

To work I see you trudge at a snail's pace.
As reluctant as Shakespeare's wan schoolboy...

Your Thinsoup Offering! belied daily,

--by your *ignoring* of requests-for-info,
--by your *dour mien* in the corridors,
--by your overheard *braggings about blow-offs*,
--by your private *commending of colluders*,
--by your public *criticism of this place*...

So, O how you at times do *Talk* it up;
But, Ah how you never do *Walk* it!
No; you pursue, via flippant acerbity,
your dedication to **high care-less-ness**:
that goal and achievement already.
Not for you the sauced Savor of the STOCKPOT.
You'll serve the piping-hot Steam of AROMA.

[IV]

From self-control you barge free also.
Good grief, after talking with the DEAN
(during *his* Annual Deptl-Visit)
on some sensitive subject or other,
you smilingly "guessed that this time,
you'd restrained yourself pretty well."
You seemingly amazed at this mild outcome,
that you'd avoided typical boil-over.

  { MIGOD IS EVEN YOUR **SELF** CONTROL
  AND **D**EPORTMENT,

  A MERE PLAYTHING OF YOUR **V**AGRANT
  BLUSTER? }

{ Whysure. *LET THE PORTIONS BURN...* }

[V]

This sour-&-sour soup of yourself...
This brew-of-you quite **taste-less**...
No one else at our Table seems to sense this,
{"For-Shame" to my S*s*ensitive Palate}
...nor would find disgustatory if they did...

So am I the only *toque blanche* around—
"Old-fashioned, fussy, compulsive..."
[*or: snottily, unreasonably perfectionistic?...*]
as I confess I still savor in our Communal Mess,
certain Minimal Daily Requirements
for a more salubrious Social Stewpot....
for a more solid Menu offered...
for more than just Décor, Service, Clientele...
for more than the whiff-&-waft of IMAGE.....

[Still, each day our Classroom Cafes
  swell to the "fully-booked" limit with patrons
  eager to dine on Lite Credits; and so,
  we're surely serving *Something* Up Right . . . .]

Art-Ful Dodger

[I]

Strange
that a colleague who awoke as a poet
quite late, blooming in his fifties,
could write POETRY **so worthy**—
   so *moral, acute, sensitive*—
   so *passionate but commanded*—
   so nearly approaching the status
   of a "MAJOR REGIONAL POET"
as I had often told him

   Straanger still, thence, that this Crafter-in-<u>words</u>,
   would be such a Crasher-in-<u>teaching</u>...;
   would **hamfist** his CLASSROOM as he did,
   would **bludgeon** and **forcefit** it so

   Still straaangest of *all*, as a corridor-voyeur, I spied it!
   At the lectern, a small thin man poises.
   Smack against the back walls,
   a small cluster of students huddles:
   (as if caught out overnight on Mt. Monadnock
   they inertly seeking mutual protection,
   seemingly stunned by the Blast)

   half-numbed by the clarion-Blatt
   which this small man automatic produces!
   as he paces the frontstage random,
   his gaze darting everywhere-but-anywhere,
   as he sure curates receivable wisdoms
   as he out Blares his pre-prepared broadside:

     "Now. *What. Did. You. Think*. That.
     Huck. And. Tom. Saw. When. They. Got.
     To. The. End. Of. The. Dock. *That's*.
     Right. There. They. Saw. A. New. Man.
     A. New **A. MER. I. Can**...."

   ....in a mazing out print of Absence

[II]

   Still heck, *not* really Strange after all!
   For **he** once told unTenured **NELDA**
   (a fellow struggling poet) that indeed,

     "Getting your writing done is easy:
     one simply backburners one's teaching...."

     So also—well heck at his time of life
     and with his ready-opened Vein;
     "triage" *veut dire* **"sauve-qui-peut"**
       since its "every poet for oneself"

Buffalo Bill's defunct, "the only man who shot 12345 / pigeons just like that"....

And Warren G. Harding, "the only man woman or child who wrote a simple declarative sentence with seven grammatical errors' is dead' "....

But burning brite as ever with his fires, is LEE CLARKSON even as he retires!
The man who held to *high standards* for maintaining—*sprezzatura*;
who <u>knew it *enough*</u>, to donate <u>mere *fluff*</u>,–
who knew it <u>sufficient</u>, nay even <u>efficient</u>, to be quite *<u>deficient</u>*,–
but who <u>did</u> all with such—*bravura*!

{Oh how now shall echo, with Glittery *Brite*-ness, our wan-dun corridor-<u>Hallways</u>,
now deprived from the regal *froth*, which LEE had admixed in,--<u>all-ways</u>}

(I) <u>INTELLECTUAL-PROFESSIONAL</u> <u>DEDICATION</u>

He who bravely bore the white battle-flag of ***Child's Play***,
(that coat-of-arms of ***Irrepressible Insouciance***,
(that garish-motley cloak of ***Irresponsible Impishness***)
right into the SOMBER SANCTUM OF AN ACADEMIC DEPT....
He who then retained said Handkerchief blanched,
kept immaculately hedonistic for a quarter-century:
kept it "Free Forever" from the soil/s of such as of the likes of
SERIOUSNESS, OF MEANING, OF EFFORT, OF COMMITMENT, OF AUTHENTICITY.....
For *He* saw ACADEMIC-ADULT ENTERPRISE for what it gloomily sure <u>*is*</u>:
a menace to a Pleasurable-Principle of ***Vacant Vacationing***;
yes a threat to the carbonated fizzing of such—***Dizzy Whizzing***!

Who would never stay for an ANSWER? Nay, *Who* would never stay past a QUESTION?
Whose intolerance of any FOCUSSED MATTER OR POINT, would whip him instant to his ***dashing sprint***?
Who did ANY THOUGHT-FULL MISSILE, stimulate automatic to his airy ***dismissal***?
Who performed ably to ***derail to mocking nought***, any straight-bore trajectory of TRUE THOUGHT?

No; every day and night, *He*'d graciously donate his fond, half-focussed, Musing ***Delight***,
enough to dishevel SOLID MATTER like some fey Sprite;
his unravelling, wry ***Interruption***; a substantially-splayed ***Disruption***...

(II) <u>QUALITY-ATTAINMENT</u>

Who achieved <u>perfect</u> dual-group membership, being both one of those
"who <u>Complained-the-most</u>—blattily-brattily, publically-vocally—about working conditions,"
and "those who actually <u>Did-the-least</u> to actually Accomplish any WORKING-THING to fruitions"?

Who achieved a <u>perfect</u> track-record of greeting
each every any and all statement in Committee meeting
of a BONA-FIDE INTELLECTUAL CONCERN,
with O that ***jauntily-dismissive disclaiming Spurn***?

Who praised highly the colleague who during the year of her sabbatical reportedly
"never darkened the door of her office" (hence avoided spoiling ***the Dance*** contortedly)?

Who said publically, "Faculty who leave *here* and move on, do *well*!"
(he content to stay and enjoy the swell, subtropical suntans in summer he achieved,
sure other pleasures to be lived, subrosa pressures to be relieved)?

Whose total amassment of professional files, remounted to only one, 1-foot-high pile?

(III) THE TRUER VOCATION OF VAPID VAPORIZING

Who obtained one of the then-scarce computers, then only played games on it, truly a *Refuter*?

Who with deft-dexterous arranges, lands prestigious foreign-teaching exchanges
("as far away from here as we can get," as if ever truly into this place he set),
all with his SCHOLARSHIP record of *zero*, so clearly in *Politicking 101* our hero?

Who even got tenured and promoted with no doctorate, even when requirements demanded it?

Who thus gained such "political" Affluence, via the dark basements of—*Inside Influence*?
(O on that subject he clearly could, and hence surely should, have written up "the Book".....
tho that would have required for once a non-*flighty*, STEADY LOOK.....)

(IV) COLLEGIAL DEMEANOR; DEPARTMENT-DEPORTMENT:

Who (with bobbed spouse **"BARBE"** ever attendant)
would always talk Poormouth, "no travel funding such a nuisance,"
but always paroled so with that *upholstered Insouciance
of the congenitally-wealthy* (that gushing delight oiled healthy)?

Ever speculating on the ISSUE-IN-MENTION, with delighted myopic beaming *Half-Attention,*
grinning satisfied-secure ear-to-ear, able to spread to all, his Madras-clothed *Genial Cheer*
(no "victor likes the defeated less" here—and yet, did he flaunt what he held near-and-dear?
for, Who tried to spook doctoral-candidate *Me,* with tales of the program's atrocities?
Ever inspecting thus from his tatersall-Tenured Position, those in inferior situation?)

(V) FELATIONSHIP WITH STUD-ENTS

Who allegedly and with scant detection (at least with no Collegial insurrection),
did carry "hands-on instruction," upon the young male athletic objects of his afflection,
to a monstrous *Delectation,* and right in the classroom!, and to the knowledge
of most students in the college? But *he* held to his *standards sinister,*
and so neither the Law, nor "Mr. Ad-Minister," got such Blunt Frontings abated...
Was *He* fated to remain safe-rated, in such frank relation to "Physical Education"?

And heck, *his* final exams—{that is, *if & when* given—no DUTIFUL RATION should shorten *Vacation*}
were a Scandal: empty sheer Vacancy, no pot, no pan, no handle:
He assigned just a Mockery: one jump-thru Paragraph, a one-digit-sized dickery-dockery
they could surf with no fidget, just enuf so *he* could say that "they did it".....

(VI) SUMMARY, & RECOMMENDATIONS

Who thus loudly his Treasure, of dedicated unalloyed *Pleasure,*
trumpeted resonant in the pallid HALLWAYS, to kaleidoscope our wan spirits always?

Oh and if any would accuse *ME* of being too unfair and HARSH,...
   ...Well then we could just employ today's so-humanitarian or at least "egalitarian"
   standard of "well whos to say say after all" plus "well you cant say any one faculty colleague
   contributes more than any other" for that would derail Collegiality in our workplace-MARSH!

And so by that so-"collegial" Criterion, we can say that—compared to *Others'* contributions,
(e.g., my own modest but solid fifty published pedagogical language-arts ARTICLES....)—
   ....**LEE CLARKSON'S** contribution of Aerating our musty CORRIDORS with his Flaneur's Flavor of
   paisley-pastel-madras scintilla-*sportwheeling*, is worth exactly just quite as much the same weight-
   or-Valorized-Valence as mine, right down to each little PARTICLE...

For, in some vacuumed Hallways of today

   [wherever such *splay* may stay to play, via **LEE**-Lieders wry,
   they've got *their* Values Clarified; WAN DOUR SOLIDITY stays defied],

ozonated airiness pastels the Day

"You say that he—*became* an 'unconscious and unintended **parody of his own self**'? Yeah but heck, he always *was* that....!"
[-- St. Pfred, Kronikles, Ch. 18, Par. 14, L. 2, *Authoritized Edition*]

But how best to play the character of our **NATHAN**? The actor selected must be skilled indeed. Yes, "pronouncements from a podium," but all for a vital High Seriousness [*o but surely short of Arid Stuffiness...*]

See, in the "military seenario" of our Culture Wars, **NATHAN** has willingly volunteered to command-eer the roll of **Chairperson of the Department of DEFENSE.** He'll rigorously-vigorously defend our **"Traditional Humanistic High Culture"** against its imagined real enemies indeed, even to rolling out the "can[n]on" of the **Great Books** because the best defense is to be offense-ively pro-reactive to the Threats which Surround Us! [*o but don't say retrospective myopia w/ elitist aesthetics serving Status*]...   And yet always, manner must support matter: while not lacking the Human(e) Touch, still Seriousness of Content & Purpose must be conveyed with Seriousness of Manner, not to mention the roll conveying high— Status... The question will be: does the Commander possess the Personal Leadership-Force, to parallel his Profound Convictions and to install them among the populous? [*o but don't say us the unaware hoi polloi multitudes in need of unwashed enlightenment*]

See first, **NATHAN** (well his character anyhow, & what a character) must convey [*o but don't say require*] rigorous-vigorous defense of, commitment to, and respect for "our" **received, revered, and rich grand humanistic "western-euro-paean"** literary-cultural heritage, this **selective distinguished tradition** to be preserved and transmitted as valuable in deed [*o but don't say enforced upon us Nonbelievers*], indeed as if it was the first and finest [*o but don't say "the only one worth anything anyhow," altho it is*]

And second see **NATHAN** must do so in a dignified serious manner befitting this important matter. O his **rigorous righteous reserve** in conveying same, his **gracious gentility** w/ **mannered modesty,** his **verbally bowing in cultured tones,** when he danes to address us in the rank-file thru his internalized mega phone! "Rank Has Its Requirements," non? [*o but don't n-ever say "dead-wooden, poker-back, dry-stick" here*]

But let **NATHAN** be seen as complex, as having maturely "balanced opposites," grasped the Brass Wring of the Golden Mean where by "no one item in excess" (or even access)! That is, let him show the "Human[isticTradition] Touch" or Saving Grace also as he leads us on, er ah leads the tropes, er troops {Nobel-esse has its obleege, eh ja?} He is patiently-patent—*to a point*—with our own frequent mistaken objections and shear non-comprehensions; hell employ his *"Dismissive Wave-Off"* only when need-led. [*o but don't say "conscendikation from Youder Mountane Height"*]

Finally, however, let Kontroll win the day—as it must in Battles of great port. Let **NATHAN** be shorn to possesse ultimate Command, via his tactic/strategy of the *"One-Way, Force-Fit, Intrudicating Delivery-System"*! *Let him tune out all our own erroneous let alone different "alternate viewpoints"* on the Big Issues of our Cultural Salvation (and Aesthetic Refinement). Let him hold to the line via his "armoured" approach of "bunkeredly-frontating" others "all ports battered down," neigh of cresting over them, and responding to virtually all comments of ours, by his perfect-ed *"Non-Listening Over-Ride of Closed-Eye Dismissal while Intoning Yes-Yes and Mm-Hm betimes"*!.....
And if this means that Seriousness and Sobriety must triumph after all, via a "Gravity Feed" as it was, well then Levity, Humor, Comedy, alas even the Light Touch, must be casualties in this combat. [**NATHAN's actual "laugh"** (albeit rarely heard) resembles only *a gentle-genteel Hiccup or swallowed Hobble of Painfulness* against such "undisciplined squads of e-motion" as might regrettably threaten to freewheel inappropriately.....]

...and so let the selected Actor, intone forward from the Pod-iumm the Command Conference of Impervious Defense! Our Mutto: "ONE-WAY FORCE-FIT, Saves the Day, Conserves It!

...The *Script*: the 3hree Very Treue *Scenes & Acts* of the *Drama* of
"our **NATHAN,** THE [En?-] CHANTER / CANTOR":

Robert Frost's **"POLISHED"** *imagery*.....
    Henry David Thoreau's **"INSPIRATIONAL"** *counsel*.....
        Ralph Waldo Emerson's **"ENRICHING"** *insights*.....
            Herman Melville's **"ASTONISHING"** *symbolism*.....
                & Nathaniel Hawthorne's ***"especially-*UPLIFTING***"** moralities*.....

(II)   And Delivered To Us On YOUR SUMMER EUROPEAN CULTURAL TOURS Which You Led Us On :   {admittedly, *excellently*-organized; . . *& Yet*, . . :} :

-----The **TRULY IMPRESSIVE** Palaciae of the RICETAG...
-----The **MAGNIFICENT** view of the BODENZEE from a **CONSIDERABLE ELEVATION**...
-----The **RENOWNED** center of the GERMANE lead crystal industry, "where we will watch craftsmen
        etching glass with *h i g h - s p e e d* cutting wheels"...
-----The **OUTSTANDING** ceramics at VILLEROI and BOSCH...
-----The **MOST SCENIC AND CELEBRATED** region of the RHIEINE...
-----The **SPECTACULAR** flower-gardens covering the **SPACIOUS** island of MICHELIN...
-----The Cathedral a **CELEBRATED** example of Romanesque architecture; the Church an
        OUTSTANDING example of "NEON-GOTHICK"...
-----The **EXTRAORDINARILY-BEAUTIFUL** doomed church at ST. BLAGUE—newly-redecorated in
        the **CLASSIC TRADITION**...
-----The DOITSCTHUSS Museum, one of the **WORLD'S GREATEST** museums of science and
        technology. **"THERE ARE DEPARTMENTS WHICH WILL BE FASCINATING FOR EVERYONE."**
    {{ so if your not fascina-ed, its your own fault because your culturally-challenged }}

-----The **WORLD-RENOWNED** collection of **HUNDREDS, PERHAPS THOUSANDS**, of, well,
        {{shabby, gaudy, meretricious, kitsch? }} porcelain figurines...

-----The **VERY ATTRACTIVE** accommodations at our **HOTEL** include its *heated, indoor swimming-
        pools* (two of OUR OTHER HOTELS also have *heated, indoor swimming pools*)...

-----The **EXCLUSIVE** "DRY KONIG" **RESTAURANT** w/ its **REMARKABLE** menu of **SELECTED**
        local specialities **COOKED TO ORDER** and its **PRIVATE, RESERVED DINING ROOM**...
            {{ dare we hope for young serveuses "avec siens comme des pasteques,"
        plus youthful jovenes "w/ washboard abs & pecs to die for"? *Not This Trip…*}}

-----**"WE'LL ENJOY SEVERAL HOURS OF TRADITIONAL GERMAN ALPINE MUSIC WITH
        YODELLING"**... {{See you vill listen; undt miraculously you vill Enjoy }}

-----**"AFTERWARDS, WE'LL ENJOY STROLLING THE STREETS OF INDIGENOUS, UNSPOILED
        ROTWEINBERG IN THE EVENING"**... {{ Once again, that seem to mean you-all }}

(III) Then Ooooh, Those PERSONAL "SIDE TRIPS" of YOUR OWN,
Attainable Via *Your Own* **Dedicated Commitment** to the *Life of Academe*

sparkling historical **silver** chalice.....
    scintillating official **lead-crystal** decanters.....
        glowing authentic walnut **antique** cabinet.....

Hence, onward & upward
To yet more exclusive
Upgraded loftier
Entrees to VIP-type
Inner Sanctorums
--Which now speak less
of the dour studies
Of LUX ET VERITAS

On crackling parchment,
smell less of the lamp,
--Than of the GRAND LUXE
post-TENURE *carte blanche*
a susurrus on plush velvet
worn like a crown
such triumph of Academe's
SUMMER VACATIONS
which, invested properly,

become true "field research"
the fruit of our labors
in royal-purpling vineyards:
the re-finement of the High
Cultural Renaissance

    in the tip-top 5-star cupola
    on the Grand Tour steamship
    of the *IVORY-ESSE TOUR*.....

The "CFL Syndrome": *A Threat to Academic Personnel?*

[*Remorphed from* **DSM-III**, the <u>D</u>iagnostic <u>S</u>tatistical <u>M</u>anual of mental disorders; American Psychiatric Association, 3rd ed., 1994, pp. 18-08:]

14

(1) <u>SYNDROME NAME</u>: "Compulsive Fulminating Logorrhea"

(2) <u>DEFINITION</u>: <u>The tendency</u>, when in interpersonal interactions (dyads, or small groups; at work, or after hours) <u>to make **one's own** talk (and ideas) **not only prevail over, but indeed to dominate, the contributions** of the others</u> in the group... In extreme cases, to **override and truly engulf the conversation**, by a ploy of vocal "surfing" which functions to **control** group interaction in to produce massive gain of **megalomania** for the CFL PATIENT—even as such verbal "cresting" also, of course, *stuns, stunts, and blunts* any true interpersonal action for the unfortunate OTHER MEMBERS of the group)....

While harmful everywhere, CFL can become *especially deleterious in college-and-university environments*. This is because <u>true education increasingly valorizes CFL's harmonious opposite, the so-called **"fairminded" thinking style**</u>, which favors "listening truly to the other conversationalists, and responding maturely in ego-free, circumspect, cooperative fashion" (Decussor, 1990: 23).

(3) <u>SYMPTOMS</u>: This uncontrollable [?] "tendency" to "permit" [!] one's own "contributions" [?!] to dominate individuals and to mangle group communication, exhibits **many variables**. (1) The CFL patient tends to speak *more often, longer, louder, faster, and more intensely* than do the other speakers. (2) S/he more frequently both *interrupts the ongoing*, and *suppresses the emergent*, inputs of the others. (3) The behavior is "pathocrescive"; it *tends to increase and intensify* (to spike or fulminate) over the course of any group interchange (such as a one-hour committee meeting, a two-hour seminar or dinner-party, etc.) (Bombast, 1991: 35-6).

> So, soon enough, this more-*barbaric* "stacattoing" of CFL overrides and tends to suppress certain **more *civilized*-mature group traits such as: natural group pacing; communal interchanges; equal participation; and natural whole-group evolution of subject-matter.** The too-frequent "merry-mahyem" result has been called the *"deleterious vitiation"* of small-group interaction or even the *"steamroller-brutalization"* of same (Scofflaw, 1981: 424).

(4) <u>ETIOLOGY</u>: Causally, the CFL syndrome is still poorly-understood—or in any event still-vigorously debated. The "Realist" school claims CFL is caused by sheer **aggressiveness**—not to say overweening, insensitive, egotistic, self-indulgent **boorishness**. But the "Psychogenic" school sees this apparent hostility of CFL as stemming from a fundamental **insecurity** of self vis-à-vis Social Others. This latter school sees CFL thus as a classic <u>defense mechanism</u> as classically defined: "Always the purpose [of defenses] is to *reduce anxiety, avoid pain, or dismiss self-criticism*" (Blindsider, 1999: 2).

> And indeed, the content or subject-matter of group discussion is quite irrelevant. The latent operating factor is the CFL patient's need "to *establish control <u>over</u>* the others, masquerading of course as if to *offer contributions <u>to</u>* the others" (Bamboozel, 1996:68). In an extreme case, the patient was observed repeatedly to speak his/her fill—for the moment!—and then to "graciously" <u>nod or wave</u> to another member of the group who for some time had been trying, of course unsuccessfully, to interject their own thoughts, however minor and unworthy! In seeming to say *You May Proceed Now*, this "regally-kinetic kinesics" seemed to display true "charade-cooperation" as ego-aggression in fact (Hustings, 1993: 44).

(5) <u>EFFECTS</u>: Upon the *group as a whole*, paralysis commonly results. CFL can "torpedo" ("brutalize") true intra-group interaction, as discussed above. Upon *individuals within* the group, responses vary. (1) PSYCHIC INSULT is common. Some members become "bludgeoned, beat bleary-and-ragged" by the CFL's unremitting torrent of "loose-lipped lecturing." And indeed, CFL does most harm those "Cooperative Personality Types" who envision optimum group interaction as consisting of the aforementioned "fairminded" **equal-sharing of individual viewpoints and then creating of meanings slowly emerging through a meditative pace proper to the given occasion, with true empathy valued and indeed normative among all the responsive-but-also-responsible participants, who value not only turn-taking for civility, but also genuine hearing of others' viewpoints for closure.** (The "fairminded" goal is workable truth, not conquest; the method is the above turn-sharing, not mini-lectures.) Upon this group symphony, the CFL patient can indeed wreak discord. In fact, the ideal interactive group suffering a CFL individual has been described analogically as "a string quartet whose harmonic interanimated emerging improvisations risk being utterly fractured, shattered, indeed splattered by the oomphing tuba-blatt of the CFL 'soloist'" (Rodomontade & Persiflage, 1995: 54-55).

(2) DOGGED TOLERANCE also occurs. Other group-members may show less disturbance to disruption by the CFL individual, whether being *more mature about* these rough-and-tumble irruptions, or simply being *less sensitive to* them.

(3) FELLOW CFL-SUFFERERS present in the same group may, however, exhibit competitive behavior which would be risible if not so disjarring and disjuncticated. The currently-silenced CFL person may perch tensely or lean forward apopectically frustrated, exhibiting the classic "Trauma of the Up-Staged," until inevitably breaking forth in a "duelling-banjos" riff which seeks to "override the overrider" thus in a fashion initially comic, but soon all too familiar to, veteran CFL researchers (Stonewaller, unpublished telephone conversation, long distance, dialled direct, 1998, 17 mins.).

(6) INCIDENCE & DISTRIBUTION: May affect males and females equally. Some researchers, possibly biassed, seek to correlate the syndrome's distribution with (1) *"macho" males* of the traditionally-dominant and chauvinistic-paternalistic type, and also with (2) the New York City area *Jewish and other ethnic* subcultures. These researchers, however, have not supported this speculative theorizing of theirs (which in any event is POLITICALLY INCORRECT) with rigorous empiricism. (On this, note that *the single most spectacularly* "abrasive and brutalizing" case of CFL *on record in the literature*, was neither of eastern-seaboard origin, nor of Jewish extraction—but rather, occurred in "*a locale uncomfortably close to home ground*" (Billingsgate, 1999: 531).

(7) PROGNOSIS: Not surprisingly, prospects for cure are distressingly poor, since the "psychic economy" of the CFL patient "profits" so massively from perpetuating the (mis-)behavior.

And indeed, few field-researchers can fail to be impressed by the power of the syndrome to gladly-and-gleefully *feed the ego* of the CFL patient, and in double-handfuls, too. Soon indeed the observer perceives how each time the "bodysurfing" CFL patient successfully invades the others' spaces, disrupts and controls and then obliterates group-pace, and the like, s/he seems to *cathect powerfully* with the sheer *pleasure of conquest*. Hence the fever-chart acceleration noted earlier; bizarrely, each new risked-and-attained success-of-excess, *not only satisfies, but also renews the demand for*, the desired goal of audaciously overriding the others. Thus, the CFL sufferer is at one stroke *both gratified by, and stimulated into* even more, intense "dominiation" ([sic]; in Mountebank, 1993: 22). The seasoned CFL-observer soon perceives the "scripts behind" this lunging saltation: among them lie "Why Stop Now," plus "Wow, I Got Away With Launcing This Verbal Blitz, Let's See If I Can Do That Again Even More Audaciously And Ride In Cresting On Sheer Thrill of Boorish Triumphing, Wow, I Can And I Did, So Let's Try For One More Time, And Now Let's Do It Again And Again." Thus does such increasing invasiveness dismally *catalyst its own self*. In the trenchant analogy of Smithereen, "In the china-shop parlor of civilized conversation, the CFL individual can be present only as the bullish brunter that s/he is" (1997: 34).

(8) PROPHYLAXIS: What of patient awareness, attitude, and ability regarding, if not cure, at least treatment? Unfortunately, by the time seen clinically, the typical CFL sufferer has become numbed against even *realizing* his/her inappropriate behavior, as well as immobilized against *controlling* said actings-out. This is logical, for in these thrashing-and-tramping "semi-conscious repetition-compulsions," the dual etiological explanations of Boorish Pleasure and Hamfisted Defense surely conflate. And indeed, when such "over-wresting" of others proffers such satisfaction and safety when it serves both pleasure and compulsion, what counter-measures can hope to eliminate, or even reduce and control, the syndrome? Small wonder, then, that current treatment seems woefully-ineffective.

Earlier, some had recommended the tactic of **"group-countering,"** whereby the other group members responded to CFL inundation by the "levees" of defensive-affirmative counter-attackings. Subsequent trials, however, disappointingly confirmed that such is the self-refuelling mechanism of CFL to vitiate, warp, torpedo, decimate, and otherwise royally screw up any **mutually-satisfying genuine, mature, harmonious group-interaction**, that such "fire-extinguisher" techniques by others merely dim or deflect temporarily the "firestorm-torrents" of CFL. Hence the **"group-countering"** ploy seems to provide not even *palliative* relief. Or to employ a final analogy, group intervention cannot safeguard a group soil being seeded for self-paced cultivation, from the risk of trespassing tramplings upon it. No; for any significant or lasting progress, let alone cure, therein *the patient would have to minister to herself*.....

"...And Even In Your Illness, You
More Healthy than Some Others Who Remain...."

15

i.

I ring the doorbell of your beseiged domicile
(an Englishman's home his castle against challenge...)
I complete the appointment I made to visit Malady's work
in Its very process of deconstructing
this Oxbridge learning which was imported
to serve this yankee Dept well as it indeed did **and better than many others**
     ...until now you are shelved in a hospital bed in your dining room.

I see how some internally-derailling crowbar has obdurated the jaw, prised the mouth,
chiselled the teeth in the air in a fixed frieze, pursed the lips which formerly

spoke dexterous interchanges with the best of us **and better than the most which remain now.**

Now, while your breath still dusts and brushes your pulmonary corridors
(in the automatic ventilation of a library/classroom being vacated empty),

now when your bed-clothes replace the jacket and tie
you no longer disport with crisp-verve dispatch in our corridors
     but which now pause pre-marginal in a dark closet upstairs from this.

You down in a rocky grotto of pain and more pain as you lie across the chasm from us:
we can peer & shout but no longer contact **(though some of us never did).**

As Mortality spears Its railroad-spike pin in to specimen you,
you arguably the best of us, you surely as good as any of us,
to lift you right out of our midst with Its erring aim and canny care to select
     you the least deserving one of any of us to be awarded
        this premature attention-to-attrition:
        (this conversion of "your corridors" back to "our corridors").

Somehow this insurrection of the primitive-prior- eventual invading your Citadel of Intellect
can only report to me of you as lost, can overly remind me of **you as best**, of your now-finished
empolishments, of your remembrance-worthy (even *pro tem* unforgettable) achievements.

Of you as having soared so much better than most of us,
surely better than too many of your Deptl "colleagues".....

ii.

.....the *lightweights* who wagger-stagger a-wry,
the *deadwood* who lurch and stumble on
(or tilt standstill toward sanguine retirement),
whilst the good such as you stalled out youngish;
leaving too many a-wry-flipped fripperies, the genial-leaned tiltings,
a number of overdriven *yammer-outs*, the ponderosed *dismissiles*,

(though admittedly also a whole platoon of prosaic but patient plodders,
those who still do yeopersonfully husband and household our Academic Store...)

all whom aside from your memory remain.

iii.

One thing sure tho. You *almost* still ready, even here-and-now, to speak and spark **better**
than some of the rather-too-many, surely too-dour, slick-slack *malcontents* who remain

" I Think There Are Other Ways..."

[i.]

To survive at being a Deptl Chair,
a deft ploy helped save you there:
a suave tactic to help you quiet
any intrapsychic riot

you'd feel, or any distress
when students you address
who bring their explosive complaints
when they feel some course is tainted:
--when *my* course: with wrath they paint it:

My assignments, they weep, are confused;
"...and such a workload; we refuse!
and the instructor's attitude
is not one of greatest gratitude

that we actually attend, then stare
in solemn seat-time from our wooden chairs!
He asks us hard to work,
to learn to "think"—not shirk.
  But peskily he says *we* figure out
  what from the course *we* are to take out!..."

To this you bring your strategy. Just say,
to me the offending teacher, **"WELL,
I THINK THERE ARE 'OTHER WAYS' "**
.....
[by which I the over-reacher
can push my students to perform
optimally, yet within the norm
of most other, easier, courses remain?
i.e., *true gain but with no pain*?
...or anyhow, will keep complaints more sane?]

So say to me today (and past and future days)
"I THINK THERE ARE OTHER WAYS"
But *never* explicate so I could see
just *what* those fabled Ways *might be*...

[ii.]

.....and so **you sacrifice** [for your Calm;
to lavish interior Balm;
to keep yourself Anxiety-Free],
certain other values. Three:

{1} Instructor - Morale, his sense of being supported
by the institution in trying to do the best job
possible even when faced with the recalcitrant
students of *today*—the "motivationally-
challenged," I'd say....

{2} Preservation of High Standards, of the quality
education about which the University talks
much, even via pushing students to their
maximum, since true change involves often-
painful *growth* (a state which they'd *loath*).....

{3} Freedom of Individual Instructor Teaching -
Styles & Educational Philosophies, (such as
"teaching thinking") even when these do not
accord with the current-traditional or
conventional paradigm ("transmission of
knowledge"), the one more customarily *used*,
hence for students an easier sea to *cruise*.....

[iii.]

But no, I will not blame **this** Chair too much.
(whom complaints too often touched)....
The Chairship, heavy task and bitter brew,
is shouldered aptly, only by the few
who to moral duties called seem true
and who volunteer to let intrude
three years of such yeoperson servitude
disheveling their scholars' habitude:
you value well your studied Renaissance lore.
Your first term served, you said you'd do no more—
three years of Chairship burdens more than bores.
  But, when no other takers knocked upon the door,
  you dutifully kept on minding well our store!

So *kudos* to your six years of ragged days.
To carp and quibble here, seems out of phase.

[iv.]

Still, the only import of *your* famous phrase

"I THINK THERE ARE OTHER WAYS"

was cisive into *me* like augur bore,
was thus to send to *me* an old "What-For":

"Please not again, I you implore,
make me have to call you upon my floor,
make me have you darken my oaken door,
to settle out such student-stirred-up gore
before such brew might overflow, get fore-
ward-onward sent to CHANCELLOR's Store....."

The Philosophers' WALK [or, Sh-AMBLE]

[1.] "*Sometimes* their reason—*at other times* their prejudices or superstitions; often their social affections, not seldom their antisocial ones, their envy or jealousy, their arrogance or contemptuousness: but most commonly their desires or fears for themselves—their legitimate or illegitimate self-interest....[and] class interests, and its feeling of class superiority." [--*J.S. Mill, On Liberty*]

[2.] "...the major *obstacles or blocks to rational thinking*: prejudice, bias, self-deception, desire, fear, vested interest, delusion, illusion, egocentrism, sociocentrism, and ethnocentrism." [--*Richard Paul, philosophy/critical thinking*]

[3.] "We **are**, *indeed*, '**reasonable**'—just exactly as 'reasonable' as our *emotions allow* us to be..." [--*current-traditional*]

(I): Home-Groan Homilies:

"**Philosophy,**
is *marvelous*....

....it can get you *anywhere*
you want to go....."

Holding classes in the Student Union,
HE leans toward his students..
HE so attentively intent & concerned,

that *you just know* (or soon learn),
that HE, just, wants to *help* them;,
to *see* it, to *get* it **just, right!**

O Philosophy
can get you *anywhere* you want to go:
you can "**rright-Reason**" your way to
anywhere

heck HE can, absolutely-fabulously,
decimate the querulous forts
of "EXTREMIST FEMINISM"
{which of course *is* Feminism}

Helped by Albert Ellis' ammunition
of "***Rational-Emotive*** [Psycho-] ***Therapy***"
[which reveals that it's our [bad] *thoughts*
(and not those unruly Emotions)
which cause our psychic torquings]
HE can just *think* right, to act & *be* right
  [stay sunny up daylight never night,
  think HIS feeble-faible-ous flickering sight
  of Cave-shadows be day-night...]

"can get you *anywhere* you might"....
  [A slandering Gossiper of him made light,
  Said Heck HE can even ankle HIS way right
  into ***another mans wife*** at night,
  so justified of mental moving watertight]

[Platonic, I merely marvelled that he felt that best
his students *by **exclusive multiplechoice*** he'd test...]

Philosophy O, & Right Reason so
can get you *anywhere,* high or low!
  [cling to the Summit, fear Below,
  skate iffily on film, HE'll never *Know*]

(II): Konference Kapers:

.....& not 10 mins. after **YOU** in **YOUR** Keynote
Talk had condemned "**Selfish,**" & touted
"**Fairminded,**" **THINKING,**
  {..."**Selfish**" being the using of brainpower to win
  over one's opponents instead of objectively seeking
  The Truth (or *toward* a *valid* truth...) ...&
  "**Fairminded**" being the acknowledging of one's
  Own Biasses and also hearing The *Other* Side
  empathetically-willingly-nondefensively,}

.....**YOU** then wheel out **YOUR** Grand Scheme
of "Sources of Knowledge" or somelike--
but at core, it's a paean to clean **Reason**
as the **only** way we really **do** think things....

& then when *I* raise *my* hand to suggest
that from this arsenal you've *rather omitted*
the whole big engine of ***Rationalizing***
as one more propulsion of thinking
which, like it or not, *exists*....

...O how, then, at once **YOU** turn defensive,
to full-blast right back to me publically
(in full-bore, scarce-"Fairminded," fervency)
a "lively and vivid" Correction:
  an *impassioned* defense of *no-passion*
  an *emotional denial* of *emotionality*
  an *unreasonable* touting of Reason
  as not only The Only Way **To** Go,
  but also as The Only Game We **Do** Play.....

....Well, ya know, I really wondered,
whether any *other* of the Conference attendees
(yeah the other 159 of 'em, beside *myself,*)
espied this as a grand "irony of ironies"

namely, a *usurping* of Reason
right within Rationality's very citadel
by that old Fifth-Columnist **emotion**!,
infiltrating, Of All Places,
Reason's own-very "sanctum sanctorum"?!

.....Afterwards, a woman to me did lean,
and disgustedly hiss, "*Never* have I seen
more **closedmindedness** than *his* scene!"
  [But she, a Woman;, perhaps not serene?;
  maybe "Rationally-Emotionally" epicene?]

I, was dead-right, of-course;
spot-on accurate as always....
(Tho heck, "Nobody's always prefect"....)
Still, "**What DID *YOU*, Know?**"

  No test can testify to scrutiny,
  an "**expert's** *true* **expertise**".....
  "The *larger* spheres will always stay
  subjective, to the utmost day".....

LEONARD, OUR FRIENDLY CUSTODIAN...

...OF CORRIDORS [AND OF CUSTOMS] QQUOTIDIAN...

"HE WOULD LIKE TO SEE ME CLEANING LATRINES:
I WOULD LIKE TO SEE HIM REMOVED TO SOME OTHER PLANET"
[--W. H. Auden, "Horae Canonicae, 5. Vespers"]

<u>You</u> boorish blue-collar babbitt
you jolly-raucous america-firster
[your car festooned with stickers
--"Proud To Be An American"
--"Proud Parent Of A Navy Son"
   your work-cart decorated
   with christian cross & the
   american flag of *course*]

you've had **four years now** to relearn
that I am "the same person I always was"
since that summer you espied in my office
perhaps the sub-versive *Logos*
   of the GAY-LIB EDUCATIONAL MATERIALS,
more probably those per-versive *Ikons*
   those PIX OF DUDES, massive & tender
   [the majestic drawing by michelangelo
   the cezanne, eakins, cadmus swimmers
   a toothsome poster from filmdom]:
...green graphics I posted to oasis a bit
the hot dry desert I inhabit

<u>but</u> for four unchanging years now
your glance has been filmed over sour
with that fathersmilk cataract of queer-fear!
   strong malegaze sudden gone distant
   hostile & fearful at once
   accusatory but stunned careful
   as a forest animal at glades edge
your study ilk seems scared crapless
by me whom youd brand as featherweight!
you think i could torpedo your *son*?
you think id monkey with *you*??

<u>but</u> i *do* seem to be *No Educator*
since for **four full years now**
my continuing genialities
my constant attempts toward rapport
my extra-mile phatic chatting
   { "...be gentle and keep
   talking and acting free...." }
are met with Bigotrys obstinance
yes are lessons forever lost
on your great stone prognathous fartface

<u>but</u>, tho *you* havent learned a *thing*
(your sidewise shunnings now permanent),
still *you have* taught *me, so* much
about "NON-VERBAL COMMUNICATION"!
(all of ch eight in intro-to-speech)
--yr "PARALANGUAGE" gruffs things forever
--yr "PROXEMICS" defends you with armor
--yr "KINESICS" moves arthritic always
while to all *other* corridor-colleagues but me
your simian visage still barks out
that air-horn macho of your greeting:
   "GOOD MORNIN THER SIR
   HOWS THE WORLD TREATIN YOU
   THIS MORNIN"
[....you, all-unaware, pinging the 3 or 4
other fags & dykes on "your" floor!]

<u>so</u> should I slap a pink triangle (w/ glee)
on your work-cart so that the images you see
are an unholy trinity of three?
but no, a lost lesson it would be indeed,
you forever knowing only zilch & *ze-*
ro about what "america" is & should be
and in fact *your* best niche in History
   **would be to sport a brownshirt
   in the Fatherland in the Thirties**

<u>and</u> i cannot say i prefer
your daily & dour dust-off
of me as a sub-human "non-person"
to the "response" of a *few* of my colleagues:
their "liberal tolerance" veils thinly
their "annihilation by blandness"
...but, such decorous half-hiding of distaste
will at least soft-cushion its impact,
is at least CIVILITYS SMALL OASIS;
unlike *your* pitting & pocking SIROCCO
which spackles the never-cleaned grime
of *your* always-smudged & soiled Corridor

onto my diurnal Veranda...

which you *can't* make *fully* SAHARA...!

"SON - of - ERNIE"
In His OFFICE....

[I]

"Swarthy." "Quietly Commanding."
Well, I mean, *the self is assuredly masculine*....
"Likes the women a lot" (p-addles about
in the Secretarial Pool,;
in his natural habitat thus,
it would seem..)

Strong. Strong-
ly addicted to *tabac*
en form de OOPS EXCUSE
MY FRENCH! tobacco in form of
fags OOOPS EX-CUUUUSE MY
BRITISH! <u>cigarettes</u>.
Probably the strong brands.
His presence Commands.

Oh, & he's the Deptl Hemingway Man:
"Yeah, Hemingway's the man...."
Articles on Papa by you his fan.
Well, you match Ernie's own Sports-Tan
& also his emotional expressiveness, man

Over Thirty & Unmarried,
& the reason's plain to see:
"likes the women a lot"
or so it would seamly

And, athletic!
(At the Dept'l Retreat, had to handle his pacifying baseball glove body-part-close.)
Office festooned with framed photos of sports heroes—
though <u>I</u> for One { but "you know *me*, Al-bertine!" }
would rather work at <u>my</u> desk without
an 8" x 10" image of some gross All-Star lout
swinging his outside bat in <u>my</u> face—
I would nature-ally prefer snaps of, [say],
ALLEN GINSBERG, oh and [say] the young star
FABIAN! in his hot & fresh-faced prime—
...but which quite inexplicably are the very ones there
which **Ernieson** permits to decorate his Office Door lair.
Which Fluff however's counterweighted well by the Joshy stuff:
the yacky "Commendation" the Secretaries wrote him up,
his **verility** holding them in *de-rigeur* Thrall?
to prevail the Boy-Girl stuff after all

[II]

O, but <u>he</u> "knows" *me*! For, one summer day,
<u>no sooner than</u> down the corridor my longhair flying,
in my windsuit of brief gymshorts & tanktop
(I transgressing *sartorial* norms *also*, in my middle age),
{having quite some time ago utterly re-closeted
my dour masculine-armor suitings,

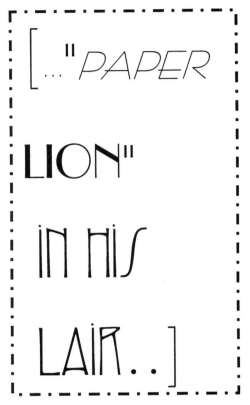

[..."*PAPER*
LION"
IN HIS
LAIR..]

tho never to debut into drag either}
did I characteristically fling & bop,
saying "Hi" easily enuf, my voice free from Gruff,
to him in his privy orifice entre-taining the two 2 Secretaries,—

Well, no sooner than *that*, did his talk suddenly for the nonce halt,
then fall to a whisper, clearly firing off an [by-me-unheard] slurry **jest** at *my*
(A) androgyny, (B) gender-unRoleing, (C) frank faggotry, Select Several!
For, right then out of the door, leaned "SARAH" (her pretty head coiffed with NotMuch inside)
to grin a silent **jeer**, at my so unsportsManlike
& Light-in-the-Loafers, "Mister Natural" **Queer**-
ness! (**ERNIESON** thus gaining his macho-points at my expense, steely;
{{but i *luuve* it o **mary**, how *Utt*erly *Faaaaa*bulously "Retro-Fit"/**FIFTIES** *reeaallly*!!}}

But this is now, the Out-'n'-About Nineties, so I did quickly to him Intercom back,
the best three of "T. Hachtsman's" cartoons from Gertrude's Follies (as in Stein & Toklas)
the trio which pinwriggled to the wall, "Hemingway's Homophobia" for once & all:

> Was it something that we said?
> Or was it something in his head?
> We threaten his manhood.
> He thinks we're no good....
> Larry, Phil, Dusty, Bernie; Every-
> body Knew But Ernie....
> Tell me Pussy Is That the Reason?
> Perhaps it's homophobia season.
> Did he say "Golly Gee! Homosexuality!"?
> Why did Hemingway run away?....

And *my* boomeranging there his served volley with such Flair,
did seem to make his Gruff Haut more rare,
did seem to make him greet *me* with more care,
{ not that *I*'d paw with that lame bear.... }

And "sexist macho pig" *(sotto voce)* to me did purr
my colleague-in-arms "KATE," when to her
the above Macho-March Role-Strut I did report:

...could she, for one other, see *Cavort*, as *Contort*....?

[III]

Well heck, never down at the Paris cafes
did the likes of MARCEL, OSCAR, and TRUMAN
lie down together & mediate
w/ the diss-likes of **Ernie**
  [who, it is said, when spying fairies in his café, would shatter
  available wineglasses at a furious rate & rent & tatter]
....let alone ever co-habitate....

Still, our "Junior Papa" here apparently does teach, write, and committee very
"SENSITIVE" well, for onto the moving belt of the "TO" Tenure-Track he ascends
"DIVERSITY" in his turn, so there must be
"TODAY" some **there** there, *wouldnt you say gertrude*??

[IV]

Me?, *I* just **keep on truckin'**, Babe,
afloat via both cool Zen & warm-brothering *gai* Yen;
and, corridor-cruising, *I* slap a High-Five toward fab FABE,
that lambda-lamb-bro who's dis-guarding the Paper Lion's Den

CRISPED UP INTO the WRY of PSYCHO - DESICCATION ...

Seems that the machine of Intellect
needs more than raw-electric I.Q. ...
Needs also some oil, salve, or balm
to smooth its action; a ration
against *decadent desiccation*?
Against the seeds of *stunting*
embryonic germs from the beginning?

Oh started off SPRIGHTLY all right,
young instructor, mid-twenties,
LIVELY RESPONSIVE, married then,
good IDEALIST, discussed directly,
social issues of moral value,
(e.g., "the media's distortion of gays")
before it was easily the fashion...

Always well-WITTY; but then became
a bit more dryly arch & waspish?
resisted a closer friendship with me
he agreed would be "quite logical, considering"
and "couldn't really understand why
we weren't closer as friends,"
a distance I then judged was my fault;
though self-searching found no such mote
that should have wrenched closed the gears
of interactive Colleague-friendship

Divorced. SHARED WITH ME WILLINGLY
my inquiries about "Alternate Life-Styles,"
nay even certain of the variant Paraphilias
but *shied away from my invitation*
to further Scenario I came to think
was "wholly appropriate considering".....

Humor became *more jaded and flippant,
cynical-weary* beyond his years?
from *some high ground of dismissal*,
some *arch-ing back-wards in-flexible*?

Willing to disqualify Seriousness now,
mocking Ritual, and deCamping
from Seriousness by *stagy poses*
among others so Dispossessed

Sought too-distant country retreats
to "get away as far as possible"
from people, but why?
Already seemed too *long-distance awry*.....

But during a cross-country road-trip
with a mutual friend, allegedly "distanced"...
So was *wafted lighter away*
from focus, serious stancing,
unanchored by *evaporation*?

Nor grew Idealism's garden.
Removed from his car's rear fender
A bumper-sticker for the Cause
which a wry-radical friend said he'd implanted.
Removed from the same space later
a one-inch micro-edition of same

Avoided attending my presentation
on "teaching thinking in English"....
his excuse patently red-faced,
but why such need for evasion?

According to a friend's child, his student,
he now became dogmatic in classes,
at least on this social point, that social issue,
or the other social concern....

Serving as interim committee-chair,
demonstrated appropriate modulation,
judicious reasoned balance
(along with saving wry humor),
but why this *hesitation-balk* elsewhere too,
this *refrainment from revelation*
even in interpersonal spheres later?

Why *crisp up awry? Dry out brittle?*

Seems the machine of INTELLECT
needs more than raw-electric I.Q.;
needs also some oil, salve, or balm
to smooth its action—a ration
against *decadent desiccation*?
against the seeds of *stunting*
unseen-embryonic from the beginning?
  Nor education, nor life-living, is antidote
  to *malaise* portended outward
  from idiotrinsic wellsprings

Well the army of INTELLIGENCE
the crusade of EDUCATION
the enterprise of ACADEME
must be campaigned by footsoldiers
all too inhumanely-human
this raw material of Homo Sapiens
whose "sportscar"-brainpower
is careened by wild-child juggernaut
the common tragedy being that

in his case and that of others to see,
as I myself have experienced scarily

  sheer *CEREBRALITY*,
  non-guarantees *MATURITY*

Ill-Rounded CHARACTER

[Characters in fiction are "flat" (types; caricatures; "constructed around a single idea or quality") or "round" (exhibit multiple traits, even contradictory and conflicting ones). Round characters represent the complexity of reality better than do flat or type characters.]
[--from E. M. Forster, <u>Aspects</u> of <u>the</u> <u>Novel</u>]

i.

A credentialled scholar-teacher,
who quickly became Full professor;
politically, an idealist-Seeker;
of local wrongs, an Expresser...

But never came to life in class?
Your students wore that gaze-of-glass
in your office-conferences dour.
Your evaluations even poorer.
And rarely a title that I'd mention
had you read; had you full intention?

ii.

A married family man
with a four-child span;
then divorced, but remaining greatly supportive of his ex-mate...

But who split, to explore "sexual fantasies"
for 13 years with younger "Ruth"...
Who never discussed that spate with me,
although self-defined as sharer-of-truth.
And when I inquired about their pairing,
He thought I meant only erotic sharing!
(Whose daughters later charged abuse...)

iii.

In "New Age" revelry,
proud to be "vulnerable," to "disclose";
A Buddhist convert (tho why on the Q.T.),
and a masseur: oil on the clothes!...

But forever such a control-freak,
that when daily tensions would peak,
you'd employ your Meditation,
but alas only in band-aid fashion...

iv.

An intended male feminist,
he'd see his flaws realistic...

But "CATHERINE" would insist
that to her you became sadistic...

v.

Saw the great value to me,
of my own psychotherapy...

But except for a few dry-hour runs,
you stayed self-assured <u>you</u> needed <u>none</u>...

vi.

To me, *truly was* a Best Friend:
concerned *and* supportive without end
he *did* Care *and* Counsel blend...

...Until—was I maturing apace,
but at too threatening a pace?—
tacitly you locked your door to my face,
with no explicit "Closure" of grace...
Hear this: if <u>you</u> didn't like that <u>I</u> am GAY,
that's <u>fine</u>, but <u>say</u>: don't just Waft Away!
Later, even said you had no interest
in giving my case <u>any</u> inquest...
Told me to please keep free
of any psychological comments to Thee!

vii.

Thus, for all the good residual
in head above, hand-heart below,...

You stayed an Unfinished Individual,
"leaving no footprints in the snow"...

viii.

Is it more pity, short of hate,
that toward you is appropriate?
How to reckon up your fate?...

How much does one have responsibility
(if one is to be called mature & free)
to face and fight one's disabilities
which impacted others harmfully?
<u>Could</u> you have come yourself to see?

...How separate is "mere" Pathology,
from poisoned Evil on a spree?

In the Novel of the Life we lead,
you a tangled volume one <u>could</u> read,...

Your character us others did perplex.
Sadly for all sakes too complex.
On us others and on your self a hex.

ANIMAL RITES:

...OR, THE ENDANGEROUS SPECIE

i.

**She has to save the world,
the whole world.....**

pre-ageing into a dourly-certain settlement,
she suffers the little creatures who suffer.
---rabbits as cosmetics test-subjects;
---chickens be/headed toward our tables;
---calves raised in narrow closets—
who come to her to be defended.

Publically in our office-corridor voluntarily,
she dresses-down a colleague's fur coat!

**...She has to conserve the environment,
every bit and piece and patch of it**

--She bandwagons us to sign ardent petitions.
--She excoriates our styrofoam cups.
--She counsels us about our diets,
  says mushroom not pork should give protein.
--For a pet, she rejects the cat;
  disappreciates my tiger's wildness,
  favors the more docile (needful?) house-rabbit
  to receive her intense (selfless?) mildness.

ii.

She has to save the world, all the world
...But in her calm-driven, dutiful fervor,
I feel she's melting down true EDUCATION
upon her bessemer-alter of INDOCTRINATION?

Does she mistreat her students "like animals,"
abuse them toward IDEOLOGY thus?
She does feedlot The TRUTH on hunting:
In a world of subtle complexities, students
can now know that this issue's quite simple.
Did you know it's amazingly one-sided?
Oh, she "discusses only the anti-hunting side,"
because students (she says) come in pre-fortified
with knowing the *pro*-hunting's arguments:
vile and snide stands she can deride....

[*But* by Minerva, do they *really* know,
all about, & why, what they *think* they know?
--far more likely they just blat out
what their culture's FOLKWAYS tout...
...here, she and I do "face-off" once more,
two Great Goals of Education tangling sore?
In my classes, difficult social issues we view
by scrutinizing all sides in equal purview;
the better, not to arrive at one-sided Truth,
but to sharpen the Pure Thinking tooth.
Wherever *my* students end up is fine,
just so they know how to draw the line
of Clear Thinking on the best straight roll,
for *their* goals not mine—*my* course's goal...]

Thus with my "insightful bias" do **I accuse**
that within the very citadel of ACADEME,
there dwells a Fifth-Columnist of ORTHODOXY.
There, a Vegan foodstuffs upon a PROPAGANDA
which lacks the vital B-12 of balance...

"*I WANT TO STOP HUNTING,*" she proclaims.
(**...not only noble, but proper to disclose it.**
But, to pursue it via classroom-as-platform?
Tho Extremist myself, I demur as Purist here.
My passion: I'd monitor Pure Passions.
I ask: in the abattoir of her classroom,
Does Validity get bloodily slaughtered?)

iii.

--It's as mere "coffee-table trivia"
that she dismisses a History of Hunting,
rejects it for library-acquisition.
It's seemingly sober and scholarly,
(from Harvard University Press no less)
but maybe too objective for her thus:
That issue drew between the two of us
another tooth-&-claw fray in the corridor!...

--When she said that she'd award grade of "A"
to a well-written pro-hunting student paper,
I hyaened grossly to her face! Thus became I,
so *reasonably irrational* against her dismissive
of Validity which questions her PET MISSIVE.

[My Full Disclosure, Admission, Confession:
As gay "semi"-activist, I must confirm yes,
I <u>do</u> "deal with homophobia in my classes."
But only in the Thinking Unit, whose goal
is <u>not</u> to spoon students *my* biassed TRUTH,
<u>but</u> how to **think** clearly, accurately,
about *any* half-known and delicate issue...
So, I surely do assign the gay-lib propaganda
(PFLAG pamphlets; Carl Wittman's "manifesto")

but also anti-queer statements as well...
("Dr. Laura" the ranter; Cal Thomas' smug banter).
Predictably, I dismantle the biassed latter,
their stereotype-defending chatter,
but I also scrutinize the suspect former.
For the Gay Task Force's line, tho well-meaning,
still sprouts Questionable Leanings...
.....The goal here, that each student arrive
not at an IDEOLOGY but at an **Ability**.
Not at a sanitized "tolerance/acceptance" connived,
but at the skill to **think** through with facility
one's *own* solid stand free from debility.....]

iv.

---She seems genuinely vexed and perplexed
if others critique as extremist
her office-door "educational" materials.

---All colleagues by now give her a wide path
thru the woods of her peregrinations.

---In the "fur-free zone" office she encamps.
(Having curiously had the walls repainted
from sun-daffodil, to greyed-down off-white...)

v.

But she has to save the world entire
-True all is not right with the world.
-But no it never will or can be saved.
-But is all right within her own world?
-And if that ever would be made right,
if she could ever save her own self's world,
would her dour need still break through
to try to save the world, the whole world?
Would not all then be right enough
with the world she seeks to save,
  for her to save only her own Garden-part,
  and not the Planet entire, let alone that
  via her scrupulous-scurrying SALVATION
which (ironic) endangers true EDUCATION?

vi.

[Nor do I think that **I** always rode free
from the Malady maybe infecting JUDY.
Too well I know now, how my earlier teaching
too often exuded some bilious preaching
of IDEOLOGIES not yet done leaching
through my own soil, so to purity reaching...

"Having been there," I can only commend
the journey toward a Personal Ecology:
Distill noxious pollutants, breathe more free...
<u>This *Getting Clear*'s</u> <u>a</u> <u>trek</u> <u>without</u> <u>an</u> <u>end;</u>
<u>but</u> <u>start</u> <u>it</u> <u>now,</u> <u>as</u> <u>every</u> <u>milestone</u> <u>mends</u>....]

[1.]

Serene as a queen   with oceanliner dignity
SHE glided "stress-free" ; she'd seance "tranquil-calm" apparent...
but actually, self-stunned into the relaxation
        (but I saw this, only-too-late-r)
of an arthritis of *defensiveness*
of a panacea-façade of *protection*...
but against what darkness?
        (But who suspected anything such, back then?)
against what danger?
        (...**Only** <u>HER</u> *suicide* **two years later, could semaphore all**)
against what demon?
        (Some Colleagues still comprehend little of it)
    against the undertow which dragged HER down,
    which ripppled even then HER surfaces....)
        (as I see now in terribly-tardy retrospect...)

Such a calm unbroken mask YOU wore,
    (as if maquillaged tranquil in heavy makeup)
as *might* seem to befit YOU the Poetess of the Simple,
"just the moment itself seen pure-quiet-intense,"
this indeed YOUR motivation:
        (I now comprehend only with Hindsight)
but no freed journey to the Arcadia of Aesthetics,
but a failed escape-attempt from,
the **Demon of Depression** which did devour YOU...

So the whole roster of YOUR Reactions gone so swirling contorted,
    of YOUR Responses warping so wayward-haywire-batbrained,
of YOUR Reasoning-strands twisting all so loopy,
now visible (too late) as the actions
of a genteelly-desperate dogpaddle
to seek to float above the Undertow,
an attraction later lethal....

So troubled SHE was by everyday's ripples
    which however (I should have read sooner and better, alas)
were no balmy breeze-from-above to blush the waters,
but boiling riptide from below to scar turbulent...
    WE mostly missed HER listing drift
    WE all but overlooked the shift
    of HER wayward rift toward beneath.....

[ii.]

And how to say? Expository as Essay, or dramatically as Story? Well, no matter.
For the waves crash shorewards to the seemingly-inevitable sorry-ending clatter....

Abstracted Up into the Cloudy Country of the Conceptual...:

-Utter **misperceptions**, some so apparently based upon gross projections onto others of one's own unconscious hostile and depressed feelings...

-Vast **generalizations** supported only by scant or insufficient-unrepresentative evidence samples, or evidence apparently misinterpreted via defense.....

-**Premature conclusions** easily slid-into, with no suspending of judgment or withholding of final conclusions....

-Statements whose **unconsidered inferences or logical extensions**, *actually disqualify* the original stated position and, indeed, support the *opposite or opponent's* views…..

-Statements **illogically contradictory** to other statements made elsewhere in *one's own* discourse….

-Statements whose **convolutions** defy even more of this sort of categorization of *logical confusion, wandering unreason*…..

…or, Precipitated Down to the Concrete Terrain of "Specific Instances":

-Says SHE **"sort of assumed"** it was I who posted all the anti-administration complainings plus all the anti-student jibes on the bulletin board. (When in fact I didn't. I complained less than many did. Or commented via a sunny satire which others liked. Plus, I for one always savored teaching… Ah, well….)

-Says a male nude photo in my office might have been off-putting to students. (When genitals were covered> When artistry was present? And anyhow when it was posted mainly during the semester I was on leave?)

-Said I re-duplicated a notice (of student writing awards) SHE posted—"I recall an interest in the bulletin board" (Well yes. If you post a newspaper article of student writing awards *plus the half-page ad for refrigerators on the rest of the newspaper page*, it's not as visually-appealing as you yourself, the artist, should have done, is it now? So I halved the length, doubled the focus…)

-Says a photo on the board showing two camels copulating, *"is indicative of my sensibility."* (Whoa, I'm more suave and raffiné than that! Plus it bore LEE CLARKSON'S distinctive, telltale orthography anyhow!)

-Says SHE became "wary of me" after hearing that I vigorously criticized the work of capable-but-underperforming students. (She prefers to give them "sympathy," and "verify their abilities"… *Okaay. Fiine*…..)

-In fact said I was "depressed, anxious, hostile," and contributed to an atmosphere of "turmoil, conflict, and malaise." (When all the others said I was never more sanguine and exuberant now, after my own earlier sick-leave…)

-Says my presence was everywhere, with artwork, cartoon-faces, and the like, becoming "too dominant in a space used by many," and that I should "clean up the clutter and **calm down.**" (While partly too true indeed—one can unintentionally over-contribute, at least I did—still, others appreciated the attempts at embellishment. Plus, I'd scarcely think that CHINESE LANDSCAPES, OLD BOOK PAGES, and WOODCUTS are irritating…..)

-Says that the visual on my office door which **the administration charged was pornographic**, was **"innocuous to the point of obscurity."** (Exactly *my* point, *my* logic! Therefore why their censorship? And why not a legitimate complaint on my part? Let's hear it for *Bat-Brained Logic*…)

-Says my boxes and bookcases in the corridor, while moving offices earlier, also caused "turmoil and conflicts," and many complaints. (….This even after I had reminded her that I had no other choice. I worked as fast as I could. And I actually posted a short public note of apology on the offending materials…)

-Admits SHE removes material from the board which "bums HER out" negatively, replaces them with so-positive items which "give HER a jolt of energy," but "worries whether SHE'd be accused of censorship" in so doing. (An insight at last, but no—not when we truly understand you. Simply self-medication….)

-Asked, "why don't you [= myself] seek more soothing surroundings?" (Something SHE herself could create for herself, *neither* externally, *nor* internally, it seems; alas…..)

___ __ _ --- -- - ≡≡≡ ≡≡ ≡ ∼∼∼ ∼∼ ∼ ^^^ ^^ ^ *

[iii.]

And so, lacking Tranquillity and seeking it in vain, propelled by Defenses not decided direction,
SHE drifted on until right into HER Maelstrom-End... And only later and too late did I fully see HER pain.
See how HER calm gliding walk, was but weak clench against shock."
See how HER seeking outer Peace & Quiet, was HER thin shield against inner Riot.
...and, see how HER "haywire-batbrained" Misreadings of (so-valuable, so-unworthily-insulted) **ME**,
were only-too-faible Copper-Armorplate against such vile-gnawing Serpents in HER particular Sea ...

So I confirm my too-tardy surmise, of HER regrettable Awrys, and alas only-in-hindsight...
   ...but I radar now **my own** ongoing blindsights? *Why* this my own propulsion-compulsion,
   this thrust to shake-and-worry out, HER Misinterpretation, of my own (Oh-So-Good) Intentions?
Yes, *why* must I distill out from *Seewasser*, all this false-gold here of HER Projections & Transferences?
How I here had to so-nastily strain to sieve and diss-splay, all her skewed deposits of reality, but *why*?

YOU now sun-set calmed from all; I semaphore salute from afar. I in wisped fog must yet cross safe a bar.

"IN & OUT OF THE ROLES— but Never Free of the Grease-Paint...."

{{ i. }}

BUT your <u>Floating-&-Gliding across the boards of
the Deptl PROSCENIUM-corridors always **IN ROLE**</u>—
   [for isnt Life so much like a Drama after all,
   for gosh "arent we all like people in a Play"—
   except should you be self-Staged each,all,every day?]
Your <u>Smile so "glad-eyed" but always fixed so
   showy-defensive,</u>
Your <u>Continuous MONOLOG</u> so glad to UPSTAGE <u>us,</u>
to STEP pre-emptively upon any of <u>our</u> LINES
(we colleagues not your troupe, just your audience!),
and your <u>Eyes</u> scarcely ever meeting ours

{{ ii. }}

...You never contact *mens'* boy-blues anyhow.
When you and I talk, your eyes orbit hysteric.
You prefer to parade onstage the piddling poodle
of Feminist lines RECITED as if from Script...
[*Why* does just simple male/female dialog,
for *you,* embody some *insufferable* analog?]
So you try fine, to step on <u>my</u> every line;
nip off <u>my</u> projected thought to ought,
you grossed by a gentle, if stubbly, "Male Extruding"?
This *might* seem like the needed, proper Feminist
   correction...
except, via your so-over-reacting SOUND-SYSTEM
   erection?
(My simple request for, say, some literary reference
   or other
provokes you to a Theatric of Disarray-Display--
bestirs in you, petticoats of ruffled Confusion,
as if I'd cruelly stentorianed "NO, Ma'am!
(Or created fluffling bustle of worse Intrusion.)
Or alarmed you as if I'd banngged on the backstage
   sheet-metal which creates thunder in profusion.
(All my affect thus affecting you so unsoundly,
you by my sound-effects alarumed too roundly?)

{{ iii. }}

You've GOT YOUR PART DOWN so pat,
that *not only* I can't "interrupt"
   [to Grab Power as of course don't all Males do...]
but also we can't even AD-LIB contribute
to your one-sided SOLILOQUY,
can't penetrate the suit-of-armor wicket
of your ongoing racket;
   you made yourself quite impenetrable to
   treacherous rapier-ripostes and such munition,
   but in the process also invulnerable to true
   DIALOGING-DUETS in addition?

{{ iv. }}

You do sole-loquacity in STAGE-WHISPER Asides,
never free from the pancaked-on protection
you seem to feel you need against—**detection**?
Or your pirouetting DANCE I think must lance
on some hard ice-rink of—soft **terror**?
You masqued by the MAKEUP, an uneasy takeup,
propelled by an Ur-script of—**fear**?
   And, not the least, does some BACKSTAGE **Beast**
FRIGHTWIG - Puppet you all Season?

{{ v. }}

Oh, you <u>can</u> ACT NATURAL-ly "Gracious"!
(You can and might be Real, but don't/won't/can't?)
(Your TRAGIC FLAW, of which you're non-sagacious?)
For, I have seen you play "Mature"—but only, alas,
as a second-ary MINOR SUPPORTING ROLE (lost lass?).
Yes; for, at one Info-&-Introduction meeting,
"all business" to forward Departmental-greeting,
you <u>did</u> face us out-of-ROLE, *only this once* free
of that protective armor of GREASE-PAINT...
and really great: (not too prim-demeure, either),
just wholly PROJECTING the new-to-you role
of "Own Mellow Self" at <u>last</u> (**tho it *didn't last*...**)

{{ vi. }}

So why not get OFF BOOK, UNDERSTUDY <u>yourself</u>?
That *just might* lead, to your BIGGEST BREAK YET!
<u>Don't</u> TYPECAST yourself as your Ruled Roles only.
I wish you well: ease down "OFF-STAGE" at last.
Wear your Skin thin; yr STAGE-FRIGHTS safely past.

   {{ Nor can <u>I</u> here throw stones (or rotten tomatoes):
   <u>I too</u> have OVERPLAYED melodrama; one hot potato,
   broadcasting overSHOWiness as defensive perimeter,
   soreing <u>myself</u> too high by any altimeter,
   during <u>my</u> WAITING-IN-THE-WINGS APPRENTICE-time
   before LANDING that MAJOR ROLE of—My **Self** }}

So here's the last PROMPT I'd give you:
Walk naked from PROPS and BUSINESS at last.
Try for less fury from the thin-tin thunder-board,
seek more **sound effects**, than just SOUND-EFFECTS.

...'cause you might have it in yourself to develop a
   true role later—or now...

& ALSO 'CAUSE, IN *ANY* CASE, THIS-HERE
"HALL of *ACADEME*" OF *OURS*, ISNT THE
BLOODY *THEATRE* DEPT ANYHOW, IS it now

--Images, *Choisis Et Cheris,* de ~~VOUS~~

MOI - **Meme** *Si* "GRANDISSIME"!!

--Reflets Au Miroir *Vrai-et-Fidele* de

~~VOUS~~ - *MOI* - **Meme**, *Si*

"MAJESTIQUE" !! ....Mais, RestantToujours,
Surtout et Partout, **Si** ["*Comme-Il-Faut*"]

"**MODESTE,**" **Sans Doute**...c'est bien le

"ME - **Myself**" *magnificent!*

[**1.**]　[**on interviewers of himself:**] It's not that they mean to be malicious. They are just dumb and out of dumbness they miss things. <u>I could do a much more devastating piece about myself than they could,</u> and I wouldn't mind doing it. At least it would be the right kind of devastation.

[--Gore Vidal, in <u>Sexually Speaking</u>, 1999; underlining added]

[**2.**]　....As an example of what we must try to examine [**how an individual stage-manages the impression he seeks to make on others**], I would like to cite at length a novelistic incident in which Preedy, a vacationing Englishman, makes his first appearance on the beach of his summer hotel in Spain:

But in any case he took care to avoid catching anyone's eye. First of all, he had to make it clear to those potential companions of his holiday that they were of no concern to him whatsoever. He stared through them, round them, over them—eyes lost in space. The beach might have been empty. If by chance a ball was thrown his way, he looked surprised; then let a smile of amusement lighten his face (Kindly Preedy), looked round dazed to see that there *were* people on the beach, tossed it back with a smile to himself and not a smile *at* the people, and then resumed carelessly his nonchalant survey of space.

But it was time to institute a little parade, the parade of the Ideal Preedy. By devious handlings he gave any who wanted to look a chance to see the title of his book—a Spanish translation of Homer, classic thus, but not daring, cosmopolitan too—and then gathered together his beach-wrap and bag into a neat sand-resistant pile (Methodological and Sensible Preedy), rose slowly to stretch at ease his huge frame (Big-Cat Preedy), and tossed aside his sandals (Carefree Preedy, after all).

The marriage of Preedy and the sea! There were alternative rituals. The first involved the stroll that turns into a run and a dive straight into the water, thereafter smoothing into a strong splashless crawl towards the horizon. Quite suddenly he would turn on to his back and thrash great white splashes with his legs, somehow thus showing that he could have swum further had he wanted to, and the would stand up a quarter out of water for all to see who it was.

The alternative course was simpler, it avoided the cold-water shock and it avoided the risk of appearing too high-spirited. The point was to appear to be so used to the sea, the Mediterranean, and this particular beach, that one might as well be in the sea as out of it. It involved a slow stroll down and into the edge of the water—not even noticing his toes were wet, land and water all the same to *him!*—with his eyes up at the sky gravely surveying portents, invisible to others, of the weather (Local Fisherman Preedy).

[--William Sansom, *A Contest of Ladies* (London: Hogarth, 1956, pp. 230-32]

[--Erving Goffman, <u>The Presentation of Self in Everyday Life</u>, 1959, pp. 4-5]

1

Brief - Vue: The 23 Ways In Which **YOU**
Always "Know Exactly What To Do,"
To Show [tho **Never** to Show **Off**!]   {"ooooh..."}
YOUR OWN FINEST SELF ("How True")—
And To Always Be **OUR True "Teacher"** Too:

(I) As <u>YACHTSMAN</u> you can Take Command—but only to serve well, not wave-swell:

1. Only the true professional can snatch dignity from defeat—can show that **foulling up can be unembarrassing after all**--and *you* show us how

2. Who but a flexible leader could *so-maturely "command" his professional colleagues* when they show themselves up as "difficult and immature" on board his sailboat during a storm??

(II) As TOWN-CITIZEN you can guide, in fact "teach," but always unobtrusively:

3. In the <u>restaurant</u>, you *save a life*—but *unostentatiously*, and so you also save your *modest, unassuming image* too—while (again modestly) setting **a role-model** for the observing diners

4. At the <u>doctor's</u>, you show us *how true teachers can teach other professionals*, about **modesty and even efficiency**, in their own realms—but of course teaching *discreetly and gently*!

5. On the <u>street</u>, *you model true modesty*—you **refuse a "good driver award,"** but *quietly*

6. In the <u>café</u>, you the "educator" *knows to praise* under-appreciated law enforcement (even if the policemen involved don't seem to fully appreciate **your empathetic comprehension** of their work)

(III) In the world of BUSINESS and COMMERCE, you lead with the deft touch.

7. As a <u>job candidate</u>, *you can "teach" your interviewers even before getting hired*—although of course *subtly and via example*—about **the importance of attention to little details**

8. <u>Entering your own office-space</u>, you can demonstrate that **"all-business" is really best for all**, even though the responsibilities of your job involve *seeming* to neglect the waiting-room throng

9. And even "<u>abnormal sexual irregularities</u>" cannot faze *your* ever-calm **workplace-strength**

(IV) Even when meeting CELEBRITIES and EXPERTS, you retain calm cool balance:

10. You "teach" us how **"less is maturely more"** <u>when talking with movie stars in public</u>

11. You show us how <u>the *true* artists</u> (yourself and another) understand each other <u>implicitly</u>

(V) You can negotiate PLURAL WORLDS: CLASSES, & INTERNATIONALLY too:

12. A true "educator" can *suavely* "teach" <u>lower-class trailer-trash</u> that **they're also worthy folks**

13. You can *so-politely* turn first to <u>help confused foreigners</u>, not impatient colleagues

14. YOU can *generously donate* **true aesthetic respect** in Japan where OTHER tourists <u>misbehave</u>

15. You can *affirm* to <u>Oriental shopgirls</u> that **some tourists, at least, appreciate high art culture**

(VI) And as TRUE EDUCATOR AT WORK ON CAMPUS—how your leadership shines!

16. You start to learn—*humbly*, of course—that <u>your influence as a teacher</u> **reaches far indeed**

17. <u>Jealousy of a more-"popular" younger teacher</u>—via your *self-restraint*, you show **how to avoid such immaturity**

18. <u>Interdisciplinary work is difficult, misunderstood</u>—but (*typically*) **you can help there too**

19. You can let <u>your valid but "unusual" work-methods</u> **"teach" others**, *not* embarrass you

20. You can <u>descend to lighter word-play</u> among your colleagues, even being able *maturely* to risk misunderstanding

21. Forever *unprepossessing*, you are indeed surprised—at first—to be <u>elected Univ. President</u>

22. Even though the "chief," you can *generously donate* <u>"human-touch"</u> **enthusiasm for athletics**

(VII) In sum, we can predict your calm expertise <u>*even*</u> in CRISIS OR DANGER SPOTS

23. Who can <u>land the ailing commuter-jet safely although not a pilot himself</u>—and **why?** And what is one's *proper, mature* response to the praise showered upon one afterward?.....

---

2 — *Full - View*: <u>All</u> the Details which Share

How Well ~~YOU~~ **I** Can "Show Us The Way,"
"Generously Donating" ~~your~~ **MY** "Mature" Care,
All While ~~You'd~~ **I'D** "Stay Away from *Our PRAISE*," ~~you~~ **I** Say—
[but away from true *SELF-KNOWLEDGE too*—that *We* see, *Every Day*]

[I.] UNDER SAIL, BUT "ALL AT SEA"...

(1) YOU KNOW HOW TO RESCUE YOURSELF, AND SNATCH FAILURE RIGHT OUT OF THE JAWS OF DEFEAT—VIA THAT **CALM DEPORTMENT** WHICH SURPASSES AND CONQUERS MERE IMMATURE "DISAPPOINTMENT":

Although superficially, you <u>do</u> seem to be RE-ENTERING THE PORT'S HARBOR <u>in utter defeat, even embarrassment, if not mild professional disgrace</u>, since you are <u>not</u> re-entering as the sailboat race's winner, <u>not</u> even as an also-raced, <u>but</u> are being towed back ignominiously as a no-finish *casualty*, disabled due to <u>your own inept seamanship</u>, (because the afternoon's gale not only dismasted your craft but also flooded out its engine—events, by the way, which a competent sailor's skills should have handily prevented)...

...*nevertheless* AS SOON AS YOU PASS THE BREAKWATER ENTRANCE AND APPROACH THE CROWDS watching from the docks, <u>you</u> (perching on your boat's debris-littered foredeck, grasping the mast-stump for balance in the cross-chop) <u>begin to understand</u> the situation somewhat <u>differently</u>—as being only *superficially*-sordid after all. First, a <u>subtle insight</u> starts to tell you that **"there are, in** effect, 'things that you know, that others do not know,' perhaps things about "HIGHER AND LESS OBVIOUS VICTORIES WITHIN, BUT ESPECIALLY ABOVE – AND - BEYOND, APPARENT DEFEATS," and the like... Second, you quickly realize that this subtle insight may be evident to the onlookers as well. Perhaps your smile communicates this to them, a musing smile which plays about your lips even as you hold on and submit to the "indignity"; also communicated by a thoughtful gaze of yours toward **"some further, still-unreached, little-known, little-sought, but valuable horizon,"** your whole demeanor of smile and gaze showing you utterly free from the embarrassment and chagrin which might be expected from, a more-conventional sailor perhaps more cowed-and-bowed by your current, but really only superficial, defeat this afternoon...

And indeed, you feel sure that the shore's crowd of people is already sensing your **"certain but obscure higher type of contest, reward, and indeed victory,"** which you may well be representing here today, your certainty of their "understanding" growing as you see them staring at you, solid, muted, possibly awed and respectful, as you pass by quite near to them now (being towed past your mooring and on back to the repair-dock), and by their occasional wave back in response to your **"generously-knowing"** waves to them in recognition of their awareness, also (if only partial of course), of CERTAIN THINGS—NAUTICAL AND PROFESSIONAL MYSTERIES—THAT ARE NOT TO BE FULLY KNOWN TO ALL, **you a true sovereign OF CERTAIN TRADITIONS ABOVE-AND-BEYOND** THE MERE PLAY AND GAMES OF RECREATIONAL SAILBOAT-RACING thus, **you having known at once what to do, if not to avoid simple mishap, to attain complex management.....**

---

(2) YOU KNOW HOW "EVERY SEA-DOG HAS HIS DAY" OF "DUTIFUL, RESPONSIBLE, SELFLESS SERVICE TO OTHERS" (WHICH OF COURSE REQUIRES AN UNFLINCHINGLY-FIRM COMMAND OF THEM....):

When a sudden major local emergency arises and dictates that YOU MUST TRANSPORT SEVERAL OF YOUR COLLEAGUES FROM YOUR ACADEMIC DEPARTMENT ACROSS THE 65 MILES OF OPEN WATER of Lake Michigan on your 26-foot sailboat (and all of your colleagues either total landlubbers, or inexperienced sailors), you sense, at once and as never before, **the complex dimensions of COMMAND,** as involving indeed the **"rights, duties, and obligations"** of RESPONSIBILITY FOR THE WELFARE OF OTHERS while being in a POSITION OF AUTHORITY OVER them...

For, at once you begin to worry apprehensively about your "situation-assigned" crew; you worry whether those professional academics who are so

expert, so authoritative, so *authoritarian,* in one realm, will be able to function well in another here. Specifically, will those who are so accustomed to *lead* within the Department, and lead forcefully at that (they often finessing you into a subordinate role on committees, etc.), be able to, in effect, "*follow* the (new) leader" in this new (and dangerous) situation?

But **at once you know what to do.** You're relieved that it is not due to any any *self-aggrandizement,* or *drive-for-power* (let alone any *immature vindictiveness*) on your part, which leads you at once to "take command over them" suddenly and completely as soon as the lake-crossing is mandated. Far from it—it's simply the time-honored need, whenever At Sea, for **the Skipper to be in complete command,** in order, of course, to avoid any indecisive or uncoordinated responses to sudden weather-worsenings or gear-failures which could quickly spell disaster in falling-domino fashion (that major Peril Of The Sea about which, non-sailors of course innocently know nothing). Nevertheless, you do find it an "interesting" secondary outcome of your assuming Command, that as the usual roles reverse between you and your colleagues (pro tem "your" crew), that these Others who habitually ignore, overlook, minimalize, or otherwise devalue the valuable things you have to contribute in Departmental meetings, are now **going to have to be taught, and accept, certain procedures in your world**—a "subservience" (?) which, however, their very expertise, or rather their ingrown, ingrained academic *egotism and arrogance,* may make it quite hard for them to accept!...

But you then quickly realize reassuringly in turn that it is, after all, only YOUR PRIVILEGE, DUTY, and OBLIGATION, and not any naked "RIGHT," inherent in **COMMAND,** which requires you to, after all, **"serve them better than they may know, by commanding them more forcefully than they may wish"** (or than they may, of course, ever be able to understand, let alone appreciate fully, as you must suppose). And therefore you begin the pre-crossing briefing by "drilling" them—**your true full voice of command and leadership-potential released at last,** if alas here rather than in the Department!—by first instructing them simply in "HOW TO MOVE ABOUT THE BOAT SAFELY IF AND WHEN STORMY WEATHER ARISES" (**"Plant your feet solidly; use your hands to grip also; and keep your weight-center low"**)...

Still, your private opinion at once opines that just as soon as the always-choppy Lake waves begin to beat up, all you're *really* going to be saying to your "Crew" is the usual: **"Do not talk to me except in emergency until this blows over,"** you installed as the HELMSMAN supreme, hand on tiller, body braced against the boat's tosses of pitching, rolling, and yawing (do they, such assured cognoscenti-experts, even *know* these terms!), your eyes skillfully scanning the rigging and the horizon continuously, your whole body affrontingly-drenched with the firehose-impact spray and spume of Great Lakes storm waves which amaze even old blue-water salts, all of which "comes with the territory" of COMPETENT CAPABLE COMMAND IN ALL WEATHER SITUATIONS...

while the others, your once-proud "colleagues," no longer your "crew" if they ever were or ever wanted to be, will no doubt <u>not</u> be "moving about the boat safely" or in any other way, but will be huddled belowdecks like the ignorant cattle they are, well no, or perhaps rather more like the vulnerable cargo which any landlubbers are at sea while In Weather, the honored responsibility of the Skipper, whose awesome and total responsibility for safety of ship and souls aboard carries with it such a mandate for total command-and-control also...

.....**you the Skipper indeed knowing these things**, and others, which of course they cannot know, and you only maturely leading them forward, you to be "eye-of-the-storm calm within yourself even as you are storm-tossed outside," and you know <u>you must</u> <u>*never immaturely disparage*</u> those once-proud, overly-sheltered academics now truly "out of their element" (through no fault of their own, although culpable for <u>their resistant, surly, insulting responses</u> to this real-life situation—*and* to your efforts to minister COMMAND to them!), and <u>you must</u> *never exult or lord it over* them either (which would be even worse)—**your own "true mettle,"** as well as theirs, also being tested, you suddenly realize, in these circumstances, and <u>in multiple ways too</u>, all of which of course you quickly welcome and embrace, and in the "double-handful" fashion of the TRUE MARITIME LEADER.....

[II.] OurTown's Top Citizen

(3) YOU CAN SAVE A LIFE SKILLFULLY—BUT CAN ALSO DEMONSTRATE **YOUR SELFLESS, EGO-FREE DEPORTMENT** PUBLICALLY ALSO!

When <u>a DINER at a table near yours in the busy, crowded RESTAURANT begins to choke</u>, suddenly and horribly, on a piece of food, the OTHER DINERS probably do <u>not</u> think it all that "remarkable" that <u>you can (and do) rise instantly</u> (though with neither fanfare nor fuss) **and step deftly over to calmly apply the Heimlich Maneuver,** that "bear-hug" which of course **dislodges completely the near-lethal chunk of beef from the potential victim's airway <u>and thus you save his life</u>** (but you simply fulfilling "anybody's" social duty thus)...

However, the OTHER DINERS probably <u>do</u> think that <u>your subsequent behavior</u> is indeed a bit more "remarkable"—because **just-as-instantly** (and just as fanfare-free) <u>you step right back to your table</u> **and sit down and resume your conversation, sort of "easily and nonchalantly,"** kind of **"as if** <u>nothing had happened really</u>," certainly nothing

of import, let alone of skilled social service on your part...

And yet the drama concludes well, as YOU YOURSELF gladly notice that first, not only have THE OTHER DINERS <u>noticed **your dutiful competent heroics**</u> and are discussing it, but second, especially that <u>**YOU YOURSELF have not noticed, or at least remain quite properly oblivious to,**</u> the OTHER DINERS' attentions (including their apparently-admiring pointing, staring, and whisperings at the tables all about you), but also that third, <u>these diners are probably also noticing</u> and may comprehend YOUR APPROPRIATELY EGO - FREE AND DECOROUS, UNASSUMING SELF – DEPORTMENT, **how indeed you knew not only what to do and how to do it, but what not to do, as well**... since YOUR OWN very "unnoticing nonchalance" regarding THEIR noticing YOU admiringly, surely confirms that <u>**YOU possess no need for any such vulgar praise**</u>, recognition, notice, or fame, in what was merely SOCIAL DUTY NOT SELFISH DISPLAY after all.....

(4) PERHAPS YOU CAN HELP TO **IMPROVE MEDICAL PRACTICE NATIONWIDE**—& ALL IN ONE DAY, & IN SPITE OF YOURSELF, TOO?

<u>*When*</u> YOUR DERMATOLOGIST informs you that <u>the simple procedure</u> of excising a small brown spot from the glans or head of your penis <u>is being delayed</u> due to the fact that no <u>male</u> nurse is currently available to aid the physician, and that the <u>female</u> nurse is present but apparently "culturally-unavailable" because current protocol in medicine still demands that our society's conventional "modesty between the sexes" be maintained even in medical offices, <u>*then*</u> upon hearing this, you are of course immediately glad that **you know how to reply**, and in a way which will not only free up the female nurse to attend after all (thus expediting your own specific busy schedule today), but will also helpfully "free up" general medical thinking on the matter (thus perhaps expediting medical progress tomorrow and beyond...)

For upon hearing of the delay, your **"response-of-counsel"** to the dermatologist consists of a perhaps MORE MATURE, SUAVE, AND EFFICIENT APPROACH, namely that (as you phrased it to him), **"What's at hand here is not fixed absolutes, but situational flexibility; you see, when one is in the social role of 'medical patient,' well then conventional modesty is not only irrelevant, as it is for a naked three-year-old child at a beach, but indeed may actually be deleterious, because the more the patient's body is stripped or revealed, the more that will assist the unobstructed delivery of better medical care!"**

And from the physician's thoughtful (if wordless) response and assent, you can only hope that your MORE LIBERATED, ENLIGHTENED VIEWPOINT on this matter, can be taken up, and from this small beginning in MADISON, WISCONSIN, can indeed be disseminated through the medical profession at large (albeit slowly at first, of course), as an appropriate step toward A MORE SENSIBLY EFFICIENT APPROACH to "the body-in-treatment" indeed.....

(5) GETTING THE IMPORTANT WORD OUT BY "INDIRECTION" OFTEN SEEMS BEST EVEN IF NECESSARILY-"ANONYMOUS"

When the POLICE OFFICER stops your car to inform you that she is awarding *you* the city's weekly **"On-The-Spot Good-Citizen's Good-Driver Award,"** she having observed you that day driving around the city not only lawfully and skillfully, but also with especially flawless COURTESY AND CONSIDERATION for other drivers (pausing for them when they were changing lanes; entering or exiting parking spaces; pausing to load and unload; and the like, and thus putting group traffic-flow ahead of your own desire to arrive), your response to her stopping you and awarding you thus shows that **you indeed do know exactly what to do,** MORALLY, in such situations...

First, you of course **speedily** *decline* **the honor**, but next you make clear to her (*and* to the newspaper REPORTER riding in the squad's back seat and observing everything for a story) exactly **why** you are firmly (albeit modestly) *refusing* **the award**. *Not* due to any *false, bogus, or ungenuine,* "modesty" (not really be selfless after all thus), but rather, due to your IMPORTANT IF OVERLOOKED BELIEF that "HECK, EVERY MOTORIST SHOULD DRIVE LIKE THIS, WITH CONSIDERATION FOR OTHERS AND HELPING THE OVERALL TRAFFIC FLOW INSTEAD OF RACING TO GET SOMEWHERE ONESELF, AND HENCE NO ONE PERSON SHOULD GET ANY SPECIAL RECOGNITION FOR SUCH BASIC MATURE COURTESY AND CONSIDERATION WHICH SURELY EVERY DRIVER SHOULD DEMONSTRATE!"...

And you are soon gratified, for not only does the OFFICER (though initially speechless), seem indeed to comprehend your SURELY MORE MATURE, GENUINELY "SELF-EFFACING," CITIZEN-RESPONSE (**proper "value-system"**), but also the REPORTER, also seems to competently grasp your probably-rare, the regrettably-rare, **rationale** of RESPONSIBLE AND "MODEST" CIVILIAN DUTY, as you are happy to phrase it to the note-scribbling reporter, before you drive off having sublimated *Vain Fame* for **truer, modest Citizenry**....

(6) THE **GOOD CITIZEN**, ALSO, MUST OFTEN LABOR & CONTRIBUTE **UNRECOGNIZED, UNREWARDED**

When you start chatting with YOUR TOWN'S POLICE OFFICERS on their coffee break at the downtown café, you're sorry that their duties call them to depart *before* you've had time to confirm to them how fully **you** RESPECTFULLY APPRECIATE law-enforcement officers, how you POSITIVELY SUPPORT them, **your attitude** surely too often insensitively-*un*expressed by too many other citizens...

You try to convey your ADMIRATION, saying, as for instance, "WHEN I DROVE A FAST CAR I VIEWED POLICE AS ADVERSARIES BUT NOW I KNOW THAT YOU GUYS KNOW EVEN BETTER THAN I DO, THAT '*COUNTY HIGHWAYS AREN'T PLAYGROUND-RACETRACKS,*' DUE TO SEVERAL SPECIFIC CONDITIONS, WHETHER GRAVEL ON THE ROAD, A WOMAN AND CHILD BICYCLING AROUND A CURVE, A LOADED FARM TRUCK MOVING SLOWLY, AND THE LIKE....AND I ALSO KNOW THAT **YOU GUYS ARE THERE TO PROTECT ALL CITIZENS, NOT SIMPLY TO DISCIPLINE CHILDISH BEHAVIORS**"...

Thus do you graciously donate **your mature respectful insight**: "HECK, ALTHOUGH WE TEACHERS ARE ALSO STRESSED ON THE JOB, THERE'S NO COMPARISON WITH WHAT YOU GUYS GO THROUGH, WITHOUT WHOM HECK, THIS TOWN WOULD SLIDE BACK INTO BARBARISM IN ONE WEEK..."

And your feelings being so PERCEPTIVE and also EMPATHETICALLY - SINCERE, you can only believe that despite, and beneath, their gruff, bustling exterior, and sort-of "embarrassed" reception of your INSIGHTFUL COMPLIMENTS (not to mention their early exit from the corner café that day), that they surely did both recognize and appreciate your CONCERNED CITIZEN'S COMMENDATIONS, it being rare indeed for them to receive such SOLID, and INSIGHTFULLY-INFORMED, SUPPORT from *you*—instead of the usual *in*difference, *non*-appreciation, or actual complaints from *other, less*-insightful "citizens".....

[III.] YOU CAN SINGE SUCH ON-THE-JOB LIEDERSHIP

(7) YOU KNOW OF **ADVANCED TACTICS** NOT [NOT *YET!*] TAUGHT IN **JOB-HUNTING SEMINARS:**

During the final phase of your SECOND INTERVIEW FOR THE NEW JOB in a fast-track business (when of course each and every small action of the candidate counts all the more), you and your top-level interviewers are walking down the corridor to the elevators for lunch—when **you pause** and, although never interrupting your flow of speaking, **easily pick up from the marble floor, two pieces** of scrap paper which you then just as effortlessly place in the next wastebasket you pass...

And *although* you realize that many others would think this small action of yours not only meaningless but even inappropriate and hence damaging to your chances, *nevertheless* **you instinctively know** you correctly exploited this minor opportunity which mere chance gave you, to demonstrate how **you can easily, effortlessly attend to things small as well as large**—a skill which you wager your interviewers will surely the more recognize (all the more, or maybe even for the first time?) which demanding jobs in general require, and which you especially possess and can offer.....

---

(8) YOUR **FORTHRIGHT AND "DEDICATED" ACTIONS** DO CONFIRM **YOUR ABLE "EXECUTIVE SELF"** TRUER THAN WOULD MERE WORDS, OR MORE "PLEASANT" ACTIONS—EVEN THO INVOLVING SOME RISK OF UNDERAPPRECIATION OR MISUNDERSTANDING:

You're quite aware that *although* your deliberately-chosen "mode" or "style" of RE-ENTERING YOUR BUSINESS OFFICE (after some important mid-day errand away from it) does carry some risk of giving some **"wrong impression"** about you to the people in the Outer Office or waiting-room (these people including both the *secretary* fruitlessly waving papers at you as you pass, papers which need your "immediate" attention or signature, and also including the many *clients* impatiently sitting in chairs awaiting the perennially-delayed appointments with you)—your manner-of-Office re-entry being **"risky"** indeed because it is *not* merely to walk in casually, normally, accessibly, *but* is to burst in and to stride brusquely, intently, directly to the door of your Inner Office and to disappear right into it, all the while in a kind of "radio silence" if not "orbit," you aware of nobody but rather simply looking straight-ahead-plus-slightly-down in an "all-business" mode **as if indeed focussed upon "a major new problem preoccupying you and you alone"** such that you not only don't *pause* for anybody, you not only don't *look at* anybody, but you don't even *speak to* anybody except to the secretary as she waves papers fruitlessly, and indeed all you say to her is your standard *dialog* of "HOLD ALL CALLS, MISS NIMS, AND DO NOT DISTURB ME UNTIL I'VE STRAIGHTENED THIS THING OUT," whereupon you instantly vanish into the "sanctum sanctorum" or Central Command Post which is your Inner Office...

Nevertheless, this "brutally all-business" mode of your office re-appearance is a "scenario" which you do continue to perform, **"risking"** indeed to *seem* to neglect secretary (bad), insult clients (worse), and indeed even aggrandize or trumpet or imperialize yourself (worst)... because **you are also quite aware** that such a **"thoroughly-professional" mode or style** probably conveys to the onlooking crowd, the better (the more useful fair true just) *impression* after all, namely, the *image* that **you do know enough, and care enough**, TO **"TAKE CARE OF BUSINESS"** INDEED, TO **ATTEND FIRST TO THOSE TOUGH PROBLEMS** ONLY TOP MANAGEMENT CAN MONITOR, to RESOLUTELY PRACTICE "THE TOUGH TRIAGE OF **PRIORITIZING**," to "DO WHAT - EVER IT TAKES," thus demonstrating an **UNUSUAL COMPETENCE** which can only benefit the clients in due turn, even though it means that **you must bear the "weariness and stress of high command"** as it were with a certain ALL-CONSUMING AND DOGGED DEDICATION which, although it is of course just as *appropriate*, as it is both *rare* and *thankless*, does indeed risk (as noted) being both *mis-interpreted* and *badly-received*, in THE COMPLEX WORLD OF BUSINESS TODAY.....

---

(9) THE **TRULY-"MASCULINE" GENTLE-MAN** CAN HOLD STEADY IN SITUATIONS *UNSAVORY* TO *NORMAL* MEN—BUT WITHOUT "TAKING CREDIT" FOR SUCH **SUAVE**:

When YOU RETURN TO THE DARKENED OFFICE AFTER HOURS, in the evening, on a sudden errand, *although* you expect to find nobody still there, *nevertheless*, as you pass an ajar door in the corridor, you catch a glimpse of THE YOUNG (MALE) OFFICE CLERK in apparent "INTIMATE CONGRESS" with THE YOUNG (AND REGRETTABLY ALSO MALE) TRUCK DRIVER, their "limbs entangled in supreme embrace" or the likes of such.... well, *although* you are of course "taken aback" by this primitive grossness, *nevertheless* you are glad that your BASIC VALUE OF TOLERANCE of "variation" nay of "deviation" and the like in human affairs, lets **you behave "properly" after all**, lets you automatically not only **know what to do** in a *"sale histoire"* type of case like this, but also lets you effortlessly do it...

Thus you instantly put on a show, you create a drama, of the **"suave, mature passer-by who neither condemns nor approves irregularity, but simply passes by, quite oblivious and non-perceiving—or tolerating if forced to,"** you starring well in this, simply by **expertly (albeit intuitively, "naturally")** STARTING TO TALK LOUDLY TO YOURSELF IN ABSENT-MINDED MUTTERINGS; MAKING SCUFFLING NOISES LOUD ENOUGH TO ALERT BUT NOT TO ALARM; THEN WHISTLING A BIT, EVEN CURSING SOME LITTLE VEXATION OR OTHER; AND SO ON, before soon breezing on out nonchalantly, your unexpected errand completed (or postponed if necessary under the unusually-stressful circumstances)...

And so you can depart the Office doubly glad that no only did the derelict duo never suspect that you even noticed their transgression, but also that your own NATURAL MATURE GENEROUS TOLERATING of the "pathetically-aberrant," need not be known to *them*, in order to be modestly-enough satisfying to *yourself*.....

[IV.] YOU'RE FIRST AMONG ALL...

(10) TO RESPOND FORBEARINGLY, TO THOSE WHO HAVE SERVED US WELL—SUCH SHOWS TRULY-"LOYAL" APPRECIATION:

As soon as you realize that YOUR AIRPLANE-FLIGHT SEATMATE IS A FAMOUS HOLLYWOOD STAR (as stellar as, say, Woody Allen, Dustin Hoffman, Mary Tyler Moore), **you know at once what to do—and what not to**. You will speak to the celebrity, but only one line of affirmation (such as, for instance, **"My college students will never forget your Willy Lohman"**) and then you will at once turn away, and indeed will converse no more during the entire journey...

This tactic of yours demonstrates SENSITIVE CONSIDERATION; it avoids what must be a common breach of etiquette by the *less-sensitive* populace, who would monopolize the celebrity's private time, whereas you can avoid this breach simply because of your perhaps higher-than-average RESPONSIBLE EMPATHY, which sensitizes you at once that *not only* are celebrities bombarded everywhere by *less-considerate* fans' buttonholings of them, **but also** this attentiveness must surely quickly grow stale for the wearied stars—and so therefore any TRULY "RESPECTFUL" fan must demonstrate instead, your type of PROPER CONSIDERATION and hence FORBEARING RESTRAINT OF CONTACT...

Your realizing this point of GOOD CIVIL ETIQUETTE, helps you to become less disappointed in not allowing yourself to discuss certain important artistic matters with, someone who is an equal to you at last in perception of these matters, namely the talented star at hand. This value of POLITE TACTFUL FORBEARANCE must be its own reward, because not only can the surely-grateful star-seatmate hardly be expected to *thank* you later for your *non-intrusiveness* during the plane flight, but also because you are surely MATURE enough yourself to realize that this disappointing loss of "shop-talk with the star" is, though not totally "okay" with you, is anyhow the price of your CORRECT BEHAVIOR, a duty-tax on your HIGHER AWARENESSES which must thus be its own reward.....

(11) TRUE PROFESSIONALS "APPRECIATE EACH OTHER" CALMLY, *WITHOUT* VULGAR NEED FOR PRAISE, CONFIRMATION, ETC.:

It was not only YOUR CONSIDERABLE KNOWLEDGE about photography specifically, but especially your valuing of COOPERATIVE EMPATHY AND RECIPROCAL CONSIDERATION in actions generally, that led you—when THE FAMOUS PHOTOGRAPHER CAME TO SHOOT YOU in your "copier-art" studio—to "COOPERATE so FULLY" (let alone EXPERTLY) with him during the afternoon's hour-long shoot, in order to be a "good photographic subject" *indeed*—maybe even a *great* subject... (This, for an article in a major regional magazine, "at last," on your innovative, if too-long-overlooked, type of visual art projects...)

For **you knew at once** what surely must be the demands of being the "perfect photographic subject," which you wanted him to know that you would be. To be RESPONSIVE, yes, but especially CONTROLLABLE; infinitely-PATIENT; and above all to be quite "SUBSERVIENT" to **his own ideas and not yours**, about his shoot's composition; framing; focal length; etc. And so you initated this role of the "good-subject" by reassuring him ["Take your time; I'm putty in your hands"]. And you maintained this role by such surely-CONSIDERATE ACTS as voluntarily freezing in a pose you judged to be especially good (whether he said they were or not)... by performing actions and processes slowly... and by repeating actions (even when he said you didn't have to—no doubt motivated by his politeness, plus surely the fact that he had surely never before had such a KNOWINGLY COMPLIANT subject to photograph)...

But despite all your contribution, *he never did acknowledge, after the shoot* that you had turned out in fact to be (as you fancied he might have phrased it), "a perfect photographic subject—much better than my other subjects ever know how to be," and the like... Although naturally disappointed, you soon realized that he perhaps omitted that praise (or rather simple validation) of your PROFESSIONAL PROWESS, not due to the simple lack of time, but to the simple fact that **between true professionals, the practice of simply taking skillful performances for granted, and not praising or expecting to be praised for, them,** is itself as properly-"PROFESSIONAL" as the skillful performances themselves, and therefore to **"voluntarily cooperate and defer subserviently,"** as you surely did this afternoon, thus is not, after all, to *degrade yourself* and your TALENTS IN PHOTOGRAPHY into an abyss of anonymity and non-recognition after all, as you had mistakenly, though only momentarily, feared earlier.....

[V.] How Stately You, Can Move In Diversity:

(12) The **TRUE EDUCATOR,** Does Well to **Champion "Social Equality"** as a Value, where *Others* Might *Neglect* Same:

Soon after YOU MOVED INTO THE MOBILE HOME PARK, you're glad to have your initial fear quickly dispelled, your fear that your new neighbors (being of the "*lower*" socio-economic and educational classes in the trailer-court subculture) might view you *distantly* and might even *misunderstand you to hold some "superior" attitude toward them* simply because you are a "university professor" whereas they work menial jobs (if at all)...

However, your find your fear has dispelled, right after your very first chat with your immediate neighbors, during which, it would seem, **you instinctively knew enough to punctuate your conversation** (whenever relevant or even possible) with **"reassuringly-equalizing" phrases** such as,

"Well, a graduate degree doesn't mean you're smarter, It's just a union card you've got to have" [laughter as usual)], The only real 'school' is real life isn't it, Some people up at the College have their degrees but are only book-smart and not street-smart, But I just keep my mouth shut about all this when I'm up there, But I'm sure you all know all about this, being people of the real world...."

And you feel confident that this **"down-to-earth equal" stance** of your first chat (your "introductory lecture," of course so-to-speak), has surely dissipated any *haughty elitist distance between you and them* which they might have incorrectly inferred; you're sure that **your so-natural folksiness** has replaced their *suspicions* with your rare but valuable NATURAL, MATURE, EMPATHETIC, UNPRESUMING, RAPPORT which you value. So much so, in fact, that as the initial chat ends (perhaps too quickly, but the others seem to feel that they must return to their abodes and pressing duties), you feel confident in predicting to yourself that the next or second chat will go well; that indeed, you could by next week have *these peons* **"sitting in a circle at your feet and eating out of your hand,"** (again, so-to-speak, as not you, but some of *your elitist colleagues,* might well inappropriately phrase it...)

(13) You, as **THE TRUEST HOST,** can Proved that **Rare,** *Genuine* **Welcoming** of Needful Foreign Visitors:

When you observe that THE VISITING FRENCHMAN IS HAVING DIFFICULTIES in making himself understood to the teller in YOUR SMALLTOWN BANK, *although* other Americans might be unable to comprehend this delicate, potentially profitable, "emerging situation," or might well mishandle it, *nevertheless* you are glad that **you know instantly and instinctively what to do** for the important causes of NATIONAL, CITIZEN, HOSPITALITY and heck, of UNIVERSAL MATURE "POLITESSE" (which is "politeness" in French)...

That is to say, **you know to speak up at once,** but not to the crankily-confused teller (as other Yankees unknowingly might do), but rather **first,** only to the justifiably-fuming Frenchman himself (in your fairly-fluent French, of course). With **a proper blend of forthright initiative plus of course respectful, almost "old-world," deference** (the two of you not having been introduced formally), you inquire of the Frenchman, *"Pardon, Monsieur, est-ce que je pourrais vous aider sur ce chapitre-la? J'en serais tres content de le faire, mais bien sur c'est a vous"* (Of course, this means "EXCUSE ME, SIR, MAY I BE OF ASSISTANCE TO YOU IN THE MATTER AT HAND? I'D BE HAPPY TO DO SO, BUT IT'S UP TO YOU OF COURSE")...

And thus by this ploy of **"proper prior attention,"** you do your small part to confirm the essential HOSPITALITY function of giving PRIORITY of attention to FOREIGN VISITORS to our nation, you realizing sympathetically how *lost* they must feel without such CONSIDERATE ATTENTION by a knowing native, not to mention how instantly gratified they must feel by even a little bit of **appropriate** ASSISTANCE from a **competent** (albeit of course anonymous) citizen, regrettably rare as such REFINED TREATMENT will probably be, you fear, in the Frenchman's subsequent dealing with many well-meaning—but *essentially unpolished*—fellow Americans.....

(14) Sometimes, Your **APPROPRIATE CONSIDERATION** Surprises *Even You [VOUS VOUS-MEME, VOTRE OWN SELF]*—Tho It's All the Natural Action of a More-Ably *Dedicated Educator* Perhaps:

When YOU VISIT THE MOST FAMOUS ROCK GARDEN IN KYOTO, Japan, *although* clearly most of the other visitors (tourists, couples, school groups) seem to feel that just a few minutes suffices to experience all of this richly religious-and-aesthetic shrine, *nevertheless* you yourself end up LINGERING FOR ALMOST AN HOUR, and this *because* you quickly realized that FULLEST APPRECIATION of the place (exquisitely-placed rocks amid freshly-raked gravel) truly requires a more protracted, indeed a REVERENTLY RESPECTFUL, pausing—so much so, that NEAR THE END of your hour-long communion (having received no new insights for many minutes now, hence preparing to depart), WHEN YOU SPY, at the courtyard's far end, a cluster of <u>monks</u> apparently pointing toward you, apparently discussing you and your long presence, and probably with with appreciation, <u>you then find yourself doubly-satisfied</u> that your SUPERIOR PATIENT ATTENTIVENESS has not only probably achieved for <u>you</u> a GREATER APPRECIATION of the AESTHETICS, but has also demonstrated to the <u>natives</u>, the MORE-RESPECTFUL RESPONSE and indeed SUPERIOR DEDICATION which—this afternoon at least!—will reassure the (surely-often-disappointed) garden-caretaker <u>monks</u> that <u>not all visitors *neglect* "going the extra mile"</u> in order to **generously donate** the APPROPRIATELY-REVERENTIAL AND UNHURRIED REACTION which a shrine of this quality surely merits.....

> ### (15) THE **GIFTED AESTHETE** DOES WELL TO ""GENEROUSLY DONATE"" HIS **GRATEFUL APPRECIATION** TO THE *BUSINESS* WORLD *ALSO*:

When (while vacationing in Hong Kong and Singapore) <u>YOU STARTED YOUR SHOPPING FOR "CLOISONNE"</u> (those elegant Chinese vases with their lustrous designs of brass and colorfully-fired ceramics), it was <u>originally</u> simply just for <u>prudent pragmatism</u> (=to identify the better-designed vases) that you soon adopted **your idiosyncratic procedure of scrutinizing the vases,** <u>not only close-up</u>, as is usual for usual tourists, but then <u>also **from a middle distance**</u> and also **from various angles**—front, back, side (you stepping back several feet, then circling round the vase, the better to view it "synoptically" from various angles)—all of this scrutiny, of course, to see better, prudently-and-pragmatically whether a given vase's design would "wear well" after all, would meet your aesthetic standards which are as high as your aesthetic capabilities...

It was only <u>later in your shopping that you became glad enough to continue</u> **this "synoptic scrutinizing"** not only for wise purchasing, but also for PROPER POLITENESS, in that **your painstaking, multi-angled examination,** once instituted, <u>quickly seemed to impress</u>, even perhaps slightly awe and amaze, the young Chinese shop-girls (shop-women actually), one of whom asked brightly "Are you an artist?"

For you soon discerned that they appreciated **your more in-depth scrutinizing** of CLOISONNE, <u>*not*</u> because it was all that <u>inappropriate or mysterious</u>, but simply that **careful considering** is quite <u>rare, unusual, novel</u>, and indeed <u>most other tourists</u>, of course, did <u>*not*</u> donate the same RESPECTFUL APPRECIATIVE ATTENTION to these ethnic treasures—which lapse of theirs and leap of yours was affirmed when another shopgirl's

reassuring you that "Most people, they just buy, they not take time to examine as you do."

And as soon as you understood how most other consumers acted *carelessly* regarding CLOISONNE, you were glad to keep on **graciously donating** your PROPER VALIDATION OF TRADITIONAL AESTHETICS to try to counterbalance its <u>absence</u> among the apparently-*insensitive* mass of the *other* <u>affluent-but-*uncultured* tourists</u> visiting the CLOISONNE shops, you thus glad to be doing **your artful part,** however small, toward RESPECT FOR INDIGENOUS VALIDITY (although always MODESTLY, of course, *without* letting the shopgirls realize you were, in effect, doing so....)

[VI.] YOU THE "EDUCATORS' EDUCATOR"

> ### (16) YOU CAN REMAIN **MODEST,** ABOUT YOUR UNEXPECTEDLY-*FAR-REACHING INFLUENCES* AS A **TRUE TEACHER:**

<u>What amazed you (initially) was that it was only casually and in passing</u>, a few months ago, IN YOUR COLLEGE CLASS ON "THINKING ABOUT SOCIAL ISSUES," <u>that you had mentioned the matter, nay the problem, of **the current dominant fashions in young college womens' hairdos**</u>, specifically the actual (though, sadly-unrecognized) **absurdity of the current style**, as having become (as you phrased it) "overly complicated-up, indeed twisted, piled, frizzled, splayed, teased, and in general tortuously-crenellated," *a false fashion* which of course sacrifices TIMELESS GOOD TASTE as well as CLASSIC "LESS – IS - MORE" AESTHETICS, (both of which would require specifically the proper matching of hairdo to individuals head-shapes), sacrifices these values to "the *unthinking tyranny* of fashions, trends, styles, modes, behavior, thinking" (this being the class' current subtopic, and hence your passing mention of hairdo-horrifics being quite relevant and germane to the course)...

That initial amazement of yours actually came A FEW MONTHS LATER, <u>after</u> your casual remark, when you read (in a regional college newsmagazine) about the unexpected, the surprising, indeed the wholly-unanticipated (let alone unexplainable) **new trend** of most college women now **changing their hair-styles back toward the more classic, simple, natural modes** which favor each woman's face and personality-types, instead of conforming to *imperious Fashion's* demand for the current mode, even if jazzy, overdone, and mixed-up as had been the current "style"...

Your amazement arose, of course, at how such a small action as your one-time, offhand, casual mention of the hairdo-tangle today could effect such a large change (even though your mention did reflect the unarguably superior, or at least correct, insight that it of course did). But then, of course, your amazement was only initial—temporary—short-lived, for with the clear-headed MODESTY which is more your trait than is irrational EGOTISM, you quickly realized that you were undoubtedly only one cog in the wheel of major social change, (albeit this time a kingpin or pivotal one, in just the right place at the right time); that it had become overdue for everyone to realize that **the prevalent confused-coiffure style was indeed absurd,** and hence to be abandoned...

Still, you found you were glad enough to have been able to **graciously donate** (and "behind the scenes" as it were) a MORE MATURE PERSPECTIVE in these matters of TASTE AND INDEED VALUE than today's young possess; your CALM CONFIDENCE IN ILLUMINATING THE RIGHT OR ANYHOW BETTER WAYS soon becoming reward quite sufficient enough, you being able to rest quite content in modest anonymity, you not driven to seek valorized *validation* for your leadership, let alone (which would be even worse) any "I-told-you-so" vindictive *vindication*, surely an immature need.....

---

(17) BEING MORE MATURE, *YOU* CAN MORE MATURELY ACCEPT, *OTHER* TEACHERS' STILL-DELAYED MATURITIES:

During YOUR FIRST TEAM-TEACHING (a short Intersession with another teacher from your department), you quickly discover that YOUR TEACHING STYLES DIFFER—he from the outset getting more "fluidly" or "directly" connected with the students, he achieving a more informal, direct rapport which causes them to respond more than they do to you, in a rich rush of responses.... But as soon as you perceive this disparity, you also reassuringly realize simply that "teaching and learning styles differ," you being by this time in your career-growth, you'd hope, FAR TOO MATURE to feel "threatened," as it were, by the (younger) teacher's *only apparent, only superficial*, greater "popularity" with the students. Also reassuringly, **you see at once what to do**, to correct the problem, or let us say to correct and balance the picture. And that is of course **to generously donate** to the team-taught class the MATURE MODEL of a slower, more low-key, perhaps more STEADILY-MELLOW and "considered" approach, to counterbalance the *too-lively* one; a kindly directing of student to "pause and reconsider and think through" their statements (and indeed their reactions to the other teacher's statements too!), yes to "discipline" their thoughts a bit more as you "re-state what it was you thought they said," to fine-hone thus the valuable but

overlooked (and only apparently "dowdy, dull, boring") skill of IMPROVED INTERPERSONAL COMPREHENSION—all this to sagely and skillfully counterbalance the less-experienced teacher's perhaps-*too-"seductive" "vitality"* with your own "overseeing" or "curating" approach.

Not only that, but you find you're also MATURE enough (again, at last!) to remain not only "unthreatened," but also actually undisturbed, by THE FINAL OUTCOME of this dissonant mismatch of two teachers' styles in one classroom which should be one's private domain after all; AN OUTCOME which occurs AT SEMESTER'S END (after an increasingly-unharmonious series of class-meetings despite your best efforts in rebalancing), which occurs AT COURSE-EVALUATION TIME, when you're initially astonished to discover that, for all your hard work to the contrary, **all the students rated the young upstart teacher as a "much better instructor" than they rated you!**

But your MATURITY, both sanguine and seasoned, tells you that, *although* your ADVANCED AND MATURE TEACHING PLOYS do *not* seem to work with these "*less-mature, beginning-level*" students, **nevertheless** it is your duty to persevere in such MATURE STANCES SOMEHOW, steeling yourself to derive such (quite-thankless) rewards-and-fulfillments as one can from KNOWING ONE IS DOING THE RIGHT THING (even if it's the more demanding, less immediately-appreciated, thing) for the students in the long run, foregoing the surely short-term reward (or "instant gratification") of easy praise from *a bunch of indolent, unappreciative freshmen seduced by shallow showmanship...*

In consolation, you anticipate that, in future semesters and years, an impressive number of students will be sending your way comments and notes of delayed realization and appreciation, at least from the **tiny** minority of **able-and-engaged** students in that class after all, as they gradually realized what WAS OF REAL VALUE (against what was merely "*entertainment and popularity-seeking*") in that team-taught class after all—that "long-ago *and never-again*" **fertile fiasco**....

---

(18) BUT SOMETIMES, EVEN YOUR MATURE ACADEMIC PEERS, NEED THAT "EXTRAORDINARY" ASSISTANCE WHICH [MAINLY-OR-ONLY] YOU CAN, IN FACT, DONATE:

Although you soon sense that the atmosphere of THE FIRST "EXPERIMENTAL JOINT DISCUSSION MEETING between the Departments of your own home field, English LANGUAGE & LITERATURE, and of the visiting SOCIOLOGY & ANTHROPOLOGY Department, might be turning a bit *unfocussed, diffident, disconnected,* indeed, even a bit *hostile or dissonant... nevertheless* **you know instantly what to do**, because you are MORE AWARE than most academics that the workaday images each academic discipline holds of the other are actually inaccurate <u>stereotypes</u>, which regrettably influence "we" (the humanists) to see "them" (the social scientists) as "merely" *reductive and mechanical empiricists*, and "they" (the social scientists) to see "us" (the humanists) as "merely" *ethnocentric and belletristic impressionists*, a quite-profitless "two-culture war-wound" which **you know you can at once help to begin to heal**, by the simple (but rare and difficult and under-appreciated) ploy or tactic of demonstrating true "CROSS-DISCIPLINE EMPATHY," <u>which therefore you indeed do begin to practice, by consciously</u> (although of course quite <u>*unobtrusively*</u>) <u>sprinkling into your comments on the issues under dissonant discussion,</u> **such key terms of the Others, such professional jargon of the social scientists** (even though your more-*parochial* <u>fellow English professors</u> probably don't know, use, or appreciate such terms)—terms such as "PARAMETER," "VARIABLE," "A FUNCTION OF," "SAMPLE," "DOUBLE-BLIND," "ORDER OF MAGNITUDE"; all salient terms which you feel confident that, by your salting them into your talk, can only help to <u>heal the wounds, ease tensions, re-build bridges</u>, although all of course quite <u>subliminally</u> (or to use the social scientists' own language, via "tacit," "covert," or "latent" means!), for any *obvious* ploy <u>would surely derail your subtle attempt to reassure the social-science faction</u> that at least *some* humanists <u>can</u> **"speak your own language and even understand you,"** and even if not as well as *you* can here today, we "belletrists" can at least **"democratically validate your rationales,"** in a MORE MATURE AND UNDERSTANDING FASHION OF TRUER INTEGRATION than is usually done, indeed via your **"generously donating a trans-disciplinary rapport"** thus.

And you can only believe that this, your whole <u>attempt-at-rapprochement,</u> has somewhat **succeeded** in this first, difficult meeting, even though THE LATENESS OF THE HOUR precludes your assessing how well you succeeded in your "fence-mending" attempts during casual post-meeting talk because right after adjournment, all the visitors <u>seem pressed for time and have to depart hastily,</u> due most probably to time, as so often.....

with others in the Union, or even attending a committee meeting in the Seminar Room), BY MEANS OF AT ONCE DICTATING those productive "green ideas" <u>into the microcassette recorder</u> you always carry on your person for that specific purpose of "inspiration-saving," ***nevertheless*** even as <u>this procedure proves efficient for yourself</u>, you have gradually sensed that <u>it may be proving eccentric to your colleagues,</u> who "may not quite know what to make" of your pausing to record a cryptic statement [such as (for instance) "VITAL TO DO A POLY-POD DIP-DOWN NOT ONLY TO INSTRUCT BUT FIRST TO ALERT AND EVEN TO CONVINCE; USE FOR VEGETARIANISM AND METRIC CORE-EXAMPLES, AND DOUBLE-VIRGULE REF TO CONSCIOUSNESS AND OF COURSE ALSO MULTIFUNCTIONALITY AND OH ALSO CREATIVE-CHANGE 180 DEGREES...."]

And your <u>awareness</u> that your colleagues were *baffled* thus, now gives rise to your <u>apprehension</u> that they may be massively *misinterpreting* your scholarly ploy of "on-scene idea-nabbing." Might they even be inferring (of course inaccurately) that your talk-taping may indicate "<u>harmless eccentricity</u>" on your part? Let alone worse yet (Minerva forbid) "<u>studied ostentation or affectation</u>"? Or (and worst of all) an <u>attempt to "impress others</u> as brilliant or industrious, but necessarily obscurantist"?

And yet, a bit later, your initial apprehensions miraculously relax considerably, as you steadfastly and encouragingly realize that such "public creative work" is simply one mundane tactic for the important GETTING ON WITH DOING PROPER IMPORTANT CREATIVE WORK" NO MATTER HOW" it must be done, **what you know you must keep on doing**. And so, if you must *seem* egregious, outlandish, maverick, and the like to <u>some</u> in persisting in your work thus, well then you'll just have to suffer unwounded the arrows of being misunderstood by *those less-"amplified" intellects in your midst*—although at once you find <u>you don't at all mind sharing</u> (by public modelling thus) <u>this "strategy of continuous cerebration"</u> (as it were) so that *the untutored others* may gain more confidence in, or really just appreciation of, TRULY-PROFESSIONAL METHODS AND GOALS thus, productive even if initially unconventional.....

---

(19) TRULY AND NATURALLY **CREATIVE, YOU** CAN THEREFORE *UNEMBARRASSEDLY* MODEL THE PLOYS OF SAME, EVEN [OR ESPECIALLY] IN **PUBLIC:**

Although IT HAS RECENTLY BECOME TOTALLY COMMON AND NATURAL TO YOU—when you are in the true "creative" or "producing" cycle of a difficult piece of writing or research, a challenging intellectual endeavor—TO SAVE THOSE SUDDENLY-EMERGING IDEAS <u>just as soon as they strike your mind</u>, NO MATTER WHERE you are (whether you're just crossing the Campus Quadrangle, or sitting at coffee

---

(20) NOR DOES THE **TRUE PROFESSIONAL** SHUN OR SHY AWAY FROM ""GENEROUSLY DONATING"" THE **"LIGHT TOUCHES,"** EITHER [ALTHO *ONLY* WHEN-&-AS *APPROPRIATE*, OF COURSE...]

One day chatting in the Faculty Lounge, YOU CASUALLY AND QUITE UNINTENTIONALLY "SCRAMBLE" SOME COMMON PROVERB. Perhaps it was **"Well, it's just water over the bridge,"** or perhaps **"Well, you can't break eggs without making an omelet,"** or something similar. <u>You instantly notice</u> that your colleagues did indeed respond with **some** jocular enjoyment to YOUR MALAPROP-MANGLING OF A

CLICHÉ thus. Almost as instantly you decide, because they responded so gratifyingly (or rather, "gratified") to the verbal flourish you had treated them to, to "salt in" to subsequent casual conversations, in the Lounge or elsewhere, additional such tortuous or tortured mis-phrasings (just as casually, although from now on intentionally, although of course covertly).

You also instantly realize **your rationale** for doing so—for dropping in such "mals mots" (as **"Well, Rome wasn't burned in three days,"** or **"Well, he knows which side of the bed his bread is buttered on"**). You know your rationale is not at all any desperate "*ego-gain*" or immature "*showmanship*," but simply **to enhance workplace collegiality and atmosphere,** via VALIDATING WORDPLAY IN THE WORKPLACE, AND ALSO COLLEGIAL INTERACTION—in an English Department which you feel could at times could *indeed sorely use* your (or of course anyone's) "help" in "livening up" the Lounge interchanges, but also in directing same toward **more legitimate linguistic finesse and language-appreciation** (instead of just the trivial, gossipy topics of the others—about which you have not been informed *nor do you care...*).

You also understand at once that you are motivated to enrich, not by "*excessive self-centeredness*" let alone "*self-advertisement*" or the like (as jealous or rather unappreciative others might misconceive), but rather by **the altruistic motives** mentioned above, for "each group member should contribute according to his or her specific abilities" and the like (the others supplying *trivial* daily information).

This MORE MATURE STANCE of yours, also allows you to realize and handle well the fact that subsequently, your colleagues now seem to *lack* the earlier laughing appreciations of your subsequent forays into "fractured phrases," when indeed even your arguably-finest one, **"Well, a burnt frog can look at a dead prince,"** engenders no gratifying response, although their silence vindicates to yourself the fact that here indeed is a department *which could use* a bit more of linguistic relaxation and even word-play (although you also then instantly realize that such professionalization is unlikely given your colleagues' prevalent topics of conversation involving no ideas at all but rather, *banal chitchat* as about their parties and other activities to which of course you had not been invited anyhow as usual, although to no regret on your part...)

Soon, however, you just-as-instantly realize that quite possibly your colleagues might be really appreciating in your absence the "verbal flourishes" to which you are generously treating them (although such is really too Utopian for you to hope for, or rather might be *immaturely inappropriate* for you to wish for!) So *although* you realize that even if colleagues aren't consciously "gratefully cherishing" your bon mots such as **"Well, when we get to that bridge, we'll jump,"** (a possibility *almost too ego-gratifying* for your mature and effacing sense of self to contemplate or to feel comfortable with), *at least* you can suspect that they may be "fondly recalling" the phrases behind your back (or let us say out of your presence) as representing the best kind of "PROFESSORIAL ABSENT-MINDEDNESS" generally, and your own "MILD ECCENTRICITIES" specifically, both of which combine to **enrich the mosaic-diversity of the Department,** albeit thanklessly to you, although you also realize that it is always "lonely at the top" for a brave innovator to forward minor matters of PROFESSIONAL TASTE, MORALE, AND REFINEMENT (as well as certain other major, and more important, if equally-ignored, matters also of course)...

So you retain your clear vision to the end, and you conclude by realizing that your role is one who risks—*one might indeed say wittily!*—**"Beating his drum underneath a bushelbasket and falling into a pit at high noon looking for the truth with a lantern"**—incidentally, an especially-deftly twisted phrase itself there, which surely awaits its future limelight-time in the Lounge (albeit of course only appropriately fitting the occasion, never imposed amateurish....)

---

(21) AND EVEN WHEN RECOGNIZED PUBLICALLY—AT LONG LAST!—THE *TRUE* LEADER CONTINUES TO SERVE *MODESTLY*, STILL:

Nobody was initially more surprised than you that, in the midst of the growing crisis of needing to REPLACE THE UNIVERSITY'S PRESIDENT (who departed suddenly in modest disgrace), the entire FACULTY SENATE closed contentious ranks and RECOMMENDED for the interim, pro-tem Presidency none other than the very improbable YOU YOURSELF! But your surprise eased when the SENATE explained that they sought **your own brand of** GRASS-ROOTS LEADERSHIP, your personal style of **replacing the usual academic power-struggles with the** "FAIRMINDED" APPROACH OF INTERRELATING WITH OTHERS, whose goal consists of MUTUALLY ACHIEVED EXCELLENCE, *not* conquest of others to make one's own power or policy prevail, and whose method consists *not* of combat but of OPENMINDEDLY, EVEN "VULNERABLY," COMMUNICATING, *not* repressing or defending one's own biasses, *but* admitting them plus EMPATHETICALLY AND RESPECTFULLY *not* ignoring *but* TRULY LISTENING TO THE OTHER POSITION's point of view...

In addition, the SENATE'S "appreciations" seem to validate your long-term efforts, confirming that that over the years, others had indeed noticed **your own modest, low-key, but dedicated and continuous practice** of THIS MORE MATURE, HENCE MORE COMPETENT AND MORE APPROPRIATE, PROFESSIONAL, ABLE, TYPE OF INTERPERSONAL RELATIONSHIPS, and that your philosophy had indeed "sunk in" or "taken hold" (despite your frequent private despairings otherwise!)—so much so, that your obvious and absolute lack of any expertise in the practical "nuts-and-bolts" of University administration skills, let alone fund-raising and publicity, did not seem to matter, given **your "gift"** (appreciated at last!) **for this "RECIPROCAL EMPATHY,"** a gift of yours which *although* you of course know is **the one and** only vitally-"moral" way to interrelate in academic settings worth the name, *nevertheless* one which you feared would remain utterly unknown to, or inaccessible to, others—due (you hated to say publically) less to their cynicism toward your "idealistic" approach, than to *their basic interpersonal immaturity* at bottom...

And that fear of yours was indeed gloriously banished a few months after your temporary appointment, when, *although* you had agreed to assume the limited-term, even "lame-duck," interim, pro tem Acting Presidency only on the condition that it was indeed temporary (you quite aware that you were scarcely fitted for higher-level Administrative work even despite your considerable abilities on lower, specific areas—you being neither one to "sell yourself short" out of false modesy, nor one to "overinflate" yourself through any regrettable narcissism or even megalomania), *nevertheless* the Senate and whole Faculty and even the Trustees unanimously elect you as the new and official, "permanent," President!

They want you to continue **the virtual transformation of the University** by what they have all now come to realize (*at last!*) IS **the workable salvation of true mature functioning** in any institution of higher education worthy of the name, YOUR FASHION OF OPERATING being at once MORE OBJECTIVE FAIR AND DISPASSIONATE (**no hidden agendas, no power-ploys, no games, no ego-struttings, no politickings**), and also MORE SENSITIVE INVOLVED AND RESPONSIVE (**no bureaucratic facades of status and rank**) than most other approaches. And the enthusiasm of the University for your leadership is so strong, that they wave aside your now-modest demurrings, your equally-gentle mild warning about how "any one approach, mine included, is incomplete" (dare we say that they see—*at last!*—that "your own approach" is indeed the only one best approach?), and thus they install you for a reign (no, one should say run or period of dutiful serving) which may well go on and result in MAKING MODERN EDUCATIONAL HISTORY despite yourself.....

---

(22) AND, TO BE ABLE TO **RETAIN** THAT "*NATURAL, HUMAN* TOUCH," ALSO COMPRISES A VITAL COMPONENT OF **TRUE GREATNESS**:

And then *although* you are truly the President now, and hence quite busy, *nevertheless* you do continue YOUR HABIT OF ATTENDING ALL OF THE UNIVERSITY'S VOLLEYBALL GAMES that you can fit in, that game being your favorite spectator-sport of all (because of its instant continuous action; potentially-seamless teamwork; and amazing reversals of fortune and skill within one game). And *although* at one particularly intense game, the school newspaper photographer candidly (and perhaps "irreverently" or impishly) CAPTURES YOU IN YOUR FREQUENT, CUSTOMARY MANNER of an unrestrained, surely "undignified," posture of robust, jubilant cheering

(with your limbs awry and mouth open in a rictus of emotion—you being truly moved by the game's dynamic verve thus), *nevertheless*, far from being embarrassed by the resultant photographic image of you as "making a mild fool of yourself" (as many lesser folk might well think you did, for all you know), you find that you are actually gratified to see this "undignified" image published in public, because it surely validates certain EDUCATIONALLY APPROPRIATE VALUES, not only the SPIRIT OF COLLEGIALITY, and natural loyal TEAM SUPPORT, but especially a CONFIDENT, UNTHREATENED INFORMALITY even from a person in your most high and formal status, hence giving a naturally-relaxed impression of **"being strong enough not to have to be concerned about superficial images others have of yourself,"** surely one more valid contribution which you can **graciously donate** as only one small part of your so-personal EDUCATIONAL LEADERSHIP STYLE thus.....

[VII.] SELFLESS TO THE VERY END...

---

(23) ...*NOR* DO YOU NEED TO **EXULT PUBLICALLY**—NO, NOT EVEN AFTER YOUR "ULTIMATE VINDICATION" AT LAST!

And then, *when* THE PILOT of the small regional commuter aircraft SUDDENLY FALLS INTO A COMA just as the plane is nearing the short flight's landing field, *although* it quickly becomes clear that nobody of the 16 passengers aboard—yourself included—knows how to fly (let alone land) a Piper Cub (let alone a complex prop-jet), *nevertheless* it **is**, after all, of course nobody other than you, who ascends to the throne (or rather the cockpit), and truly "saves the day" (=achieves the safe landing of the aircraft) after all—and *not* because of any specific aviation experience, *but* because of **your general ability** (although until today the regrettably under-appreciated and under-utilized!) to TAKE CALM COMMANDING COMPETENT CONTROL OF CHALLENGING COMPLEX CIRCUMSTANCES exactly such as this one.....

The Procedural "BIBLE" for THE UNIVERSITY'S STUDENT CENTER ...& esp. for all the "bonafide" Professional Career-Personnel there:

> "....a profession is not, then, an occupation, but a means of controlling an occupation....professions are about power,....their high degree of power and control, which is employed ultimately to benefit the practitioner (and profession), rather than the client (or public). Professional knowledge and practice serves first as the guarantee for an unequal power relationship between practitioner and client, while also serving as an important basis for claims for autonomy and reward for the practitioner."
> [--Key Concepts in Communication, p. 184]

[{(1.)}]

Before, I understood only darkly; but now,
I see the *no-face* behind your EFF-FACE-MENTS.

How Thou erect unto Thee Thine FAÇADE
of *apparent, superficial*, Achievement...

How OUTWARD APPEARANCE will be All.
How **Substance behind** IMAGE, would fail...

How no real **Achievement** stands tall.
How for you, true **Dedication** would pall...

How high goals are not worth your toil,
How resources not worth it to pool...

You'll remodel your **CENTER** in FACE-SAVING
"warm" lannonstone, wood panels, chrome.

You'll front the OUTFACING with a cluster:
a "fine" info/services FLUSTER.

You'll blossom up these ACCOUTREMENTS
on the Veneer-layer of AFFORDMENTS.

You'll mask thus the internal absence,
no Backdrop of **Responsible Competence**

Just prop up the *hollow-vacant-showy*
hollywooden Stage-Set SCAENA

of your own little DRAMA OF APPEARANCES,
behind which no core of **Commitment.**

All to hoist your own career-advancements
up that rickety, low-Status ladder

which is a career in Student Services,
your cohort scrambling for a foothold

to go from "nowhere much" (*as you sure see it*)
from somewhere in between, and so what.
For Ye there seem to follow well,
the "Second-Raters" UNIVERSAL *LAW*

in the Tawdry Business of Today,
and that *RULE* which obtains now is this:

> "THE LESS IMPORTANT YOUR ACTIVITY,
>   OR THE LESS APPEAL & STATUS (*as you see it*)
>   OR THE LESS USE & VALUE (*as you see it*)
>
> WHY, THE MORE YOU MUST SUBSTITUTE SHOW,
> MUST MUSTER APPEARANCE, OF A REALITY;
>
> THE LESS TRUE SUBSTANCE BEHIND,
> THE MORE NEED FOR OUT-UP-FRONT IMAGE...

All your *PLEASANT-PROFFERED SMILINGS*,
merely a *fluorescent* sunshine upon us,

cannot disguise the paper-thin VACANCY,
the absence within of **Integrity**...

So forward your outward "SERVICES,"
but interior, loll disconnected...

Oh, "comply" w/ all GOALS & MANDATES,
but only to the LETTER, prodded Reactive...

[{(2.)}]

...never by the Spirit self-started Proactive.
NEGLECT, thus, the **CENTER'S** visuals.

You could embellish your Hallways,
and aid student taste simultaneous...

...but no; spurn my offers of **good visual arts**,
(with a Face so *PLEASANT-VACANT-DISMISSIVE*)

...while you still blitz the restrooms with **paid ads**!,
let the unshorn **bulletin boards** fester raucous.

> By Athena!, even **Hardee's lunchrooms**,
> even the **local Clinic's waiting-rooms**
>
> let alone **the Public Library's lobby**,
> sport better visuals than **your CENTER**!

But "art" isn't on your OFFICIAL GOAL-ROSTER.
(Then later it is—*but you'll botch it.*)

You reject my series of **Cartier-Bresson**
(the French photographer world-famous

for his decisive-moment images)
in favor of **a series of brown-faded photos**

**"showing the University and the town,
as of a 100hundred years ago"!**

(*This* is some brilliant, original *breakthru*,
to best serve *Aesthetic Education*?...)

[{(3.)}]

Oh you administer things Behind-Scene
with such a vacant, hollow SHEEN:

When I write <u>requesting the return</u>
of the file of visuals I'd presented

   ...whether they were of known artists
   juxtaposed in creative pairings:

   (Van Gogh—*with* Hiroshige/Hokusai;
   The Fauves—*with* Art-Deco posters);

   ...or lesser-known but powerful
   statements of visual integrity:

   (Bonnard, plus Vuillard, interiors)--
   (such pairs as refresh with their power)—

   such brilliants as would sparkle
   both your halls, and the students' vision)--

--<u>Neglect to reply</u>! then, I asking again,
<u>invite me</u> to come search thru your files

(which naturally serve up no trace
of my pr-offered contributions)

but through it, <u>do "MANAGE</u>," so "supportive,"
embracing things while effacing,

via that *VAGUE-VACANT-PLEASANT, GAZE* of yours,
which accelerates my hastied departure!

When <u>I submit</u> my quite-adequate **copier-art**
for your **CENTER'S** Gallery show,

   ("Old paper Money, Stamps, and Maps")
   ("20 Trees—from Realistic to Symbolic")

I hand-deliver it to the secretary for safety,
but, <u>report later you "never received it"</u>...

When I check, then deliver a duplicate set,
<u>never return the dupes w/ "thanks-anyway"</u>.

In fact, <u>don't even return the samples *at all*</u>,
though I requested same once again...

Then finally <u>mount visuals</u>, but hamfisted:
spurn Art, splay the **chaotic but—trendy**

(All continuing to adhere so well
to your vital DOCTRINE OF APPEARANCE:

of "warm flow" to your unsuspecting Public,
but of Behind-Scene STUMBLE & SHAMBLE...)

When <u>I propose how even *informal* subjects</u>
could embody **True Visual Artistry**,

   ...that "combination of balances and imbalances,
   that "unity precarious in its order,

   (Even "Paintings *&* Photos of Italy")
   (Even "Bicycles," "Bridges," "Baseball"!)

...say No; go for "Multicultural Diversity".
<u>Select instead</u> a trendy but vapid

**Readers-Digest – or - Norman-Rockwell type
"portrait of the Negro Patriarch**

with the Offspring gathered around him"!
(Your unthoughtful tribute to Today-Now.)

...and, <u>*never* even explain to me your choice</u>,
thus denying me the enjoyment once more

of your *VAGUE-VACANT-PLEASANT, GAZE*
which facilitates my speedy exit!

[{(4.)}]

Thus put all you have into FRONTAGE,
into Forwarding the STAGE-SET,

so that, economic, you've used up all,
have nothing left for the inner,

the core **integrity** from which
must flow any **import, worth, value**

(Oh you've quite missed **the lesson**
which *surpasses* your UNIVERSAL LAW:

a strategy which could orient us all,
even if "choice careers" tilt and fall:

   A *CRAPPY* JOB—IF TRULY *EMBRACED*,
   A *NOTHING* TASK—IF *COMMITTED* TO FULLY,
   A *DEAD-END* CHORE—IF *ENGAGED* WITH,
   A *ROUTINE* ACT—IF WILLINGLY *ACCEPTED*,
   A *DISRESPECTED* DUTY—IF TAKEN ON *FULLY*...

   YEAH EVEN A "SIDELINE"-CAREER [?]
   [A "DETOUR" *BUT ONLY* **as you sure do see it**]
   SUCH AS ONE IN—STUDENT SERVICES,

   <u>CAN</u> BECOME ITSELF & MUCH *MORE* TOO,
   <u>CAN</u> CREATE OUR TRUE *VALUE* OUTSIDE...

   <u>CAN</u> CREATE YOUR TRUE *WEALTH* INSIDE.

You too care-less perhaps to see?
Your **CENTER** stays on your Periphery...
You cling committed to the PLASTIC,
Hence miss the **Domestic Fantastic**?

[This verse is "for" DOLORES DANTE, Chicago-lunchroom waitress—
and worker extraordinary, as chronicled in Studs Terkel's <u>WORKING</u>]

➔ "Adrift In Academe" ..... Or,

when the "VOYAGE" to TENURE is p-r-o-t-r-a-c-t-e-d

and becomes a "DEEP-SEA ODYSSEY":

..........When the usual **3–to-7** year "***Probationary/Tenure-Track***" 'CRUISE,' ***strays off course** "pirated"* into ***13*** *additional "'wander-years'"* of "***Intermittent/Part-time/Temporary/Terminal/Adjunct***" status:

[*drifting* in a true "Sargasso-Doldrums" plus "Hurricane-Route" before ***finally*** attaining the HARBOR of " TENURE "later"]

.....all on a JUNKET *not* of **3-7** years, *but* of ➔ ***19*** years

[{ "Of which I along have excapaded to tell you..." }]

{{ That "Slight Delay" That Occurred .... Might Furnish Informative Word..... }}

[1.] The Simple **Plot** Of The **Story**:

"In the year **1966**, at a state university, an individual (among others) is hired, on the tenure-track (in English). All the individual's cohorts except him, attain tenure in **three or four** years ("de facto" by 1969, legally by 1970). The individual is "provisionally rejected." He does attain tenure—however, varied circumstances delay it for him **until the year 1985—nineteen years later**."

[2.] A Literary **Explication** Of The Tale's **"Meanings"**:

➔ **SERVING SUGGESTION:** Decide whether this Ship's Log of "*protracted part-time status*" [as sk-etched here], can *illuminate* **(1) "human social nature,"** i.e., **"how does an individual respond to being 'outplaced,' "** *but also*, **(2) the "psycho-politics of In-groups and Out-groups..."**

The SYNOPSIS of the Salt-Stained Sea-Voyage on the Good Ship "Career-Careen":

ACAD. YEAR: (Sep.-to-Jun.)	**Status** of yr **COHORTS**:	**Status** of **YOURSELF**:
1966-67	PROBATIONARY TENURE-TRACK	PROBATIONARY TENURE-TRACK (*aet.* **29** years of age)
1967-68	PROBATIONARY TENURE-TRACK	PROBATIONARY TENURE-TRACK
1968-69	PROBAT. TEN.–TRACK: **TENURE AWARDED**	ON LEAVE for graduate work: **TENURE DENIED**
1969-70	TENURED; full-time.	TERMINAL contract (3rd year)
1970-71	TENURED; full-time.	Half-time TERMINAL contract..

1971-72	TENURED; full-time.	1-sem. TERMINAL contract.; [PRELIMS]
1972-73	TENURED; full-time.	One-year TERMINAL contract.
1973-74	TENURED; full-time.	Fall sem. TERMINAL contract; Spr. sem., REPLACEMENT for a resignation.
1974-75	TENURED; full-time.	**NO** teaching work.
1975-76	TENURED; full-time.	**NO** teaching work.
1976-77	TENURED; full-time.	[Ph.D. EARNED] TERMINAL {1/4-time, **Spr. sem., only**}
1977-78	TENURED; full-time.	TERMINAL 1/2-time Fall. sem.; TERMINAL full-time Spr. sem.
1978-79	TENURED; full-time.	TERMINAL: 1-yr. full-time contract.
1979-80	TENURED; full-time.	TERMINAL: 1-yr. full-time contract.
1980-81	TENURED; full-time.	TERMINAL: 1-yr. full-time contract.
1981-82	TENURED; full-time.	TERM. 1-yr. con; **CONVERTED** back to PROBATIONARY/TENURE-TRACK
1982-83	TENURED; full-time.	PROBATIONARY; full-time.
1983-84	TENURED; full-time.	PROBATIONARY; full-time.
1984-85	TENURED; full-time.	PROBATIONARY; full-time. **TENURE AWARDED** (*aet.* **49** years of age)
1985-86	TENURED; full-time.	TENURED; full-time.
1986-87	TENURED; full-time.	TENURED; full-time.
1987-88	TENURED; full-time.	TENURED; full-time.
1988-89	TENURED; full-time.	TENURED; full-time.
1989-90	TENURED; full-time.	TENURED; full-time.
1990-91	TENURED; full-time.	TENURED; full-time.
1991-92	TENURED; full-time.	TENURED; full-time.
1992-93	TENURED; full-time.	TENURED; full-time.
1993-94	TENURED; full-time.	LEAVE OF ABSENCE medical.
1994-95	TENURED {or start to RESIGN}	**RESIGN** to write full-time... (*aet.* **58** years of age)

DISCLAIMER: The author knows that by the 1980's, *protracted part-time teaching* had become, *rampant, endemic,* even *"permanent."* And so, *his own* chronicle (of *ultimate* tenure *"at last"*) ended better than do *many* others today. And he'd be ironically insensitive not to confirm this here...

--However, his own Navigation Log for 1966-1985, shows what it was like when **"_you,_"** were the **_single and only_** non-tenured or temporary member of "your" department of **40 or so individuals** in a state university. [Not the case today, when *multiple* part-timers abound.]

--And this solo-status meant that "you" were curiously "***both there, and also not there***":
.....in a way few-if-any of your secure, "insider" colleagues {those VARSITY-TEAM members sitting "*above the salt*" so to speak}, appreciated, or even comprehended...

.....but in a way you yourself *had to notice every day*. This **contrastive disjunction** between the cadre of 39 certified sailors snugly aboard-ship—and the one lone individual on the life-raft nearby, ***"there but not there"*****.....

.....plus, in a way that today's multiple part-timers also know: a collective not solo disjunction.....

--And so this **may mean a Tale Worth Telling**....
-No, not for any "RE-VENeGEance-ful Retribution"...
-Just for some GRISTS OF WISDOM we can extract on "**human social nature**" **generally**
-Plus heck it makes for a lively "action-adventure" tale,
   with its *conflict-action-suspense* {*"for sure"*}...   ...and "*good-vs. evil*"   {*"well maybe"*}.....]

...and so, in the spirit of the **"Micro-Story"** [that under-appreciated literary **genre** which elucidates concepts, via splendid specifics / excellent examples / instructive instances], we have:

➔ **"You know you're teaching for 19 years mainly as *part-time / terminal / temporary / adjunct* instructor** [when there was work], **amid a totally-or-largely *probationary – or - tenured* faculty, when....."**

(0) <u>The Dismal Dice-Rolled Preliminary Setback</u>. After your first two years teaching, you decide to "improve your chances" for tenure by taking a year's leave to complete doctoral coursework. *Bad estimation*: had you stayed put, you would surely have been **accepted** for (de facto) tenure—since **all the half-dozen** serious **candidates** were..... As it is, *a new and hard-nosed committee, the very next year,* **rejects all four out of the four** tenure-candidates that year. However, someone up there knew your work: the Committee disagreed so much about you alone, that you can be re-considered as soon as you've passed prelims, which you do by 1971. However, by then, the Great Job Hiring Crunch of the Seventies has of course begun to loom; and,...

(1) <u>Analogically, One feels "Exposed On The Foredeck"</u> It is *"as if"* the financial and enrollment reductions made **the academic department like a CRUISE-SHIP {or an ELEVATOR}.** "All aboard," the gangplank is withdrawn and the doors glide shut, the **select crew** safe aboard—and those who didn't make it aboard or inside, either fell into the sea to drown {or down the shaft}, or—like **yourself**—*hung and clung to the bending stanchions outside the warm dry cabins, splashed with salt-spray, trying to get inside* {or clinging to the outside of an elevator avoiding the shaft's projections.....}

(2) <u>But a better analogy might be the "Beast"</u> Now, the whole department votes upon you annually as to whether to renew (or not!) your contract. Consequently, **you come to see the "Department," its members,** *"as if"* it resembles **some kind of BEAST you have to placate.** *A ponderous galumphing BODY with gaping mouth and vacant bleary eye...*
Not that they are animalistically-obtuse, just diverse. Hence, a A "BODY" easily mis-directed by a wrong stimulus or word I might emit... Also an animal just as easily overlooking earnestly-repeated information about my job-performance I would also try to pass along every week or so as relevant... Of course, an ENTITY never to be crossed; never to be given a bad impression; never one in front of which you could be your own, developing self (whatever <u>that</u> might have been) always one near which you had to be on your best, probationary behavior. Even when you were no longer "probationary, tenure-track" faculty any more, but were in the 13 years of limbo; in fact, especially then.....

(3) <u>Your Seniors Take Proper Care Concerning You</u>. When "NELSON," the then-Chair of the Department (who knew your good work well, after a slow start the first year) announced to you the rejecting vote of the "Killer Committee" (in March 1969, two months after they had voted), he said to you, "The vote was 3 against and 2 in favor. As Chair I could have cast a vote, making it 3 to 3, and thus reversing the rejection. But that would have entailed writing a letter and so forth...." [In short, using up some political capital?] "....So why don't you resign, and then return with the Ph.D. in hand, for a better starting salary?" [In short, clear yourself from the decks?]
This person actually said this to you—that he could have "saved you but didn't," in effect... And in fact, years later, when you are still in the middle of your Limbo-journey, this man, now ex-Chair, will ask you: "What is your status now? Are you still academic staff, or faculty now?" {He having been too absorbed in his own professional affairs and achievements to have been able to keep an eye on your case.....}

(4) <u>Who (Or What) Pulled The Plug On The Project?</u> In December of 1971, at the end of your first semester of the one-semester contracts, you learn that you will not be renewed for the spring semester. In your office, you look at the notes on your desk for a developing project—article about teaching, whatever. *Suddenly, the notes look, **not** <u>alive and engaging</u> as they did yesterday, **but** <u>cold and distant</u>.* Suddenly, survival-concerns have stepped in between you and your proper professional work....
....And suddenly, you know <u>what one of the main</u>—if under-emphasized?—<u>reasons for **tenure**</u> is. Or at least what one of its important—if under-utilized?—functions can be. To snag an easy career with summers off? No indeed: **"to get your proper work done....."** (This insight will deepen in truth, depth, and poignancy in the upcoming semesters, and years.....)

(5) <u>"Communicative Clarity" from the University.</u> A tradition begins, and continues for years. The tradition of the "reassuring notification letter." During a long string of one-semester-only appointments (whether full, or just part, time), you inevitably receive from the University Administration a registered letter, requiring your signature that you have received it. It is of course the official notification that your appointment is "TERMINAL," is not meant to lead on to, or guarantee, or promise, or imply, anything "more" than that. This letter is of course to protect the University legally from any claim of "more." Since you are not at home when mail is delivered, <u>each semester after each semester you perform this ritual trek down to the Post Office</u> to receive what you come to know awaits you, this letter of TERMINAL appointment. ***"BEING VERY CERTAIN THAT YOU KNOW THAT YOU ARE <u>NOT</u> IN, BUT THAT YOU ARE <u>OUT</u>; THANK YOU"***

(6) <u>A Tiny Foretaste Of Your Future Fame.</u> In the Departmental Mail Room, you observe letters for <u>former</u> faculty, <u>who are no longer here</u>. (Usually, they've departed for other, often better, teaching jobs.) But nobody forwards their mail; it floats around the Room for awhile. You understand that *this will be the fate of your own mail—**your own name**—*when you leave, when you are *finally* terminated for *good*. (Like little tombstones, the "wandering-scholar" envelopes lie scattered below the bank of named-and-numbered mailboxes for the Tenured Faculty above...)

(7) <u>Those Who Come After You—And Come Aboard.....</u> A year after you were originally hired [1967], "GASTON" is hired. He seems a white-shoe type, a do-nothing, profoundly anti-intellectual type holding only an M.A., but seeming quite good at slick politicking. Two years later (1968), three others are hired on tenure-track: "FRANK" seems a painstaking teacher, but also with only an M.A.. "ANNA" is an older woman with the Ph.D., though not a researcher. Then there's "PERCIVAL," a jolly holder of only an M.A. in education......

All four of these people make it to tenure, the last ones to board the ship without the Ph.D.... (Years later, "PERCIVAL," who turned out to be a scandalous blow-off for years, is finally retired out to the Personnel Office.) And when "GASTON" attains tenure, about 1971 or so, you hear him say, "Well, yes, we made the varsity team"--speaking *grinningly in your presence.* (Years later he cleans his office. You observe that his entire professional files consist of one half of one filing-drawer cabinet. Your own voluminous research on student writing, alone, fills many drawers. You recall that when you were originally de-railed from the tenure track, in 1969, the then-Chair explained to you that "There were some doubts about your contributions to the department—it was felt that you would not make a strong showing....")

(8) <u>"You Must Have Thought That You'd Never Be Teaching Again!"</u> This was the response of many when—completely laid off in 1973—you assemble the best of the teaching handouts you'd accumulated or created, and then distribute packets of them to the faculty. (To share; to save...) <u>But</u> their response was given in a <u>tone</u> of **cheery levity**, of **innocent jolliness**. As if to them, the thought that one would not be able to teach again, was—merely an *absurd improbability*? (Or not something Serious...)

(9) <u>Who Is Doing What, If Anything?</u> You realize how much ahead of many of the other faculty, the 39 Certified Crew, you are in exploring and refining <u>teaching as such</u>; the teaching of **writing**; the teaching of **introductory/freshmen** courses, but voluntarily not as a chore; and the teaching of **thinking**. (You <u>do</u> know and value the fact that of course, not all but many of the others, have their own specialties, excelling where you do not.) This up-to-date specializing of yours is typical of many younger-guard or new-generation faculty. However, here you are engaged in the "revolution in composition studies," new to most and allegedly "threatening" to some though it needn't be, and then you hear "HORACE," a very old-guard member (also an M.A. only), say that he'd like to teach Advanced Composition, thought of teaching it by bringing in *rhetoric and examples from the eighteenth century*—his earlier area of specialty (in which he had published nothing at all). *"HELLO, ARE WE ALL IN TOUCH AND IN TUNE WITH THE OLD AND THE NEW IN OUR FIELDS HERE"*

(10) <u>"Many On The Bridge, One In The Bilge"?</u> The semesters of the 13-year voyage drag on unpredictably. Sometimes full-time. Or part-time. Sometimes no work at all. This meandering route makes you aware of *how differently* the permanent members, and you, "see things," live your days....

In fact, you could *almost* say that "<u>You Know That YOU'RE THE PART-TIMER When</u>...:"

---While the tenured people float along in their watertight cabin, <u>you anxiously read newspaper articles</u> about state education budget-cuts which might affect the ever-fluctuating tide of money for positions, might open up a new line, might chop off existing temporary lines.....

---While many may not even read the University's <u>Faculty Reporter</u> *[see # 11 below]*, <u>you anxiously scan it</u> to see if an English colleague has received a grant or sabbatical. If so, your hopes leap up that you will be considered for the *one-year replacement* position.....

---You are the <u>sole</u> "defunct" alumnus of the "Class of 1966," still hanging around, all the others either having been tenured, or having left for other teaching jobs. (Still lacking the Ph.D. in hand until 1977, <u>you amass a one-foot-thick stack of rejection letters for jobs</u>, then burn same....)

---When the question occasionally arises (in casual corridor-conversations) as to "when did this-or-that faculty colleague first arrive at the University," you soon learn to keep silent. Because, <u>you know full and painfully well, the starting-date of each faculty member in the Department</u>. You could rattle off *"AUGUST, 1953. JOHN, 1957. DAVE, 1960. RACHAEL, 1960. JOE, 1961. HARVEY, 1962"* And so on.....

HOW COULD <u>YOU</u>, <u>NOT KNOW</u>, <u>NOT</u> BE AWARE OF, THESE LIFELINES-DATELINES, THESE VITAL STATISTICS?

---Worse: when you are in more despairing times, <u>you find yourself calculating</u> "which six of the tenured faculty would have to perish in a car accident driving to a conference in order to clear the seniority ranks most completely for your best chance of being taken aboard *at last*?"...

---And worst: when you are in even darker times, <u>you imagine "spraying a Department meeting with bursts from a machine gun</u>, to clear and clean things up for everyone at last" or mania of some such sort. (You feel *much* "better" about this when "BRUCE," a friend and another mis-stepper, tells you he felt the same way about the **German** department at **Princeton** University.....)

--They Just Don't Understand The Outside. You come to see that the secure, protected *naivete* of some—many?—of the permanent faculty is indeed astonishing. Serene "GILBERT" (M.A.; "Class of 1964," by the way) asks you—in quite-genuine astonishment—"You mean that you would accept a *one*-year contract?" <u>You refrain from vocalizing what your mind is silently shouting</u>: *"THAT'S LIKE ALL THERE IS, IF INDEED THERE'S EVEN THAT, BUDDY.....'*

(11) <u>The "Turkey Shoot" by the Beast in the Jungle.</u> Poignancy in the 13-year voyage increases during the middle years. Then, (A) <u>you become not the only part-timer</u>; a handful of others are also teaching—and vying for any future positions next semester, and (B) the specialized Committee no longer decides in re yearly appointments, but <u>the whole department in session does so.</u>

.....What this meant, was a somewhat-undignified—*what*? Modified *lottery*? *Popularity contest*? *Turkey shoot*? Anyhow, this phenomenon of "mass semi-scrutiny" means that you are *not* evaluated <u>with full dossier open before a specialized Committee</u>, *but* rather <u>impressionistically by whoever of the faculty attends the meeting for the purpose.</u> To-wit & viz.:

-----<u>You must re-double your efforts to "make a good impression upon all</u>," the difficulty being that all are diverse, different, disagreeing. Must you become a "*chameleon on plaid*"? You find that the strain-and-drain of such "impression-management" becomes less a simple indignity, than a subliminally-corrosive abrasion upon at least part, albeit not all, of your productivity, creativity, innovation.....

-----A prudent, well-meaning FRIEND of yours advises that <u>you must "watch your image</u>," including even unto the likes of (1) conform to the prevailing dress-code, (2) don't take a nap in the chair in the Faculty Lounge (do you snore?), and (3) don't use a suitcase as an attache-case. *"THESE CONFORMITIES NEEDED TO REASSURE ABOUT AFFINITY, AFTER <u>THIRTEEN YEARS</u> HERE??....."*

-----The CURRENT CHAIR advises that <u>you must "be friendly, known, accessible</u>," even though as he knows "you don't like chit-chat"..... When you have all evening classes one semester, the Chair advises you that it's important to "be around sometime during the day," and not just for office hours.....

-----In short, you find that <u>you must "take a course"</u> right now, "WORKPLACE REALITIES 101." Its gist:

--(1) **Affinity Impulse**, or "like hires like." People prefer their own kind. This is less herd-mentality or Groupthink, than simply the in/out-group mentality. "Is s/he one of us or not? remains a mandatory question on all tenure-track "exams." [*As well it should to some extent but still...*]

--(2) **Stasis vs. Change**. People can feel insecure, maybe even threatened, when confronted with the truly new-and-different—even (or especially?) in their professions. Although unjustified (we all work, learn, and change-or-not together—or should), nevertheless this anxiety-at-complexity exists. Although desire for new experience is a human motivator, so also is the counterbalancing security, the status quo, familiarity. The old guard doesn't change its ideas, but can only retire and die off?

--(3) **Tenuring as Watershed**. Accordingly from the above, the best advice for the pre-tenured individual is: "chameleon yourself".....Can you *really* discuss such semi-maverick issues as: non-academic writing... composition studies... gay and lesbian liberation studies... interdisciplinary (integrative) endeavor... teaching critical thinking... heck, *teaching* itself, including the pleasure in teaching basic courses"...and the like? Technically, *yes*, you're contributing; actually, *naaaaah*, due to the all-too-human realities in (1) and (2) above.....

--(4) **Postmodern Irony**. This (non-correspondence) course "JOB 101" satisfies the M.D.R. of irony, since (A) here you are in the Ivory Tower removed from the "real world" *and yet* operating in the realities of it!, and (B) the University's mission, nay obligation, is to search toward truth responsibly but fearlessly ["to be in the vanguard of public reflection, debate, and civic action"—David Noble], *and yet* who thought some barriers toward such would lie *within* the U. *itself*... [See #19 below, on "Tenure"]

[27] – 05

<u>And then, each year, at times each semester, the Big Day for **the "vote"** for annual renewal, approaches... When your colleagues will pour your future over coffee perhaps.....</u>

-----Earlier, when fewer rival candidates existed for the temporary positions, you felt free to telephone colleagues who are friends of yours, the night before the Vote. Simply to ask for their support of you if they are inclined to do so. To a person, they say that they think that **"GOSH, IT'S TOO BAD THAT YOU HAVE TO DO THIS..."** (You can only agree...)

-----On the day *before* the Vote, "NORRIS," a supporter but an aging, detached member, casually mentions that he "wishes you well"—but that he's not going to go to the meeting to vote tomorrow.....

-----On the very day *of* the Vote, "VERN," also a supporter (and a successfully-tenured member of the "Class of 1966"), but a sort of head-in-the-clouds, absent-minded, poet, says to you, "Oh, <u>I thought the meeting was tomorrow</u>," or "Oh, I thought the meeting was <u>an hour later</u>," or "Oh, I hadn't changed my office clock from Daylight Savings Time!" You both **"LAUGH AND AGREE THAT WOW THAT WAS QUITE A CLOSE CALL INDEED HA HA!"** *You rage inwardly*, fearing that the vote might have been close, say a tie, and that <u>the single vote of "NORRIS," or of "VERN," might have gotten you in</u>—but <u>only if they had attended—and if you had not gotten back in this semester, possibly you might have been left out in the dust for good due to constantly-changing circumstances</u>—**"AND SO UPON WHAT SLENDER AND AMUSING THREADS of CHANCE, DOES YOUR POSITION, YOUR LIVELIHOOD, YOUR CAREER, YOUR FUTURE—AND YOUR CHOSEN CALLING—HANG INDEED "**

-----A month *after* the Vote, the <u>Faculty Reporter</u> (of sabbatical-announcing fame) lists some of your many emerging publications in the "Achievements" section. Quite soon afterwards, this colleague and that one congratulate you about them. You definitely refrain from saying what you can scarcely restrain from bursting out with: **"BUT WHY DIDN'T YOU SEE THEM WHEN YOU INSPECTED MY UPDATED CREDENTIALS BEFORE YOU VOTED UPON ME-AND-THE-OTHERS FOR THE NEXT YEAR'S POSITIONS?   BECAUSE YOU NEVER BOTHERED TO GO AND INSPECT MY UPDATED CREDENTIALS BEFORE THE VOTE, THAT'S WHY"**.....

(12) <u>The Unbearable Ambiguity Of Being—Ranked "Why-ever"</u>. One year, when the whole Department votes on all the temporary staff in "Turkey-Shoot" fashion as defined above, you end up *only fifth out of the six contenders*—and some of them, new this year. You and your faculty allies (of whom there are many by now) ponder this unusual setback:

--"Well maybe its petty jealousy of some kind for your many publications....."
  "Well heck it could be....."

--"Well maybe theyre tired of seeing the same issue come up again......?"
  "Well heck it might be....."

"Well maybe they think, this has gone on so long, so just put you out of your misery.....
  ""Gosh perhaps do you think....."

"Well maybe they take you for granted, think youll always be around ready to serve....."
  "Well wow, that it might be....."

"Well perhaps discrimination exists against single people even just unconsciously....."
  "Oh yes that too, could that be....."

...*We end up* **"SCRATCHING OUR HEADS AND AGREEING THAT IT SURE IS HARD TO TELL ISNT IT MY GOSH"**

(13) <u>Life Begins At The Tenure-Track?</u> After thirteen years of this voyaging in Limbo, you fear you may at last become *psychologically undone* because of it. Quite apart from being actually *legally discontinued* (because "more than seven years' service may give one a legal claim for tenure," blah, blah—despite all those superbly-clear Letters of Termination you signed for at the Post Office over the semesters...)

So in 19**82**, <u>you apply for "conversion"</u> from Academic Staff status to Faculty status (probationary or tenure-track type). On your merits as a composition specialist—which you have become, and which the "literary-heavy" Department now realizes/admits that it needs. Appropriately and fortunately, <u>**you do receive tenure-track, probationary status**</u>—regained from when lost in 19**69**....

--You perceive that *you* were the one who had to do this, to initiate it. The *Department* did **not** see fit to do this, despite your faithful (if intermittent) service since 1966. ["Personality" looms large?]

--And the letter from the Dean of the College stipulates that certain information on my performance, etc., must now be kept. Why? In his own words, "so that we may **begin a record of his achievements here.**"

> [.... "***BEGIN***" a record??

> ...But <u>what the hell were you doing</u> between 1966 and 1982? Between the ages of **29** and **42**?
> ***"MAYBE WALKING IN THE SNOW WITHOUT LEAVING FOOTPRINTS....."***]

(14) "<u>Outsiders See More Inside Than Insiders</u>"? You begin to detect that the CURRENT CHAIR is "*someone else again.*" You would not say out loud, *a "maladjusted paranoid sociopath,"* of course.....But, do Secured **Insiders** naively overlook problems-injustices, where the Vulnerable **Outsiders** see things, not distorted with "minority-*paranoia*," so much as with keen-eyed *realism*?...

One could *almost* say that "<u>**You know that you have A PROBLEMATIC BOSS, when:....**</u>"

--Despite your best efforts, you get on the Chair's bad side—simply by inquiring of others about the procedure for hiring staff, when he cheerfully "blows away" your inquiry.....

--You experience his truer nature: his saying to you, "You are in my power," right in the presence of another faculty member too.....

--You hear him say "I always run a meeting knowing ahead of time how it's going to turn out."

--You see that he's insured that the Executive Committee consists of many of his subservient favorites. You hear that one day, "CLARA," a liberal-activist teacher, ran out of a meeting in tears of consternation from his harrassment..,..

--You hear him actually say—right in the public department meeting, and sarcastically—that the College's Associate Dean, "RUDOLPH," is "The kind of person whose ambition is to be a high-school principal"... More, you then notice that *nobody* else seems to think that that remark exceeds mere "non-collegial" *incivility*, easily attains florid *unprofessionalism*....

--You raise your growing concerns about the Chair to ROSE, an established-and-respected department member. Abruptly she replies, "Well, _____ is my friend, and I'm not going to say anything against him." (Years later, after his final public unmasking, she does change her tune; a bit too late for Validity.....)

--You gradually discover that the CHAIR has planted in everyone, the false idea that you did not seek to continue employment there, but instead, that *you resigned*, voluntarily and even enthusiastically. Specifically, that you "burned your bridges behind you" thus. And for *years and years and years*, you have to correct (or try to correct), *colleague after colleague after colleague*, who say such as "Well, apparently you broke your service or otherwise harmed yourself when you resigned." ("*I DID <u>NOT</u>, RESIGN*!!" you must reply, of course to the echo of no-response...)

--In fact, at the crucial vote on you—when you come up for approval to **re**-enter a probationary, tenure-track probationary position (in 1982), you have a rival; there is a contest. Two candidates vie for the one position, you and "MATT" who is one of the CHAIR's "favorites."
Fair contest? But before the vote, the CHAIR himself individually presents to many faculty, letters-of-reference praising "MATT" greatly. He justifies this ploy by saying that "People had requested more information on MATT." (The point being once again, not the Chair's biassed electioneering, but the faculty's *unawareness of, or unconcerned non-disapproval of*, such arguable action.....)

--Later, the CHAIR comes up for yet one more renewal (after *12 years* of shambling). Elder-statesman "ALLAN" ponderously states, "I believe _____ is doing a good job." "***BUT CAN YOU NOT SEE***," you cannot yet shout.....

--Much later, after _____'s belated departure from the Chairship and your tenuring at last (post-1985), more and more colleagues, "ROSE" among them, take to saying, "Well, everyone knew about _____ all along!" "***DID THEY NOW***," you know it is of no use to shout.....

(15) <u>Inspected, Poked & Prodded for Quality-Control.</u> Over the years of your voyage, the business of evaluating "probationary" faculty (let alone part-timers) becomes more and more ponderously-rigorous (as the University creaks and groans topheavily toward supposed improved status).

--You live in genteel, refined terror of the **student course-evaluations**. Yours are much lower than the others' average, not any longer because of (1) your earlier psychological brusqueness and impatience, which you have conquered, but now to (2) your attempting to teach thinking, as against content-mastery—a painful paradigm-shift which makes disgruntled students downgrade...

--Fortunately, "3" or average between 1 and 5 is acceptable. So are your 50 <u>pedagogical articles</u> placed in a dozen language-arts journals—more by far than the sum total of such written by all the rest of your 39 peers, although again, many others did valuable things you couldn't, and anyhow, "each cobbler to his/her own last"....)

--But you also come to live in increasing *disgust* at the annual classroom visitations by members of the Personnel Committee. "Inspections..." You love sharing teaching ideas and methods, but after *visit after visit after visit*, you vow that, if and when you do attain tenure, "*NO person other than a student* will *EVER* enter your classroom again"—anyhow without your express permission....

> .....and then, on 07 June **1985**, you receive the Chancellor's letter with final approval of your promotion to Associate Professor "with **TENURE**" effective July 01.....
> [You frame a copy to hang in your clothes closet in an obverse, occult, now-whimsical "shrine"....]

(16) <u>Residual "Rubbings" Resist Resolution</u>.....

Some years later, the "Turkey Shoot" or whole-department vote is employed again. The issue is which of three adjunct teachers should be converted to the one tenure-track position available that year. Voting is close. The first vote ends in a tie for first place. A runoff-vote provides the winner, "EDWIN," with a margin of only one or two....

--In the meeting, "DAN," a youngish tenured member (he arrived after your 13-year wastewater sail) sincerely, responsibly *regrets and criticizes* this so-impersonal way of selecting the conversion-person. "Should we not wait and deliberate and study credentials, and meet again next week?" he asks...

--Outside the meeting afterwards, you turn and spatter "DAN" with cheery but top-of-the-voice invective. *"SOOOO, THIS IS YOUR FIRST TURKEY SHOOT, IS IT? WELL, YOU SEE WHAT IT'S LIKE! AND HOW GOOOOD OF YOU TO BE SO CONCERNED ABOUT IT!....."* And so forth upon well-meaning and totally-innocent "DAN"....

--But at once you see you're clearly out of line. You've violated the unwritten code of decorum, of non-boat-rocking, which your **so-"collegial"** department has developed over the years. True, this harmony <u>is</u> better than the cliques, factions, and turf wars and the like which do plague so many departments. (Even if at the cost of any honest, invigorating ideological controversies, which however do not exist....) You regret your fire-hose effusion. But it reveals how stubbornly-fierce the submerged volcanic pressure remains from your geologic "past time".....

(17) <u>"What It's All About Really".....[Take Two]</u>.

You found your insecure Outsider-status especially difficult to bear because over time, you've come to love teaching. Your job gradually became a rewarding calling, even with lackadasical state-university students. (1) Teaching; (2) teaching freshmen; (3) teaching writing; (4) teaching thinking—this quartet of passionate pursuits gratifies you.

--However, you sense that X % of your colleagues don't share those developed enthusiasms. This despite both their valid actions (their yeoman paper-grading labors) and their more-vacuous ones (their professed platitudes and then semi-private sighings)....

--In fact, you start to realize that the **"corporate culture"** of "your" department, is corroding you. Underneath that famous surface **"collegiality"** seems to lie the **"script"** of **"Ain't It Awful."** (As in the amazed, sympathetic, poor-you response: "*You mean you have **four, freshman,** courses this semester?*") And so you start to suspect: could *your* subliminal frustration, with *their* frustration at "having to come to work here every day," have subliminally tinctured your attitude toward them—and hence in boomerang-fashion, their attitude toward you?

THE SCENE is **the annual Christmas Party in the Departmental Lounge**. "NATHAN," a dignified-traditional elder member, is discoursing with "DONALD," a legitimate poet. You can't *believe*—at first—what you begin to hear (but *in vino veritas*, and it *is*, after all, in that glad glowing interlude after that first high-test eggnog). You are *amazed* to hear them say that **the so-called "PERKS" of the teaching career were a large factor as to why they entered it!** That's right; and during talk over their second 'nog (you savoring fresh-brewed coffee betimes), their conversation waxes more and more frankly, lushly appreciative of the such as *Times Off.....of lengthy Christmas breaks.....of "enriching, invigorating" hikes in the Alpine regions of Europe* [of course with the enabling fact of a **tenured** position to return to in the autumn as an imperative if tacit **Implicit Presupposition** or unmentioned **sub-text**].....*of stays in "some of the most exclusive" British.....*

--But this time you are proud of yourself. You recall your regrettable, firehose-blast tirade splashed upon poor "DAN" earlier! You tell yourself: no second outburst! Instead, you break in to their dialog, your tone calm and even, you think, "pseudo-speculative." And you say: "*Well, all that is so true of course. But you know it's also interesting to think of teaching as, well, as working in an, oh you might say an **intrinsically valid field of endeavor**. That is, I mean you do have the sense that, unlike managing oh say a bill-collection agency or the like, that whatever we do get accomplished, after all we <u>are</u> working in vineyards of **innately significant realms of validity**, that what we attempt is **intrinsically important, significant**, and surely **both challenging and rewarding in the attempt**! a three-part challenge of material, people, and techniques, **a privilege to confront**, and worth the students' time and ours.....*"

And you pause....

.....And you see how your two auditors <u>pause</u>, for an interval which fascinatingly is "just more than brief" .....before, to a person, both of them assuredly <u>agree</u> that ***"WELL YES INDEED THAT IS A NEW AND INTERESTING WAY TO THINK OF IT AFTER ALL***

(18) <u>Wee Timorous Giftie! Which Comes Round, Goes Round...And Sails Forth</u>. And now it is the year 1986. Twenty years after you first came to work at the University; one year after your Tenuring..... The Chair of the Social Committee, "TESS," comes around to solicit money for gifts for the "Twenty-Year Service" recognitions for, in effect, the successfully-tenured members of the, of your, "Class of 1966": ROLAND; WILLIAM; VERN; CLARA; GREGORY; others. You explain to TESS with some quiet intensity, as to how you are somehow *not* inclined to contribute. and why—"should liferaft-survivors feel philanthropic to those who scrambled aboard earlier?" "TESS" maturely comprehends, and then exits your office.

--Soon after, I am invited to be a part of that twenty-year folks' **celebration**. (It seems that "TESS" had thoughtfully brought the matter up with the entire Social Committee.) I decorously refrain from expressing my degree of gratitude for this act of—inclusion? --of recognition? --of acknowledgment?

--All members of the Class of 1966 receive appropriate gifts. [I receive a book. It is maritime, which is appropriate considering my avocation of Great Lakes sailboating—and my job-related writing of 135 published feature-articles in a dozen yachting magazines. My gift book is the annotated edition of Jerome K. Jerome's classic nautical chronicle <u>Three Men In A Boat</u>, lavishly illustrated. I enjoy it, and then give it to my friend JOHN in Madison, a former and loyal crew-member.]

(19) <u>Ghostly Doppelganger</u>..... During your unlucky-13-year voyage with happy if deferred landing, you often catch sight of your ghostly "*BROTHER*" next to you—he who would have been tenured by 1968, had the vote been 3-to-2 for instead of 3-to-2 against...

--He more secure, serene, able to speak up-and-out more, not just to enjoy professorial privileged peremptory declarativeness, but also to feel more validated, and surely to explore and think without fears of censure or non-renewal....

--In fact, on into the late 1990's, you have recurrent *dreams* that you were promised tenure; began to act naturally; then were denied tenure after all.....

(20) <u>And About **That Issue Of "TENURE"**: Your Own Little Contribution to the Debate as to "Whether We Still Really Need It"</u>....

--You recall what you learned in "WORKPLACE REALITIES 101." Fear of major change, newness, conflict-disagreement.....

--You review your professional contributions, all of them as solid as you could make them, many of them quite superior enough to contribute much to the profession.

--However, you are also grateful that in the 1970's and 1980's at your state-university institution, research (etc.) standards *were not yet all that high*. This meant not that you could loaf, but that you could largely follow your own path (as all genuine academic work must do), without being poked-and-prodded by Reappointment Committees as to whether this "new, different, innovative, etc." material was "really quite solid and legitimate," etc., etc., blah blah blah....You were very lucky to be <u>here</u> (at a "second-rank institution—only second-rate if it lets itself remain so—or thinks of itself as such), and <u>then</u> (before the tenuring and promotion standards bar got raised insanely high).

--This, so you could "*get your own proper work done*": surely THE main rationale for tenure itself..

[[EXAMPLE: I spent <u>most days of the summers of 1992 and 1993</u> in Room 310 of the classroom building, painstakingly processing the millefeuille-leaved research for <u>Mind-Play</u>, my emerging "big book" on thinking, spread out on eight folding tables. I still had nothing definite to show by the end of the second summer. Tenured, I didn't have to. But the book I hoped to bring off, would be a needed, useful, and enduring contribution. *"Good Work Takes Time"*... Imagine being asked, "But what have you published in the last 12 months?!"...]]

And yet, while **pre**-tenured, *you still had to "fly below the radar" in a certain way.* That is, could you *fully* participate in the Department *safely, before* tenure, thus? "Alas, **no**," in the following cases:

1. Can you share your creation of a classroom-proved "**interdisciplinary**" unit—*if* your department still regards integrative studies with *some* legitimate objections, *much* misconceived suspicion?

2. Can you share your excitement with the "process"-revolution in **composition** studies—*if* your department is, and remains, *heavily-literary*, in that Great Tradition?

3. Can you emphasize your **non-academic, real-world writings** (feature articles in special-interest magazines for boating, travel, nature, etc.) which confirm that *you can indeed write*—*if* your department still holds "POPULAR JOURNALISM" definitely **below the salt,** and if the trend toward "CREATIVE NON-FICTION" has **not yet arrived**?

4. Can you broadcast your savoring of **excellence in teaching** itself, even and especially in the required (and hated) **beginning courses**, even English 101 and 102, and can you share your many **pedagogical articles** (50 of them, in a dozen national and regional language-arts journals)—*if* in one's department "perhaps-to-be," most seem to prefer unchallengingly-**conventional** teaching of upperclass majors plus their specializedresearch (and in a few cases, their sedulous relaxation)?

5. Can you proffer fascination with the emerging "**critical thinking**" movement? But thinking is rarely taught, though teachers suppose it is. This is a paradigm-shift issue, wherein major new-and-different ideas can provoke resistance, defense, anxiety....("This is not a game for the untenured," wryly intoned one participant at a Critical Thinking conference—not the least because of student evalutions....)

6. Can you include in your re-appointment dossier, your articles on **gay liberation studies**, they being germane not only for the current "multiculturalism-diversity" trend, but also for thinking well about difficult topics? Unfortunately, the risk is too great of one member of a Re-Appointment Committee being subliminally-anxious about this hot topic.....

7. And above the Department level, can you prudently emit even a whiff of negative criticism, however constructive, within earshot of a currently third-rate University **administration** whose actual propulsions are simply good public image in the press, good rankings in national surveys, good image with their superiors?

...You feel that all the above powers your springboard to the position—insane, uncooperative, realistic— that: <u>"if there were *no* tenure, how could *anyone* ever afford to innovate? *Everyone* would have to look over their shoulder at the REAPPOINTMENT COMMITTEES who would be reviewing their work every five or so years..."</u>

(21) **The "End Off It**." *Nine* years after tenuring in 1994, and *twenty-seven* years after starting in 1966, I *retire from teaching*. (I still loved classroom teaching. But I had to continue as educator by writing. I had to complete a major work on teaching/learning thinking; a book of poetry; a student-writing anthology; etc. ...)

My <u>retirement citation</u> (prepared by the current Social Committee) is quite brief; even laconic, compared to their fulsome effusions for others, albeit quite complete. The current CHAIR, MARIANN—competent leader, also sweetly-empathetic soul—wonders to me whether the citation isn't "kind of spare or sparse." But I'm not worried. It says what it should concisely, and "all-in-small" is good writing style.

I also receive a <u>retirement gift</u> selected by the current Committee.
...It is a book about 19th-century American *cookery on the frontier, the range, the wild west.*
...Rough-raw recipes over open fires and the like.
...[Beached ashore from the ten-year gift of the boat on the English stream?]...
...Its *utter irrelevance* to me and my work is, of course *quite sufficiently "relevant"*—to *me.*
 (Tho not to MARIANN, who, bless her charitable less-harried heart, thinks the book is original, interesting...)

——— ——— —— — — ----- --- ═════ ════ ═══ ══ ═ ~~~~~ ~~ ~~ ^^^ ^^ ^^ ^ *

*Exit **ridens**; ou bien, en tout cas, en **souriant**.....en disant, "Bien faire y laissez braire"*....

[i.]

CHEAP SHOT / DIRTY POOL:
A Skewed & Flawed INTERVIEW
with a Departmental Colleague,
Fudging & Juggling its Data,
to Fabricate an Unfair Portrait,
Beschmirtszching a Hard-Working
COLLEAGUE for "Politics" Thus:

Or: How Gay Activists in Academe Seek to *Advance Their Agenda for Special Rights* by Sabotaging Empiricism! In pretending to be "surveying current attitudes," they'll actually seek out only the most atypical, extreme cases (or case!) of "Homophobia Among University Colleagues" (via the ploy of Insufficient & Unrepresentative Sampling-"Errors"). But they'll then present this *atypical* instance, *as if* it truly represented widespread phobic attitudes in the whole faculty population today... Via this "cooking the books," the GAY ACTIVISTS seek to *artificially inflate* the true [= but infrequent] incidence of academic HOMOPHOBIA, all the better to engage in their Sensationalistic Special Pleading for their Minority-"Rights" Cause! (But in so doing, they ironically only *increase* any real problems, if any do exist...)

The INTERVIEW. BRANDON talks with CORA. She is not only a colleague in his own Dept. of English, but also is herself a specialist in minority studies [Black & women writers]:

BRANDON: And so, CORA, I'm interviewing faculty on their responses to "*homosexuality – homophobia - gay liberation – heterosexism*". But this time around, I'm simply identifying issues to explore, important viewpoints not to overlook. (And as you know, this isn't for "liberation politics," but rather is for "liberal pedagogy." To find out "how can we think critically and competently about a social issue." And no

teachers have room in their course for everything!) So first, do you have any **unstructured, impromptu responses** to the gay issue?

CORA: Well, I'm just not too sure whether the gay rights movement, gay activism, is even basically valid. Because, I did hear that recently, in Chicago, in a public restroom, a homosexual accosted a nine-year-old boy and actually bit his penis off....

BRANDON: [*".....* "]

[Here, BRANDON **falls** *figuratively* **to the floor,** then takes a moment to **recompose himself**]

.....[*then*]: But **CORA**....that doesn't seem like gay sexuality. That seems like—well, atypical sadistic pedophilia?..... And not only are "boy-lovers" distinct from most or all gay males anyhow, but also they claim to cherish boys, not mutilate them?....

CORA: Well, but you see, it's sexuality all the same, isn't it....

BRANDON: [*sees it's lost for now*] .....Well, anyhow, another probe might be, "Does homosexuality, **currently receive too much attention in education—just the right amount—or not enough attention**, and why? Any response?

CORA: ...Actually, I think you, BRANDON, have spent too much time discussing this issue. There are other issues which are at least as important.

BRANDON: [*".....* "]

[BRANDON reflects silently, **"too much time? One half-hour presentation in twenty years?"** Perhaps wisely, he does not voice this reflection. Surely unwisely, he does not actually ask, "But exactly **what other important issues** are we overlooking at their expense?" But no, wait: CORA could simply have noted "just-any-issue"....]

CORA [*continuing*]: After all, we don't discuss heterosexuality in public; therefore why be so explicit about homosexuality?

BRANDON:....[*".....* "]

[*He's recalling* that, at this moment, **CORA's office door displays photos of her recent re-marriage.** (Complete with rice-shower; it's not "raining men"....), Intuitively, BRANDON does not mention this fact...]

[....*then, resuming personfully*]: Well, another survey-question might be, "In teaching, do you deal with the gay issue as a "minority or multicultural or diversity" issue at all, and if so, how?" Actually on this one, CORA, I know of course that you are into minority perspectives. You've written a book for an Authors' Series on a famous *Black* American author, and you are doing a study of an earlier *feminist* author....

CORA: No, on that issue, I just let the students make any connections on their own.

BRANDON: [" ..... "] [then] ....Okay, I see....

    [...*He's recalling* a prize-winning paper by one of CORA's students. It mentioned virtually all minorities, **except homosexuals—but its thesis required it to.** *But he also recalls* CORA's notes overlooked this...]

CORA [*continuing*]: ...Besides, I don't think homosexuals are a "minority group." After all, they choose their sexual orientation.

BRANDON [.....*after another silent pause-to-regroup*]: But . . . the overwhelming testimony, . . . of gays and lesbians, state that they don't decide upon their sexuality, they discover it—discover their "hitching posts," as your famous author said....

CORA: But you see, that's just what they say.... [*then with considerable heat*] And by the way, BRANDON, I think that you are trying to make me out as homophobic, when I am not! I really resent....

[....**but, at this p-art-iculate poing, the INTERVIEW** *cludes*.....]

___....----====++++~~~~^^^^ ^^^ ^^ ^*%!/-___

[ii.]

The Somewhat-More-Balanced
SURVEY-SWEEP of DATA,
proffered humanistically via an Extended,
or "Homeric," Analogy or Metaphor!

"Now, *even as* the biological malady of MALARIA has become resistant to current drugs (such as FANSIDAR) which now suppress but do not destroy it,... *so also* the sociocultural ailment of HOMOPHOBIA is only blanketed over, is not "scotched," when treated by the current prophylaxes.... Including such standbys as the earlier LIBERAL HUMANISM (take a tablet of "be fair") plus the more-recent powerhouse of POLITICAL CORRECTNESS (have a dose of "polite-esse oblige"), plus "AMOUR-PROPRE" or GOOD SELF-IMAGE (pop a capsule of "What, *Moi* a Bigot?")... But also including such "over-the-counters" as the DESIRE to avoid embarrassing any people with whom one has to interact closely, plus the UNEASE of communicating in civil but quite candid fashion...."

--The competent but traditional **professor** who told me that a certain gay poet "also wrote some *non*-gay poems of better import"—and that these might be preferable. He was disturbed by what he said were some of the "explicitly sexual" G/L poetry in our traditional college textbooks. [Which were *those*, I wondered, and asked him, and I did not find out...] I suggested that some of the specifically gay-subject poems indeed offered good general *universal* themes. (I should—no, could—have noted Joe Butkie's "The Trojan Horse"...)

--The **five departments** who "supported" the new Gay Studies course *but* could find no home for it in their schedule, not even as a Special Course. (True, the schedule is tight; but, **"*Not In My Back Yard*"**?)

--The **literature professor, a feminist** [with a waft of lesbian dimension herself], who said she *only recently* had thought to include gay/lesbian poems and stories—but especially for the *gay/lesbian* students themselves, whose needs she *only now* felt that she'd overlooked.

--The "with-it" **straight-male colleague** who proposed a course in modern poetry via *diversity-of-voices*. His syllabus presented "Black Voices," "Feminist Views." And many more. But no "Gay/Lesbian Notes." Seeing this, I genially quizzed him. "Which group might be left out?" He didn't know. "Oh, it's about 10% of society," I hinted. He tried, but simply *could not guess*... Informed at last, he ruefully smiled, slapped his brow, gladly added. {The "invisible minority" indeed?}

--A **Black woman colleague** (later a good friend indeed) who *criticized* my presentation on Gay Rights at the departmental Retreat on "minority perspective." She said I was too *defensively forceful* (alas I was, through residual nervousness...) But also, "*too basic in my information.*" For, "This is the Nineties, after all, and we're past all that old-hat basic stuff and also confrontation-stances!"
[Good; however, when later discussing the Gay Thing further with me, she opined that (1) G/L's are not a true minority group because they do choose their orientations, plus (2) she was uneasy because the Bible does call it an "abomination" after all. In fact, she could disclose that when a dean at her former university came out as gay and as a transvestite, she had temporary problems with it. {The lavender menace as old-hat?}...]

--A **male colleague** and I who were close friends for years, in fact for decades. Finally I formally came out to him. He had suspected, he said. Also he said that he had already "mulled it over" and that "it was okay with him." Even, that he (who seemed heterosexual to a point of clinical obsession) had been fellated once when in the military, what the heck...
So, all seemed sunny; but at once, two cloudy recollections fore-shadowed the bad weather which did arrive. (1) The only explicit references to homosexuality he had ever made to me in the prior twenty years were (A) "I think two of the men at that party were gay, though that's not a very good thing to say about a person, of course." And (B) when I told him that two women who worked as psychotherapists and shared living quarters were in fact not lesbians, his response was

the monosyllable "Good!" but uttered with enough enthusiasm to blow out the room's windows...

...And too soon indeed, the barometer did drop. In the ensuing weeks after I had come out to him, he gradually distanced himself ... selectively recalled only the most negative things about me from the last two decades ... and finally (despite his protestations of "vulnerability, self-disclosure," and all the rest) ostracized me, dropped me as a friend.

--The **heterosexual feminist professor** who said she agreed to be the contact-person for a regional professional Gay/Lesbian Alliance. A colleague jokingly asked, "Are you going to sell your house?" The professor laughed genially. I thought silently: perhaps she would *not* have laughed if feminism had been at stake.

--The **feminist professor** who (or so a lesbian student reported) was reading the new Women's Studies bulletin—came across a lesbian poem—*eyebrows shot up and she quickly skipped* to the next item.

--The **two responses** to my "zapping" a biassed presentation. My University sponsored (and touted) an off-campus speaker on the trendy (and now-mandated) issue of "multiculturalism-diversity." At the well-attended talk, I soon noted that his scheme omitted "sexual orientation" from the otherwise-long list of minority groups. Heart pounding, I did the classic Radical Protest in Public. [**I felt right On The "Edge," but of course I was only one millimeter Out There Ahead...**] I resolutely interrupted publicly, and questioned the omission. The touted speaker responded by waffling, and trying to smear me instead. But more interesting were two peer-responses later. One colleague of mine referred genially to what he called "*my big fuss.*" Another colleague asked me whether I was "one of those with *planted questions designed to get discussion going.*" This was odd indeed, since this same second colleague had recently worked on an all-University clause forbidding discrimination on the basis of—that's right, "*sexual orientation*"...

--A **straight male colleague** who was an old-guard staunch leftist, even radical liberal for social causes. (He and his wife even marched in the area's Gay Pride Parade one year.) Yet after the department faculty volleyball game at the local grade school, only he and myself left in the locker room, he *stepped into an adjacent area to change clothes.* Okay—probably he's just modest always, even when amid heterosexual males, who knows. [**Indeed—who knows?**]

--The.... but we///|\\\ \ \\ \ ___ __ ... .. --- - ~~

[iii.]

"JUSTICE"—Arrives...
also "Full Awareness about
TRUE Justice...
Or does she? And does it?

.....as for [**1**] **Actions accomplished, the achieving of JUSTICE:**....
--In **timing**, JUSTICE ... ARRIVES [*if* she arrives], **WHENEVER** SHE **DOES** ARRIVE...
Usually **not** when it's TIME for her to arrive, which surely is "always" or "already"....
[**And when present at last, will she stay?...**]
--And in **causality**, JUSTICE ... ARRIVES [*if* she arrives] SIMPLY **BECAUSE** SHE ARRIVES, for reasons "whichever"...
Not because it's RIGHT, JUST, MORAL for her to arrive, which surely it "always" was....

.....And as for [**2**] **Awarenesses attained, full freedom of thought about Justice...**
--Are "we" ever really able to KNOW reliably about "true Justice" *vs.* immoral-unethical-unjust beliefs and behavior—and profoundly mistaken ones, too...?

--Can we only "KNOW," what the **Puppet-Master** of the current **Climate of Opinion** of the times tells us are **Today's Truths** and **Today's Taboos**—the tune to which we must tango? Where invisible fences prohibit us from wandering from the current home-base norms-mores-folkways, into any outlandish, egregious, maverick "inconceivable" terrain of Another Paradigm. Such as **"true Justice"** above and beyond local norms...

--And **Then** YESTERDAY and/or TOMORROW, the **right** *of* **Now**, *may be wrong,* and vice versa respectively...

--"Yesterday's Taboo **HERESY** (or even AN ISSUE UTTERLY-INCOMPREHENSIBLE, INCONCEIVABLE) is Today's **ORTHODOXY** (a mandatory Truth) and tomorrow's **COMMONPLACE** (a "ho-hum truism," an "of-course" or utterly-unconsidered issue)."

--More technically, the truly-New/Different may be [non-/mis-/under-] seen by "us" in three flawed ways.
1. "**N**ot-Thought-Of/About" (cognitively, is simply not on the plate or in the radar screen)...
2. "Un-THINK-Able!!!" (affectively, is "of-course" Wrong Immoral-Unnatural and etc.)... or the most difficult to comprehend,
3. "**N**on-Comprehensible" (isn't even debated, etc.—simply can't be comprehended or understood via one's pervasive Social Script to which one dances strung along. As in, "You just don't get or See it, Do You?!)

"You 'Justice-Bearers' of Today: but Where Were You Earlier?" (Not that you could have been, nor I myself, or anyone, it seems...)

--**You college-university faculty who now display a "Safe Space" sign on your office doors.** (To announce a haven for gay-lesbian-bisexual-transgendered students.) By your act-ion, I am oh-too-wryly "amused." This is very NICE, and nice-of you. **B**ut I wonder whether you think you are doing it because you've personally *decided* that it is the responsible, good, moral-ethical, competent, right, and "just" thing to do. *I think not.* I think you are doing it because your Reference-Group of "liberal-ish educators," is currently defining it as a TRUTH OF TODAY that it's the "good thing to do" to display such a pink-affirmative sign. Hence you are *encouraged* and *permitted*, and probably "should," display such a pink-affirmative sign—to conform to your Group's norms and mores and hence gain self-esteem for yourself? TOMORROW, by the way, you'll probably be *required* to, such will be institutionalized, and LATER, you'll *not need to*, or at least theoretically, gay liberation will become such a ho-hum Commonplace that "why would anyone need such a sign?" **It's more-than-just-nice that you gaysign your office,** *but do not think that you thought it out for yourself and came there Doing The Right Thing against any obstacles gross and subtle, taking any principled or "on-the-barricades" risks* (whether against "guilt by association" or whatever). No; you are merely being puppetized by TODAY'S emerging **ORTHODOXY** of minority-multicultural-diversity acceptance and the like. Which got started, why? For Justice? No, simply because—due to various causes, it got started. Not because it should have gotten started, although it should have, and yes, earlier...

So, "Today," you *can* **gaysign**; "tomorrow," you'll have to do it; "next week," you won't need to do it; and of course "yesterday," you *could not* have done it... [Could I or **anyone** have? *No*...] [**True, "next year," Oppression may well have returned in full flower...**]

So, *WHERE WERE YOU "MORAL" ALLIES SO "PRINCIPLED" AGAINST INJUSTICE, THIRTY YEARS AGO? When you were needed indeed?* On the issue of the Gay Thing, you were Taciturn. Surrounding you was a miasma of **1.** historical and social embarrassed *Silence*, broken only by **2.** *queer-jokes-plus-nervous-laughter-underneath*, **3.** frank rank oppressive statements delivered non-maliciously but un-thinkingly, **4.** frank rank "guilt by association" operating, and above all, **5.** a **Climate of Opinion** which made any alternates to the totally-pervasive paradigm of "Sin-Crime-Sickness & Disgusting" image of homosexuality, not only scandalously unTHINKable or untenable, but indeed insidiously simply non-Comprehensible, as in You Just Could Not Have Gotten It, Could You Have? Your sign-display now is indeed "nice." *But you do nothing truly ideological outside of the Box of Today's Show, let alone anything truly courageous.* You are not such. Even I was not, not even when we "liberated a small-town dance bar in 1971," and the like. [We were nowhere near the near-forgotten pioneers on the true Edge, such as the "homophile" groups of the Fifties, Franklin Kameny, Barbara Gittings, Harry Hay. Let alone earlier, the Chicago postal clerk who in 1924 **dared simply to start a "brotherhood society"—and who was promptly both fired and imprisoned as a result—and with not a whisper of "social-justice outrage".....**] You are following TODAY'S TRUTHS, near the edge of, but still safely within, the new but already-institutionalized Way We Do Things Now...

[But, can I blame you for this? Or myself? Or any of us? Can *any* person view **true Justice** beyond the myopic lenses of **Today's Truths & Taboos**? Step to the Different Drummer of **true Justice** beyond the pre-scribed choreography of the PUPPET-MASTER of Current **Norms & Mores & Folkways**?.. Even in "enlightened today"?]

--**You male media columnists,** surely "heterosexual and married," **who now pretty regularly denounce anti - gay discrimination,** as in the Boy Scouts and elsewhere... And in such so-male "pulpit"-tones of so-certain if hoity, disgust, so sure that the Christian Far Right is so misshapen, etc. ... This is NICE, *but you are not Thinking. You are merely following Today's Script* which *now permits, soon will require,* yes even "normal men" to proclaim and disclaim thus. Because, *WHERE WERE YOU THIRTY YEARS AGO when you were more-desperately needed?* I'll tell you where some of your journalists "were at." You *were* writing, you *could* write, no you *had to* write, you *could write nothing other than*, such "of-course" TRUTHS then, which TODAY sees (in the oopsy-daisey reversal of 180-degree shift) as "of-course" TABOO... Classic is the following final paragraph in that in-famous 1966 Time magazine essay on homosexuality. How finely it displays the absolutely thought-less Certainty, the flywheel-momentum plowing-forward, of the NORMS-MORES-FOLKWAYS, via the rhetoric of "of course," even if it dourly " standardizes error" thus:

"Even in purely nonreligious terms, HOMOSEXUALITY represents **a misuse of the sexual faculty** and, in the words of one Catholic educator, of 'human construction'. It is a **pathetic little second-rate substitute for reality, a pitiable flight from life.** As such it deserves such fairness, compassion, understanding and, when possible, treatment. But it deserves *no* encouragement, *no* glamorization, *no* rationalization, *no* fake status as minority martyrdom, *no* sophistry about simple differences in taste—and, above all, *no* pretense that it is anything but **a pernicious sickness.**"

Oh in the above I hear no real hatred. I hear more the tinny echo of the speaker of TODAY'S TRUTHS, like George Orwell's tired party hack mouthing *un*thought cliches *un*known to be such. *But yes, that Injustice was indeed just fine and all right for all of you to say and believe, wasn't it?* Guess so, as X per cent of gays and lesbians then surely internalized it too, eh, didn't we? Didn't I....

--**You folk at the distinguished New England prep school who now warmly support a "Gay-Straight Alliance" and also welcome same-sex couples as residence-hall advisors.** And of course you now **"know"** that this is ssoo appropriate, right, Just. "Of Course." Very NICE, but I am sub-amused. *WHERE WERE YOU THIRTY YEARS AGO?* I'll remind you where. *You were putting on the first train home the very next day, any student caught in deviant sexual misbehavior...*

And of course you then **"knew"** that such ostracism was right, proper, necessary, yes Just. "How could you hold such a misbelief," is better phrased that "Neither you, or anyone else, could either think, or act, otherwise." (Or else if you could have and didn't, you are truly immoral...) *Did you Think then? You did not think*, but alas, that DAY'S TRUTHS/TABOOS did not even *permit* you to even privately consider more-Just alternatives at all, let alone courageously differ publically. I demand no psychological "reparations" let alone apologies; I simply wonder whether you know why you are believing as you do now, and whether you possibly *mis*-believe that you thought it out integrally, as against merely dancing to the Puppetmaster's new tune of Liberation...

[For, who *ever* publicly, formally defended homosexuality as "nontoxic," before 1969 Stonewall, or rather Mattachine in the 1950's? **Virtually nobody on the entire silent social scene...** Not the guilt-ridden Andre Gide. Perhaps only Robert Duncan in that 1944 article?...]

--Even **the U.S. Supreme Court...** In 1986 you could **continue condemning private consensual sodomy** (in BOWERS VS. HARDWICK), with all the "good" reasons you thought you thought up or your Dance Card told you (the "ancient roots" of the proscription; the "people of Georgia" condemn it; etc.). In the 1990's you could **uphold the Boy Scouts' exclusions** of gays [which is open-and-shut unjust simply because reasonably unnecessary, because gays are variant, unrespectable, alarming, but no objective threat.] You **"knew"** all these dangers to be present.... Even as in the Dred Scott Decision days, you surely did **"know"** that Negroes were innately inferior, just as surely as you now **"know"** that such 3/5'ing was indeed un-Just.

You knew these things. Can you know anything else? Even conceive remotely of anything else? What was true yesterday, is true today—absolutists naively believe. [Could you *even comprehend* the enlightened Dissenting Opinions by your more-liberal Colleagues on these cases? What British politician was it who said to his House colleagues **"I beseech you, by the bowels of Christ, consider that you may be mistaken"**?]

--And you **high school administrators who *repeatedly* today continue to ignore, hence literally "misbehave" regarding, gay/lesbian students** when they are attacked—verbally, otherwise—by other students, even by homophobic faculty. Some of your documented responses here, "amuse" me, but darkly. You fetch up rationalizations to the tune that "*Well, this gay/lesbian student can only expect harassment, due to his/her sexuality or deportment...*" Or, "*Well, this is a private matter between student and [homophobic] teacher, we can't get involved...*"

You ignore with that utterly-certain, never-suspecting, Righteousness which the current **Truths** donates to verbal gay-bashing; to other-minority oppressions. You misbehave (=you perform your job "unprofessionally, incompetently) You quite immorally and unJustly botch things. But, dizzied by the momentum of the Traditional Tango (or the Homophobia Hustle), you "know" not, that you do bungle.

Oh, you would *not* speak thus concerning women students, Black or other ethnic students, the differently-abled students, and so forth. But why? Because you follow like Scripture, the Social Timetable. *Not because you "know" any better, let alone even could think things through* outside the social "electrical fence" corralling you, because on this *truly you "know,"* nothing, except inaccuracies.

If and when you're told of the "other side" to things, you'd ignore and non-hear, skid defensive—unless the Other Side became the Majority Opinion, in which case "of course" gay-bashing is bad. Oh, a few folks now can hear the advance tones of the "other side," of true Liberation and Justice (or of the New Now?)... But for now, you "school officials" simply follow quite non-comprehendingly Today's Social Script. Which is (at

last!) Officially Protective of Blacks, other ethnic, women, the disabled, who else, but not yet gays/lesbians "beyond the fence." But you see no contradictions here, let alone hypocrisies, because you cannot See. (Can "we"? Can I?) Today you are saying, "That is wrong, but anti-gay is right or okay"; Tomorrow, you'll be saying, "No, anti-gay is also wrong." What changed? *Not your ability to Think, to Know.* Simply the arrival of the new social Tango...

--**You scholars, and leaders in higher education.** Anthropologists such as Weston LaBarre, zoologists such as Desmond Morris, from earlier decades—it's "amusing" but instructive now to see how these scholarly specialists were merely secretaries transcribing the Climate of Opinion of their times. Their "reasoned, supported, thought-out" condemnations of homosexuality are merely clever Automatic-Writing, their fabric-ations *un*knowingly suspect (or were they truly immoral?)..... And even **Nathan Pusey, president of Harvard University**—he who bravely opposed the demagogic Senator Joseph McCarthy during the anti-Communist witch-hunts of the 1950's...? When confronted with the nascent gay student group, he stated (I have read it reported) that if they tried to incorporate, he would close them down....

--**The Boy Scouts of America in the year 2000....** They barred gay personnel from Scouting. They claimed they were acting "morally, ethically." Few folks saw that they most certainly *both were, and were not, simultaneously.*

How? On the literal level, they marched to the tune of "morality: traditional American style," which happens to condemn homosexuality. On the higher level, they of course botched truer morality, which holds that one clearly and bravely seeks justice even amid confusions and conflicts..... In a decade or two, of course, gay Scouts will be ho-hum, de rigeur. And we'll be hearing from BSA Leadership how "why well of course" that is right" and so forth. And the liedership will truly believe that *They Themselves Do "Think" This Way.....*

--**You psychiatrists.** Earlier, you could only move to the received tune of "sickness." Now, many of you can only sing the tune of health, normality. Who can hear any distant, different drumbeats and carefully inspect for any possible connections between homosexuality and "arrested development" or say, "attachment-disorder"? To even privately think, let alone publicly discuss, such satanic sounds, is overtly and insidiously **prohibited**: *No Dancing That Tune Here Any More!* ...as vigorously now, as it was **demanded** earlier....

--**Even gays themselves.** Earlier, the concept of **civil rights, marriage, parenting** were foreign: unthinkable. *Even in the minds of those for whom the concepts were valid....*

——— —— — ═══ ══ ═ ~~~ ~~ ~ `````` ````` ``` `` ` ^^

.....and so perhaps we are all united, after all. Be we reactionary or innovative, conventional or "freethinking," perhaps we all must dance on the Puppet-Team, a chorus-line of Today's Tunes strung up by the Puppet-Master conducting an often-cacophonic Custom to we must step... Drowning out all other, "distant-drummer" melodies?.... Except of course Today, when at last we're surely aware of all In-Justices.... *If anything had been wrong, we should certainly have heard.....*

GAYS / LESBIANS *DO* "THREATEN FAMILY VALUES" *AFTER ALL* ?

---"Homosexuality threatening the family"—important but confused-and-confusing too, as in "but exactly what kind of threats—indeed if any?" *New research now knows.*

---Fair accuracy is needed. Gays do not cause divorce. And, gayness is not directly "contagious." On the other hand, "common sense" plus "received knowledge" plus "folk-wisdom" (not to mention "Natural Law") all do strongly suggest that gays/lesbians do pose some THREAT to traditional American family life and values.

---The problem has been: but exactly what kind of threat, and how? Pressed for details, the "anti-gay" folk have never been able to specify their charge! So, many "pro-gay" folk mis-label objections, simple homophobia.

---*Insight at last.* New research has established that gays and lesbians do indeed pose certain identifiable "threats to the traditional family." Multiples; nine separate dangers.

---The "good news" here is these threats arise only from within. Not from outside gay activist agendas. Only within families which contain openly-gay offspring—an overt gay son, a blatant lesbian daughter. Families with normal offspring, seem quite safe

---But alas for the family with one or more explicitly-homosexual children within the fold. Up to nine of their traditional family values may well be specifically threatened by the "opposing lifestyles," in the following explicit fashion which new research reveals:

[1] "RIGID MALE-FEMALE GENDER-ROLE IDENTITY"

This is the useful "family *value*" of separating macho male and frilly female behavior, "trucks and dolls"... But, deviant offspring may androgynously "blend genders." This threatens or at least violates this important "traditional family and social value" and harms personal identity and social uniformity.

[2] "INFLEXIBILITY TO CHANGE"

...and to growth, let alone any independent thinking. This is the *value* of strictly adhering to tradition, including approved (heterosexual) norms and mores, at almost any cost—even disowning G/L children if necessary.... But, militantly-"open" offspring can surely stress this basic value also. Disruption results; we all prefer the known-and-familiar to its opposite.

[3] "FIRM SOCIAL CONTROL"

This is our longstanding *value* of disciplining children via the usual **shame**, as in "Why, you little pervert, you!," let alone even parents via the usual **guilt**, as in "Where did we go wrong in raising a deviant child?"... But the rebellious claims-for-acceptance which today's "liberated" G/L children can make, may threaten this classic "informal social control" mechanism.

[4] "OBSESSION WITH SOCIAL STATUS AND REPUTATION"

This is our cherished *value* of respectability in our reference-groups, even if purchased at some cost. We value an untarnished social image over stigmatized identities. We naturally worry about "What will the friends and neighbors think of us if they see our little Bobby with a boyfriend?"... But inverted children who are "not latent but blatant," irresponsibly "invert" this keystone value as well, due to their essentially-childish nonconformist rebellion thus.

[5] "RESTRICTED INTERNAL FAMILY SOLIDARITY"

This is our human *value* of complicity, of preserving "uneasy silences" and "keeping secrets" (even if "open") on difficult issues. (As in, for instance, "Well, okay, but don't tell Aunt Burletta or Uncle Bruce, they simply couldn't take it.")... But again, the G/L "agenda" of extreme openness ruptures the non-chain of our interpersonal non-communication thus.

[6] The "WORK ETHIC"

Here emerges our family, and national, *value* of dutiful productivity (savings, wealth) over the irresponsibly-lavish disposable income of single or childless people... Yet another maturely-prudent norm violated by the disgustingly-distended vacation-habits of gay men (who often play church organs as well) and lesbian women (who tend to play too much softball, if not actually golf, in any event). These role-models risk seducing older g/l children into the "slackness of the sexually-satiated."

[7] "RESIDUAL PURITANISM"

The *value* of remaining uneasy, deeper-down, about sex-for-enjoyment instead of for duty after all... But G/L individuals, of course including older children today, seek to topsy-turn the tables on this ancient value which persists despite our shallow veneer of relaxation about the whole messy business.

[8] "STRICT RELIGIOUS FUNDAMENTALISM"

The *value* of placing solid Biblical literalism ahead of sloppy "situational morality" and the like. We know what the Bible says about homosexuality—some Old-Testament "sins" are minor and outdated today, but others (sodomy) remain sinful always. This leads to our *valued* practicing of "the hypocrisy which heals," or "our contradictions which become consonant."... But G/L youth now attack this value too by convolutedly rationalizing their anti-Biblical positions!

[9] Above all, "NORMALITY-AND-NATURALNESS"

The keystone *value* of all: of preserving pair-bonding in marriage, and then parenting well... But we know that not all gays or lesbians do "value" staying coupled, never mind raising children!

- - - - - - - - - - - - - - - -- - ------- ～～～ ～～～ ～～^^

Well, are you as surprised-but-relieved as we were at this list? Homosexuality a "threat" to "traditional American family *values*"? Indeed; and, incisively, thus. Case clarified and closed, at last—and fairly!

True, G/L folk will object to this. They've CLAIMED that "family values" consist of those PERMISSIVE, SPONGY, SENTIMENTAL stances of **"Tolerance," "Solidarity"** and the like. [In fact, recent research in the JOURNAL OF HOMOSEXUALITY reports that in a survey, a large sample of G/L informants (inaccurately) defined "true "family values" as: "Respect; Courtesy; Support; Kindness; Pride; Love; Compassion; Acceptance." Well, *our* study here, calls *those* "lightweight" definitions into heavy question, doesn't it?]

Indeed it does. Now we know what few people knew before this study. Namely, that **actually, *GAYS/LESBIANS HAVE NEITHER KNOWN, LET ALONE ADMITTED*, what "family values" really** mean—to **them**. Specifically, such *unnerving, even deviant,* behavior as **Insight; Independent Thinking; Flexible Adaptability to Major Change-Needs; Truer Responsibility, Commitment, Strength, even Bravery.** *Dangerous* behaviors *indeed...*

But now we all know. [1] Many social "values" are traditional, unstated, unexamined—and possibly dysfunctional. ("Culture," the norms mores and folkways, has been called "a standardization of error.") [2] Certain of our own "traditional family values"—these nine right here—can *truly* "threaten." Can *surely* threaten [A] G/L children, *probably* also [B] their families, and *possibly* even [C] other folk (though *never*, of course, [D] we & us ourselves...) Thus, knowledge is power. And [3] Values and morality exist on two levels. Lower-down, the unanalyzed "sociocultural"; higher-up, the more-solid "philosophical." EXAMPLE: the Boy Scouts excluded gays. They were simultaneously quite moral via "conventional-traditional group-values"... and quite immoral via "higher criteria..."

A MEMORANDUM from the "Central Administrative Executive Board" of OFFENBACH UNIVERSITY:

Last summer we discovered that **tenure** (=continuing employment short of immorality, incompetence, or position-elimination) **is no longer necessary** for colleges/universities. Not even for its prime purpose: *maintaining superior intellectual life and productivity.* (Hence the current attacks on **tenure** become insignificant.) Below, we explain our discovery (during June, July, and August) as to why **tenure is no longer necessary, even important, even desirable.** It was caused by **two recent and major changes or "maturations," one in the teaching faculty, the other in the administrators—an "evolution toward excellence."** These **dual metamorphoses** occurred recently-and-suddenly—all during **the last academic year** (between Sept. and May)—and were discovered by us only **this last summer** (between Memorial and Labor Days), during our own **Research**. Unpredicted even by us, this **"brace of betterments"** will quickly become welcome to all.

True, many still believe (as we used to) that **tenure** is needed to protect "free speech." That (1) legal-constitutional protections in society can't protect (2) truer free speaking, thinking, researching in education. Especially truly-new/different scholarship which is *threatening* because unpopular; out of fashion or not yet in fashion; groundbreaking hence also paradigm-challenging; wrongly judged to be wrong; and the like. **Hence, isn't tenure still needed?**

No, because last June, our **Research** told us that *much* speaking-and-researching is quite "useful, valid, beneficial, productive," *without* being "groundbreaking, innovative, paradigm-challenging, hence anxiety- and resistance-provoking." That is, much good work remains of the "prosaic" or "vanilla" type, plodding and slogging onward within the Corral with no possibility of offending anybody really (except via boredom, minusculity, and/or irrelevance). This "whitebread" work can benefit society without needing the protective armor-plait of **tenure**. **Hence how can tenure still be really needed?**

Then around last July, we next reconsidered the *other* powerful arguments *against* Tenure. **(1)** It creates "academic deadwood," unproductive but unremovable faculty. **(2)** It obstructikates administrative **(A)** Power & Control of dissident faculty, **(B)** agile adroit Flexibility to shuffle positions and resources around to meet new "needs," **(C)** access to Power Prestige & Pocketbook on the part of management. **Hence tenure becomes even more suspect than needed?**

But then it was in mid-August that we "**performed original research in the Field**," and we there discovered the **twin "morphings toward maturity"** among faculty and even administration, which have happily rendered **tenure safely obsolete hence unnecessary,** even in its main finest purpose, not for "privileged positionings," but for "professional protection": namely, **"*to enable serious scholars to get their proper work done for their students, institution, and profession, and society.*"** And these august neoisms prove: **tenure no longer needed!** Specifically as follows:

(1) Faculty Piers have become more competently mature. It used to be that a being all-too-humane, academic department would risk undervaluing innovations, due to natural Anxiety and Insecurity. [Such "outside-the-pale" challenges as [in English languages-&-literatures, for instance]: **(A)** *Composition Studies* as **not** *just* "poor-cousin service-courses" to literature... **(C)** *Publications in teaching-or-pedagogy* as *potentially* **not** *inferior* to Literary Skolarshipp... **(B)** *Non-academic writing* (magazine journalism; technical manuals) as **not** *necessarily inferior* (indeed, germane to teaching writing)... **(D)** *"Interdisciplinary," "integrative"* work **not** *"unprofessional" alien turf*... **(E)** *"Minority-diversity-multicultural"* studies as **not** *educationally-invalid.* (Alas, probationary tenure-track faculty often had to omit or conceal their achievements here. **But, fortunately no longer**)... and **(F)** *Individual personal teaching and communication styles* as **not** *necessarily counterproductive even if* "conventionally-eccentric" or the like...]

--But now, "No More Problems" here—simply because, during the last academic year however miraculously, **faculty have grown more open, mature, objective, and hence responsible and responsive!** No longer are faculty disturbulated or THREATENED BY THE NEW, THE DIFFERENT, THE PUTATIVELY-BETTER. In fact, our aestival research even seems to suggest that such supposed "laws" about human mis-behavior (such as the INGROUP/OUTGROUP or "WE/THEM" distinction) have actually been repeeled, not to mention the "AFFINITY IMPULSE" (or "like likes like" for luncheon dates, and "dislikes the OTHER"), or closed CLIQUES, fractious FACTIONS, "TURF-WARS," and NONRATIONALITY or staining with the ink of human bile, etc.

(2) And, Administrative Personnels have also become more empathetically accepting. We all knew that higher education has been adopting the "corporate" model of *top-down power and bottom-line accounting,* instead of the traditional educational model of *a community dedicated to educational and intellectual excellence.* But what a reversal this last academic year. We found (by July 4th) that we administrators today now appreciate excellence in quality as the goal, and long-term secure institutional allegiance the means toward that finest work even if initially innovative and lengthy in gestation. Even more toundingly, we found (well before Labour Day) that we administrators no longer valorize and privilege "power, prestige, and the pocketbook" as a prime goal. **Hence, tenure is no longer necessary.** Under this New Aura—er, Era, faculty can confidently accept short-term contracts and expect renewal via a fair, objective, mature assessment, by their faculty posts—er, piers—er, peers—as well as their administrative overlings!

--Now, you Out & Down There, may be as stonished (or even as stounded) as we Up Here were, to learn of this "all-in-one-year" apotheosis toward authenticity, this segue toward solidity, this transmogrification toward truth. Faculty easily open to innovations and individuality? Administrators effectively comprehending excellence as goal, and valuing long-term committed faculty for best productivity and morale?... Who knew, or even could have predicted, **this puctuated progress in civilized institutionalization?** The new order truly emerges—colleges and universities which, due to the above-mentioned improvements in *basic human nature* plus *basic social-unit interaction,* have matured unexpectedly but gratifyingly. An advance which of course obviates the need for "Tenure" in its only justifiable function: seeking "Truth or toward truth" in cognitive competence and affective authenticity.....

.....So let this Good News of these **"twin tendencies"** of this last *Annus Mirabilious* (as tified by the Summer of our Re-Search) be distributed from Us, to all SECTION CHIEFS and thence downward to the POPULOUS at large, [this could meen YOU] on a "Need-to-know" basis, including our "Need to tell them" and their "Need to be told." **Thank, You.**

"Reader #1 response":

{A} Good opening, grabs reader's attention. (No explicit thesis-statement, however— should state his point at once.)

{B} Good sense of "suspense" here to interest us in what is going to come!

{C} Well, he makes a good point or thesis from the story. And he doesn't "preach," either; good honest direct tone.

{D} Another good example to support his thesis. He's structured, using chronological or time sequence to organize.

{E} Good, he now shifts to larger overview of the issue— history, sociology. Doesn't just tell his stories—interprets them thoughtfully..

{F} The new point becomes clear. "Alcohol can cause trouble but people aren't aware of this until trouble actually does happen to them."

{G} ...and he nicely blends his self with the concepts he's discussed. He writes responsibly even if he can't drink responsibly—he can admit that he has a problem!

{H} Good job. Structured: two examples lead to thesis. Surely he demonstrates **"thinking about"** an <u>issue</u>, *not* just "telling story facts" about <u>events</u>. I guess this was Needful writing which mattered, also a Challenge to reach readers but not to preach down to them.

GRADE: **B+**, "good work; personal & thoughtful, entertains & informs...."

The Student Essay:

"WHEN DO I STOP?"

I can still remember how happy everyone was to see my cousin Joey getting married. **{A}** [1] Being only eight years old, I thought of the wedding only in terms of dinner and reception. This was a time to fill yourself with the best of food and then run it off by chasing girls with your cousins. But it just so happened that at this particular wedding I played the obnoxious little brat. **{B}** [2]

Nearly everyone had a beer in each hand and was engaged in a heavy conversation of how long it's been since they've seen each other. While everyone was so involved in their chitchat, my cousin Mike and I were carefully planning a night of entertainment. After artful plans, we chose a plan which led mistakenly to an unforeseen conclusion. Unnoticed, we helped ourselves to nearly fifteen glasses each of wine off the table. Just as quickly, our beginning fun slowly approached an end. Continually relieving my stomach sure wasn't my idea of a drinker's delight. I couldn't think of a more successful way of convincing a youngster not to drink. **{C}** [3]

Several years later I was confronted with another disaster due to alcohol but this time more tragic. A friend's car had stalled late one night on his way home. Being so far from home he tried desperately to flag down a possible ride. Unfortunately his first try was his last. Joe ended up flagging down a drunk driver who apparently looked as though he was stopping, but never did as he ran him over. **{D}** [4]

How many times must tragedy strike before one realizes when to stop? [5] I sometimes wonder if there's an answer to this question. [6] Alcohol has been a source of both pleasure and destruction since the beginning of mankind. **{E}** It seems that many people can answer this question only after something has happened to themselves. **{F}** The unfortunate part is that I cannot exclude myself from the many. Most frequently I find the question asked, but not responded to, by a person I respect—myself. **{G}** [7]

{H} [8]

"Reader #2 response": 30

[1] Anecdotal opening, okay.....

[2] ...this is getting lengthy for its probable purpose and length - limits.... getting less like good story to set point and tone, and more like amateur unedited diary - babble...

[3] Aha, a point at <u>last</u>, or so it seems. "From a childhood misadventure, I learned to not drink irresponsibly..."

[4] Another anecdote, <u>but to what overall thesis?</u> Now the point is "Excessive drinking can tragically harm innocent people." Coherence???

[5] **But** (1) the author did stop, didn't he? And (2) did the drunken driver then stop drinking?

[6] Wow, what a **bloated, cliché**-type, **textbook** sentence! Tone gets hollow, shifts into **unreal lecture-mode** here... He "sometimes wonders"? I doubt his "philosopher" persona here...

[7] Whoa! *Does the author even **have a drinking problem?*** He <u>claims</u> it—but <u>doesn't show or prove</u> it! Methinks phoney-plastic here; me smells "bull"! **This is a put-up job**, he just Had To Write A Paper To Get It Done! NOBODY HOME HERE.

[8] Part of me "*enjoyed*" the way he slapped together a paper slickly and probably didn't even think whether it would work..... part of me says *shame*, it's an <u>insincere, irresponsible fabrication</u>, a print-out job. **I wonder whether** *other* **readers spotted this phoniness—or swallowed it? Other students... other** *teachers*??

GRADE: **F** [actually, "**R**" for "re-do," he *isn't going to get away with this*.....]

[Or, for more *zip,* "**See how badly, a Maladjusted Individual Maladaptively Over-Reacted to His Group's Allegedly NON-ACKNOWLEDGING of Him**"—*as in,* "just because this Faculty member repeatedly had his Retreat recommendation REJECTED, he then grew, from that little grain of Sand, this monstrous big *Pearl of Plaint* which he then wore sorely in front of all of us!" {Heck, makes for more-lively copy, anyhow...}]

→<u>SERVING SUGGESTION</u>: (1) <u>Read</u> the **#1 LOG** chronicling the "unpleasant events." Then (2) in **#2AB,** <u>decide</u> which **ANSWERS** insightfully *better* account for the "unfortunate happenings," and which answers incompetently, evasively, etc., *fail* to explain the "regrettable history"...

Part #<u>1</u> of 2: The "<u>LOG</u>": record of events as reported by the participant:

[Parts #2 A & B later, are the "<u>TEST</u>": which answers best explain the events reported in #1 herein?]

---

(1) <u>August 1987</u>. A Department Retreat will be held, to share ideas. Should be good—we pride ourselves on our good **community**, or as we say, "**collegiality**," unlike so many other atomized departments, "especially English departments" [*Later*—it was a good time indeed.]

(2) <u>August 1989</u>: Another Retreat will be held. Theme: **DIVERSITY IN LITERATURE**. I offer to speak on "Gay Poetry"; and am accepted. *Later:* well, my talk was informational, but too rushed, I fear even too emotional (a baby-step stumble?). Well, just so they don't hold that against me for any future talks.

(3) <u>August 1991</u>: Another retreat. I offered to talk on "**TEACHING THINKING**," my major project. But the two colleagues who organize the Retreat, rejected this, and four other themes. In favor of their own suggestion (of "EVALUATION PROCEDURES"). But whether I spoke or not, shouldn't Retreat organizers democratically correlate group participation, not autocratically impose their own topics? (Or does this really *matter*?)

(4) <u>August 1993</u>: Another Retreat. And another disappointment. Theme unannounced beforehand. But when I walk in, I find that colleague ERWIN is talking on "**TEACHING REASONING AND ARGUMENTATION**." *This bothers me.* Is it egotism, because ERWIN's talk was casual, once-over, non-organized, non-focussed—compared to what I had already done in a published article on reasoning published in <u>English Journal</u>? No; less egotism—than **non-acknowledgement**. I do not demand inclusion. I only expect invitation to be considered for inclusion. A crucial distinction. Especially in view of this Dept's *supposed* trait of "inclusive collegiality."

(5) <u>August 1994</u>. Yet another Retreat emerges. *This* time, I circulate my "*TEACHING THINKING*" proposal *not only* to the Retreat managers (again), but to *all* members of the Dept. But again, another issue is selected, with no feedback from the Retreat managers as to *how* they decided. *What of "collegiality"?* (Or am I really over-reacting, sour-grapes fashion?)

(6) <u>August 1995</u>: Another Retreat—and yet another another disappointment. The announced theme is "**TEACHING POETRY**." As in argumentation, I've researched and published on how to teach poetry better via using "people-poems." But the Retreat staff says, "We're going to let the practicing poets in the Dept tell how they teach poetry." *Why?* I wonder beforehand. And especially afterwards, since their talks turned out to be anecdotal, non-systematized, non-pedagogical... Does the *Dept* really care about teaching? *Am I overreacting*...

(7) <u>August 1996</u>: Another Retreat. Theme: "**STORYTELLING, OR DRAMATIZATION**." A third setback? Once again, I have researched on the important issue of how to bridge story and essay in Freshman Composition. But again it's the same bingo: "we're going to have our colleagues who come from foreign countries, tell their stories." Once again my Passion for Pedagogy feels displaced. And once again, the organizers did <u>not</u> select the topics openly in grass-roots, democratic, group-consensus fashion. Maybe we <u>do</u> have "in-groups and out-groups" after all. (So, am I stereotyped as eccentric and excluded? Or did my over-emotional way back in 1989 presentation stigmatize me? Not considering the good performances I produced since then; so, I'm probably overreacting...)

(8) <u>August 1997</u>: I'm now "Emeritus," retired to write full-time. Still, I attend this year's Retreat—hmm, the only retired colleague to do so. Theme: "**RESEARCH INTERESTS OF THE MANY NEW FACULTY**." Another good time, and in genuine "**collegiality**," I drop a note to the Retreat organizers, thanking them, praising the presentation.

(9) <u>August 1998</u>: Ah, my "great chance" at last? On campus (by chance), I encounter the Retreat organizer in the corridor (also by chance). She says there may, or may not, be a Retreat this year. I once again (!) proffer my suggestion about "***TEACHING THINKING***," the topic I retired to write up full-time. I tell her: "Anyhow, if there is a Retreat, I'd like to attend again, even if you don't select my topic. So please let me know." She seems to agree....

....*But Two Weeks Later*: By chance again, I'm in the Dept mailroom. I happen to spy a stray notice announcing a Retreat. I was never sent one. Theme? "**ACTIVE, OR STUDENT-CENTERED, LEARNING.**" *This hits my gut like a punch*. This is *so close to, but quite short of*, the <u>true</u> teaching of thinking—a false cognate, a pseudo-approach often mistaken for truly teaching thinking. I could tell people about this! *I remain stunned.* <u>If</u> the Retreat's theme had been, instead, like "**PEDAGOGY OF LIBERATION**," or "**RELATING LITERATURE AND THE FINE ARTS**," or such, I would not have been insulted. But this is multiple stonewalling, major non-acknowledgement. And worse, I see: inept management, the wasting of an important local personnel-resource.....

   [*Arrggghhh...* <u>An analogy from cuisine</u>: Compare the truly-new "**Teaching Thinking**" movement to "FUSION CUISINE: NEW PARAMETERS, VARIABLES, DEFINITIONS, OPTIONS, ETC."...Then I'd say that "**Inter/Active Learning**" is more like just "HERE ARE SOME NEW RECIPES WE PICKED UP IN MADISON THIS JUNE"! Do the presenters know the cutting-edge work of Ennis, Paul, Resnick, Costa, Lipman, Swartz, Hatcher, DeBono, Bayer, *inter alia*? <u>Wow</u>....]

....*One Week Later*: I gripe about this exclusion to **MARION**, a savvy colleague. His instant reply: "You were and are left out simply because you are out of the loop of the in-group here." Hmm, the truth at last? Or wait, could they have recalled my inept 1989 presentation? But since then I have delivered three strong other ones...

Yeah, but then insult caps injury. I note in the Retreat memorandum these fine lines apparently welcoming individuals' input: "<u>We are a Big Tent department and generally can accommodate modifications to our agenda. . . . Join us . . . for **invigorating interchanges** and **gleeful camaraderie**</u>" [DRAEHEIM, 1998: n.p., n.d., n.p.] Whaat? I'm the camel whose nose and self remains firmly outside the collegial Tent... *This becomes absurd*.....

...and so I draft and send a memo questioning the Civility and Morality of all this. I get no responses at all...

Part #2 of II: The "<u>TEST</u>" *Which* <u>answers</u> *below,* <u>best</u> <u>assess</u> *the* <u>regrettable</u> <u>events</u> <u>above</u>?

[2-A.] The ⌐BLUE-LIGHT SPECIALS¬: **"always convenient and easily available at your service"**
{User-Fiendly, Warm-&-Fuxxy, One-Size-Fitz-All, E-Z In-&-Out, Short-Kut, Disponible, and even less...}

[2-B.] The ⌐SMOKE-&-MIRRROIRS¬: **"riskier but more potent, double-bladed incisive-cutting explanations"**   {Achtung: use with safety-shield *only*}

2A. "<u>BLUE-LIGHT SPECIALS</u>: E-Z Resolvolutions, Speedy Dispatch:
These so-handy options will easily clarify this *sad* case-study:

1. "<u>These Things Just Happen</u>."   "This little misunderstanding seems nothing more than a **simple communication breakdown**. These things happen, and are no one's particular blame or fault—(unless it's that of the writer, who initiated the communication after all, and should know how to communicate better anyhow)"

2. "<u>Get Priorities Straight</u>!" "This little affair seems merely like a **tempest-in-a-teapot** really. In fact, <u>other workplace-issues exist</u>, and ones which are <u>more significant</u> to attend to—(or surely such others *must* exist)"

3. "<u>Wrong Attitude</u>."   "The writer **unfairly trashes** his Colleagues who presented the "Active Learning" module. His action scarcely seems 'collegial'—even as *he* charges the *others* with being un-collegial! (This would amount to 'Situational Irony'; something we enjoy discussing in literature classes anyhow)"

4. "<u>Undemocratic Bragging</u>."   "The writer wants to infer that he's actually somehow, '*better*' then us others—in some way actually **superior** to his colleagues. But, such ineqgalitarian haughtiness will *scarcely* do..."

5. "<u>Baffle Them With Bxllshxt</u>?"   "The writer <u>seeks **prestige-&-esteem**</u>—and by the [*dubious*] means of presenting **mere dull-dour <u>data</u>**, as (or as if) it were some **exotic, special,** even **ultramontane, <u>arcana</u>** which only *he* [as some kind of 'Expert Specialist' or other] is qualified to present. But again, how could this *be*?"

6. "<u>No Need To Get To Serious About It</u>."   "Or the writer has just gotten **too 'intensely involved' in his material, too intensely committed to it**, to present it *objectively,* hence *usefully*. Specifically, we can't tell whether the writer mainly wants to (A) <u>prosletyze-and-indoctrinate</u> us, his colleagues, into believing his <u>propaganda</u>—or mainly wants to (B) <u>exploit</u> us colleagues as guinea-pig subjects for his <u>research</u>. No (C) here."

7. "<u>Psychiatric Disqualification</u>."   "The tone-and-tenor of the writer's memo seems to confirm that the writer is **basically unstable**, or at least **volatile**—a psychological state which <u>surely</u>—and ironically—disqualifies the writer's claim to being able to present a competent, mature talk. (Anyhow, we seem to remember that, a decade or so ago, the writer gave an overly-rushed and intense, hence an inefficient, presentation—and we don't, of course, want such repeated again. We don't seem to recall any other, better presentations of his in the meantime...)"

8. "The Strain Of Work Is Telling." "Relatedly, the memo shows the writer's **Transference** or **Displacement**. Specifically, how someone can INAPPROPRIATELY **take out on others**, some *issue* of his own. Perhaps that issue is simply that of <u>the strains and pressures of doing professional research</u> (which OF COURSE WE ALL undergo also)? Or perhaps the issue is darker, a <u>more personal</u> perturbation? In any case, however, such **'issues'** seem—AS OF COURSE WE ALL KNOW—quite INAPPROPRIATE to a Retreat program"

9. "<u>Good Old American No-Frills</u>." "We're basically a **pragmatic** teaching Department here. A **hands-on** or **shirtsleeves** enterprise. As such, we surely don't have either <u>time</u>, or <u>need</u>, for such **deeper, complex theory** as the writer proposes to impose upon us. Whom does he think we *are* any how, an haughty *Har*vard?"

10. "<u>We Can't Be 'Pants-Down' Surprised!</u>" "The so-called **Critical Thinking** Movement (which preoccupies the writer) is <u>probably</u> just another fad-trend-fashion-phase in education *generally*—as so often. But <u>certainly</u> it's superfluous to our own Department *specifically* here & now. Because (as OF COURSE WE ALL KNOW) ""*WHY WE'RE ALREADY ALL TEACHING THINKING IN ALL OF OUR CLASSES HERE NOW ALREADY*"" "

11. "<u>Dont Air Dirty Laundry Publically, It Isnt Collegial</u>." "The writer's gripe is <u>probably</u> just a *personal maladjustment* within himself. However, it <u>possibly</u> may be an *interpersonal vendetta* between himself and Retreat Managment. But in either case, such squabbling is <u>certainly</u> just **"a private, or one-on-one, matter among himself and Retreat-Management."** And as such, it was quite INAPPROPRIATE for said to be aired around the whole Department, in this public fashion thus"

12. "<u>Your Basic Over-Generalization</u>." "**Merely one 'difficult' incident** between someone and his Dept, does <u>not</u> justify **denigrating the whole group**, in wholesale tar-&-feather—as his Memo seems to infer {sick}"

13. "<u>Better Ways Exist To ~~Bury~~ —er, To Process Problems</u>." "It <u>is</u> regrettable if a group member group <u>feels</u> **inappropriately excluded.....wrongly-overlooked.....<u>insufficiently acknowledged</u>** and the like. *However*, even a such-unpleasant ***feeling*** does NOT justify such an **'unproductive'** *response* to that feeling, by the member—such an uncivil memo, etc. Surely, better, more APPROPRIATE, ways exist here. [However, kindly do **not** ask us <u>specifically what</u> such an appropriate response should or might actually **be** or consist of *Thank* you....]"

14. "<u>Modern Hectic Pace, Set Aside Idealism</u>." "Although an 'appeal to **values**,' to some **'moral imperative'** or other, may be admirable and even APPROPRIATE. Still, if such an appeal is **unrealistically-idealistic**, it risks becoming both **tedious** and **tendentious**, hence INAPPROPRIATE after all for our so-busy, demanding situation"

15. "<u>I Mean Who's To Say Who's Right After All You Know</u>." "Gosh, you know, it's a *relativistic* world out there today. Some *minor* issues are touted to be important, but only by one, or a few people—while other, *major*, issues are truly more important to larger groups and more people. So, **"Whose to say Which,"** as to what issues our Dept should confront? We <u>just don't have time & attention</u> to handle *every* tiny minor issue!"

16. "<u>Lets K.I.S.S. or '*Keep It Simple Sutpid*</u>." "Gosh, you know, something the freshmen students often say, may actually be revelant in this tempest-in-a-teapot case. Namely, that if you dont watch out and take care, its possible that <u>you might actually find yourself</u> **"<u>Thinking Tooo Much About Something</u>!"**—especially a *minor* issue such as this one. (Such has happened before; shouldnt again)"

> ## 2B. "<u>SMOKE-&-MIRRIORIRRS</u>": <u>Tuf In-Cisions</u>.
> These <u>more-obdurable</u> options are to be used *only at your own risque*.....

1. "<u>Hey No Problem</u>" Who can say, that a supposed 'Scandal' actually did occur? That is, what if a Scandal falls in the forest and ***nobody*** hears it fall? (**At least, nobody who is counted as** *Somebody*...) Maybe our hearing and judging sensitivities differ. In that case, <u>did said Scandal really occur</u>? Whew probably not...

2. "<u>The Oldd Man Out</u>?" <u>Emeriti</u> faculty (A) **are**, or (B) **are** <u>**not**</u>, to be considered still significantly-connected with (A) the workplace dimension, (B) the collegial community, of former faculty colleagues

3. "<u>True Talk Is Tough To Walk</u>" If an Event-Manager anticipates that a volunteer's presentation might pose a **problem** [whether in value? in APPROPRIATE/INAPPROPRIATE style or method? in etc.?]—then, the most competent course of action for Management would do would be to [*<u>select one of the three options below</u>*]:
<u>*either*</u> (A) <u>explain</u> candidly to the Presenter the possible problems existing, and that they seem insurmountable;
<u>*or*</u> (B) <u>work</u> with said potential Presenter (even **'collegially'**) to insure an acceptably-improved Presentation; or
<u>*or*</u> (C) <u>simply *ignore* it</u>—**never communicate with** (=never even 'get back to') the problematic Presenter <u>at all</u>

4. "<u>Rebuffs *Do* Rub Rashly</u>" If an individual is <u>repeatedly rejected</u>—let alone is unacknowledged-overlooked-ignored—this non-response can make the individual react in a <u>rough and ragged fashion</u>—whether APPROPRIATE or not, which is of course another issue

5. "Psychopathology: Pernicious? And/Or Productive..." Indeed, a person's individual psychology (or psychopathology) can tint or taint his response to social issues—for good, for ill, or for both. For instance, if in his early childhood his self was rejected, denied, non-acknowledged, he may well, later in life, either **(A)** *project* this onto situations which in fact are **not** rejecting him... or **(B)** *transfer* or *over*-react to situations which actually **are** rejecting him. (And of course he may either understand this "Repetition-Compulsion," or may sadly remain unaware of it.)... But he may also **(C)** *sublimate*: rise above injury and productively use his early sorrows into something not socially-*salacious* (unproductive), but instead, socially-*salubrious* (sublimated into valid useful "moral critique" or other form of insight. (As he egotistically *claims* to do in this case here....)

6. "Manners and Morality: a Disconnect Today" A basic **civility, empathy, responsible tact, and consideration** in large and small matters... (Such as treating all fairly, yes even including problematic Retreat volunteers?) Ah yes; such "good behavior" is a form of "everyday morality." Today, it's less practiced than formerly; perhaps less valued and important today; possibly even less realized or known-about today, than formerly. This "decay" could cause friction among today's majority, and the fewer folk who value more, this so-called **larger higher etiquette of good moral manners.....**

7. "It's About Resource-Squandering" Simply and objectively, the issue is the rather "boringly-bureaucratic" one of a **"mis-use of institutional resources."** Not Material Resources, as, letting a copying machine languish neglected in a damp basement, say. Rather, **Human Resources,** as, letting the valuable output of an employee go unused, hey. Cognitively, this wastes one's relevant expertise from being used; affectively, this may blunt-stunt-dent one's enthusiasm and morale, from being further shared. And so: here, Retreat Management can simply be accused of a mere *"professional incompetence"* in mismanaging useful resources....

8. "Lower Letter Collegial, Higher Spirit Communal." It would be a simple error to conflate (to incorrectly identify as being identical with each other) a Department's essentially **surface-and-pragmatic** *'Collegiality'* (goal being merely to conveniently avoid frictions in the workplace), with some **deeper, truer** *'Community'* (goal being actually to correctly implement integrity and the like). Thus, it would be a simple mistake to identify slick *'Collegiality*,' as being or implying solid *'Community'*... *if*, that is, it's only thin **'Collegiality'** which exists after all, and not deeper **'Community'"**

9. "Say It True: There's US... & There's—YOU" Realistically, a group may claim surface coherence ("collegiality"), or even deeper commitment ("community")—but both of them are vulnerable to, and may have to defer to, a prior, major "human social reality." Namely, the fact that **In-Groups and Out-Groups DO exist**, and then that **those people perceived as out-group** (=outsider, Other, invisible, under-represented, etc.), **will become and remain exactly that**—"out of the loop" of the In-Group. (This despite any "lip-service Lore" about how the group "collegially includes everyone" [as in like "big-tent fashion" & the like....])

10. " 'Corporate Culture': Comforting? Corrosive?" If a group posses a **"corporate culture"** of its own (and most if not all human social groups do), the resulting norms-for-behavior may remain subliminal. They may not be overt-explicit-analyzed-discussed. Even or especially if those Cultural Norms are somewhat taboo by other existing standards—*e.g., "teaching is tedious"*...

11. "The Elephant In The Room, or The Nudist Emperor..." To speak candidly if not circumspectly, **for** *most* **educators, Teaching is simply** *not* **that much of a DEDICTED CALLING.** Not a Deep Pedagogy with **commitment, engagement, fascination**, and the like, so much as an **AGREEABLE OCCUPATION** to work in, albeit usually performed dutifully... (This might mean that at a gathering such as a Dept'l Retreat or the like, it is probably *really not all that important* as to what pedagogical topic is actually selected, would it be

12. "Major Change = Growing Pains" "Paradigm-shifts" and the like surely often seem to unsettle, to disturb, and even to threaten, those on the conventional-traditional end of things. Whether this response is justified by the facts of the matter—*or not* (unease may be justified; also it might not be, hence may be poignantly unnecessary and inappropriate—albeit just as existent as if it were really warranted).

13. "Individual Dissent, May Initiate Dissonance" If an individual in a group finds that he's becoming *disdainful* of "voluntary mediocrity and/or non-engagement" of some others in the group, those others may well PERCEIVE his *distaste*. Yes, even if the "deviant" individual does NOT express his *disquiet* overtly, even if he tries to SUPPRESS his stance of *disapproval*. Further, such *"doubtfulness"* of his, may well not only PERMEATE the "intersubjective fabric," but also may "FRICTIONIZE" relationships between the "distanced" individual and the putatively-disengaged others—albeit all subliminally and hence confusingly, of course...

[_____ ____ __ – ----- ---- --- -- - ===== == = +++++ ++ ++ + ~~~~ ~~~ ~~ ~ ^^^ ^^^   ]

ANSWER KEY: *"Thats right 'R' you are if you think !"*

"....AND SOME BOOKS {by 'Unreliable Narrators'} ARE TO BE EXPECT – ORATED..."

i.

I could read you like a book?
(All is "text" now—world, people.)
But alas by your **cover/up** I **misread** you...

Seeing (1) blazingly-acute <u>intellect</u>, plus (2) sanguine muscular <u>moxie</u> to the max
plus (3) a <u>person-a</u> of empathetic understanding of *and* concern for our Dept'l colleagues
including their trials and challenges—

--seeing <u>your</u> <u>strengths</u> thus I mistakenly
thought this Rx'ed you as a reliable **source-volume**.
Surely of all, you'd have the insight plus strength
for the admittedly-difficult **Reference Question**
[well no, the "*only-conventionally-embarrassing*" Reference Question]
I had to pose to you?

ii.

I having been regularly and routinely omitted (elided, occulted) from all
y/our Dept'l colleagues' private social gatherings—all, from intimate ones to tall,
I badly needed self-Knowledge: to know my image among my "collegial" colleagues,
to "**see myself as others saw me**," to know where I might be awrying.....
And *from whom else but you* in the whole Dept—you fearless, capable, dedicated--
could I this Essential Information have sought,
from **your open, no-reserve shelves**—or so I mis-thought...

[I alone the *hoi polloi* welcome only at the public official events:
year's-end whole-Deptl party and such open-door-like events whirly—
from which (a telling foreshadowing-clue I missed) I'd always voluntarily frenchleave early]

Who other than you, with your eye, grit, and [apparent] care,
could tell me of my such warts as might be ef-facing
my contact with you-all "collegial Dept'l colleagues" mispacing?

iii.

But ah how my simple request **de-constructed** you, broke **your bound spine**...
I asked my question, told you why I asked you alone. But at once you balked.
Feigned non-comprehension "of what I was asking";
Got all *unsettled,* your pagination *rifffled.* Ended up saying you wouldn't want to reveal such,
except to someone who lived distant, not to anyone who still occupied
the daily work-corridors where you'd "<u>have to face them tomorrow</u>,"
as too "uncomfortable" you'd be thus...

And so you became a living character, like those in the Greatbooks we teach;
an "unreliable narrator," pretencing to values you don't possess.
Even though doubtless you allwhile enter Class and Teach Lit about
MORAL ISSUES, HYPOCRISY, and Failure in STANDARDS and the like.....

That is,

some Bookes

are to be read onley in Parts;

Others

to be read but not Curiously;

And some Few

to be read wholly, and with

Diligence and Attention.

[-- Francis Bacon, "Of Studies"]

Stepping up to Challenges; Walking and Practicing the Talk we Preach:
and doubtless how we, Class, can and should do better in our daily lives.….
.….Reading you thus, I'm experiencing Dramatic Irony enough.….

Because, *curse you in fact*. <u>How</u> (after your public stances loudly understanding so well the
wrong and the right things to do, your sympathetic stance of eminent understanding of others—
oops, I mean your "colleagues,' " difficulties, your strong stance implying *you if anyone* here
have the sanguine guts to Walk The Talk.….)

.….<u>how</u> after your blank-paging me thus,
<u>how</u> can you now greet me cheerily in those very work-corridors,
"Hi, BRANDON," with a pro-smile—**<u>how</u>**, after having so majorly, cardinally, grievously
failed me in my hour-and-season of genteelly-desperate interpersonal-communication need?
<u>How</u>, given your ongoing strength-and-empathy demonstrated in major screed?

And the fact that such cheerful blank "greeting" does **not** make you uncomfortable
about your Sin of Omission, shaky-in-the-clutch Failure of Nerve,
tells me all. Yes the Author of events Let Me The **Reader** "See It For Myself."

> It's as Fanshawe said in <u>Kronikles</u>, XII: "As for whether any correlations exist between:
> (1) sheer I.Q.; (2) amount of education and advanced degrees;
> (3) professional position held-----*and* (4) 'degree of emotional maturity'—
> we find that null, or even *negative*, correlations, exist..."

iv.

No *matter after all*   For after I read the quick dismal **character-cameo-sketch**
which your actions better than words told me was all you,
I consulted **the coffeetable-books** *of Better Departments* (visiting friends elsewhere),
even more informatively I plus read squintingly into *the* **microfiche** *of myself*.
This self-education both deluded and confirmed me into detecting at last the true causes
of my offhanded treatment among my "colleagues"; <u>I had brought it on myself</u>:

1. During 19 years of pre-tenure probationary status, I had learned too well the lesson of **deference**,
   needing to please all who might vote me in or out each year of every year-only appointment,

2. During years of professional development, I had grown crescively weary of, hence hostile to, the
   Dept's "country-club" type of **"corporate culture"** which daily vocalized how burdensome it is to
   teach here, which chomped on trivia not ideas, which ever said "oh yes of course" instead of "that's
   interesting I didn't know that," and the slick like to make workplace time palatable.….

.….my distastes up on which quick—I'd now guess you all had picked;
A disdain quiet, but enough—for you, my "presence" to slough...

v.

So my inquiry solved itself, and I bloomed elsewhere-otherwise.
But see—to your small-group functions, your planned and impromptu parties,
I would AT LEAST LIKE TO HAVE BEEN ASKED,
    simply for Basic Belongingness, for Intermediate Inclusion,
    for Rudimentary Rapport, for Routinized Responsiveness .….
But I thus came to need no **Cliffs Notes** to know:
(1) Your Dept's famed so-"collegial" Corporate Culture
    is inclusive only to the included,
    to the approved band of disapprovers,
    (who was it spoke of "the herd of independent minds"?)
    the conformers within that famously-iconoclastic Dept,
    the in-group of campus social critics,
    the Establishment within the Univ's "maverick" Dept
    hence all becomes "an ironic travesty of itself,"
    a so-modern **text** booked for the reflexive, sub-textual shelf...

plus (2) You yourself, a **Book** with sour moral to render;
you thus the most daring heartful upright member
of the Dept the most morally "tender"
of true rights-from-wrongs a false-indeed defender

The TEACHING Of THINKING:

...But ALAS, *It Must Remain*

"Still Only Our Little Secret...."

Being a type of drama, played out between the interviewer **CHESTER**, and the "expert," **BARTON**:

[THE SCENE: AN ACADEMIC OFFICE. THE TIME: "NOWADAYS IN EDUCATION." CHESTER TURNS AND SPEAKS INTO A TAPE-RECORDER (PREPARING FOR AN INTERVIEW), ALSO *ASIDE* TO US THE EAVESDROPPING AUDIENCE:]

Did you know that the Teaching Thinking movement is not just another fad, but much more, indeed the only true salvation of education itself? Anyhow that's what **BARTON,** a local Expert Leader in the TT movement, claims. He's graciously donating an Interview to me (still the Infidel Outsider), to reveal **the inside truths** which alone the Converts know, which we Unenlightened never realize... Sorry about that tone there, but I'm still skeptical. Open-minded, but I do privately question whether at times, the supposedly-expert INNOVATORS can themselves be far more *self-deluded,* than they claim ignorant TRADITIONALISTS are. Irony of ironies. Well, we'll see....

Oh, to be fair, **BARTON's** introductory handout-materials *are* clear enough, I suppose. I read them, and they do orient. At least I think they claim these audacious points:

1. What **is** true higher-order **thinking?** *Nothing all that new here.* Whether creative critical etc., it's "confronting complexities competently via conceptual tools." (**Cause-and-effect "explaining" of vegetarianism... "solving problems" regarding the metric system... "evaluating" pros-cons of same-sex marriage... *and* all the rest...**)

2. What are the **goals** of the TT movement (at least the purist sect of **BARTON's**...)? Well, *something perhaps too new here!* They argue for radically reversing 180 degrees, the current-traditional paradigm of education (goal="what to Know and Believe about a subject"). They'd change the goal to "how to Think the subject through—competently; on your own; now and later on too—and other complex subjects too!"

3. What are peoples' prevalent **misconceptions** about TT? *Much more new here, plus much questionable too.*

#1 "We" supposedly believe that "TT is surely already being done in formal education."
    [➔Apparently *not*: "90% of formal education omits it utterly"...]

#2 "We" supposedly believe that "TT is just another educational fad or phase."
        [➔But *no*: rather, it's *the summit salvation for all education.* For "Duty & Beauty" thus:
            **1. to dignify and mature and empower students and classroom at last, but also
2. to empleasure teachers with gobs of unanticipated satisfaction, marvellous enjoyment from the challenge!]**

#3 "We" might simplistically believe that "TT is Utopian unrealistically-unachievable among the masses, hence impractical." BARTON's brilliance [[HMMMM...]] shows us the complexities here:
        [➔**YES Unnachievable, but why? Only because of 1. institutions lag and resist,
            2. student–learners are apathetic / nonmotivated, and — get this —
            3. teacher-instructors can't comprehend, plus are resistant, plus apathetic also.**
            Teachers don't know what's Good & Fun for them—"Duty & Beauty"!
        **Hence we must TT even if 95% wasted; as the physician's oath, "Above All, Do No Harm,"
        so the teacher's creed: content-mastery is incompetent indoctrination, thinking-skills are the
        Only True Salvation let alone professional competence let alone ultimate teacher-satisfaction...]**

See what I mean about "insight vs. fanaticism"? ... (Plus, I wish he'd given some "oasis" examples to prove his "desert" of theory...) Well anyhow, stick around for the Interview: enjoy... It's not just for those interested in TT (although that's more-interesting-than-not to know about, people find). It should also be fun to see major idea conflict-and-change actually happening, with all the lively exchanges (including sparrings, defenses, excesses). Finally, I predict some irony here; I bet you a ginger ale that there'll also be a little of that circus whereby it's <u>the supposedly able Experts</u> in Innovation who <u>themselves need the enlightening and correcting</u>, and not <u>Us</u> the Conventional Amateurs.... But, we'll see.

[[AT THAT MOMENT, **BARTON** ENTERS, BUT EMPTY-HANDED...]]

CHESTER: You're right on time! I've already introduced your rationale on the tape so that the listeners... Wait, where's the rest of your demonstration-materials?

BARTON: I didn't get to tell you. I'm in effect quitting. I've realized that nobody can convey the so-different, paradigm-breaking essence of our Calling. Not even me... No public Interview...

CHESTER: But you were so enthusiastic [[EVEN IF FANATIC]]. Why can't you convey your key rationale? [[OR DID YOUR **ELITIST-EXTREMIST TONE** TORPEDO YOU UNAWARES?]]

[1.] We hear that a concise <u>synopsis</u> of the TT Manifesto *is* possible:

BARTON: We can state it, as below, but how many people truly hear it? They think they comprehend the following, but can they really? Here's an update to those materials you received:

(1) Thinking is the "*only* true real" goal of education worthy of the name. Not "what to know or believe," but "how to think it through." Three reasons why TT is the summit-goal: Pragmatically, it's needed in life. Philosophically, it's more moral-ethical—to do, and to teach-learn. Pleasurably, it's fulfilling: for students, for teachers... *"For Duty, & for Beauty"*

(2) In the past and today, regarding "TT," formal education *shortfalls*—and *scandalously* so...
-- Schools themselves, largely do *not* teach thinking. Or they *mis-* or *under-*teach it (in somewhat-obvious ways), or *pseudo-*teach it (in much more insidious ways).
-- Teachers and others, largely *mis-respond*. They give a mishmash of lip-service. They benignly (and understandably) misunderstand. They malignantly (and unacceptably) resist-deny-evade.

(3) And in the future, "TT" will simply *not* occur in formal education on *any* wholesale, broad-scale level.... And why?
--It's *different*—needs rethinking. "TT" is a major "paradigm-shift" change. Especially in the 180-degree reversal of "content and skills," because now, <u>the true content or material substance of the course, is the thinking skills themselves</u>! No more "covering content" except to support concept-acquisition. (Traditionalists see our reversal here as a major sin...)

--It's *difficult*—needs dedication. TT requires raw ability, yes, but crucially also interest, involvement, engagement. Which the vast majority of students lack. Which too many *teachers* lack also. Plus, the institutions exhibit the "drag" of inertia and resistance...

(4) But still, in a very real sense, "TT" *is* "The Answer." TT can mature education. Enhance the classroom situation. Truly "respect" and "empower" the student-learners. And, truly empleasure or reward those teachers who can enjoy this higher satisfaction, nobler enjoyment...

...and there you have it. Audacious, but accurate...

But oh, how educators *mis-*respond to this. Some disagree (which is good), but mistakenly (which is not good).
--They say, **"But we have to cover content."** This ignores that we still do, but now, the true "content[1]"—the substance-and-goal—has become the higher-level thinking skills themselves (in geography, in history, in biology...), which are supported just so much as is needed of the conventional "content[2]"—or the usual factual material, the "subject" data.
--Or they say: **"But we already teach thinking in our classes."** The Interview always clarified *that* one.
--Or **"Too much too soon for most students, who pick thinking up as they go along anyway."** (*Arrggghhhh.....*)
--Or they say: the felt-but-never-stated: **"But teaching thinking is Too Much Work, plus It lowers student evaluations."** (Well, honesty there anyhow...)

--And twelve more objections (I always did mention them in the Presentation).

--But mainly, educators disconnect. They *non*-respond. They don't even ask "But what would Teaching Thinking consist of, that we don't now do?" *They don't even know that they don't know...*

So it's for these reasons, **CHESTER**, that I must abandon Preaching to the Masses, instead offer Grass-Roots Support to the Elect Few Insiders and Converts, to defend the Truth against its enemies. *Still Only Our Little Secret*—though, ours to *SAVOR*.... I'm sorry I didn't get to notify you in time to...

CHESTER: [[CAREFULLY]] Well, but if a teacher *wanted* to teach thinking, how could s/he start to do it?

BARTON: Actually quite easily, via a two-step procedure. (1) **"Deliberate, Discover, Decide, Do."** That is, decide <u>whether</u>, then <u>which</u> thinking skills explicitly, you're going to teach. Then <u>teach</u> them *explicitly, as such, as skills*. (Most education doesn't.) Finally, <u>assess</u> how well learned. Bingo.

(2) As for deciding on "<u>which</u> thinking skills," we propose: **"Goal-to-Go."** Decide: <u>what must the students end up able to do</u>? It's been called **"outcome-based"** education: simple, improved, still under-used. That is, <u>decide exactly what mental operations do you aim for your graduates to be able to do in the post-School arenas</u> of Private-Personal life; Vocation Career on the Job; and Citizen-in-Community? But on their own as needed? <u>Then, *shape every hour of the course* toward this ambitious but exact goal</u>...

CHESTER: Sounds simple. But don't many teachers do this already? They teach **comparison-contrast; value clarification; scientific method; historical thinking; "cultural studies for a diverse world"; and more**? Your Manifesto above [[OR, IS IT A SCREED...]], *insults teachers*! You'd have to show me in what ways...

[2.] ...and, we're assured that some specific <u>examples</u> *can* clarify:

BARTON: Okaaaaaaay [[I KNEW THIS WAS COMING; ALWAYS DOES...]] Here are a few sample course assignments to show how "TT" is (1) under-done, (2) in-conceivable. Inspect these paired examples below. The left-hand ones (actual cases) represent traditional Education. The right-hand (our proposed rewrites) seek to represent our "TT" approach. Do these "dueling duos" help you see the *gross shortfallings* in Education as Usual, the potentially-*magnificent achievements* from true TT?

<u>Education One</u>: goal, what to <u>Know</u> (factual content mastery), <u>Believe</u> (ideologies?), do as **RRR** <u>rigid rote rules</u>, or simply **OOO**, one's own personal <u>opinion</u> mis-called "thinking":	<u>Education Two</u>: goal, how to <u>Think</u> through the subject, and others later on, via **"AAA"** or the "<u>a</u>utonomous (=on-one's-own) <u>a</u>pplication (=transfer) of <u>a</u>bstractions" (=higher-order thinking skills):
1A. "Tell me whether or not you liked the poem "Hairlip Mary" and why.	1A. [FRESHMAN LITERATURE: POETRY] "Here are sixteen varied short poems we have neither seen, read, or discussed before. Using them, show what you've learned about 'responding to poetry specifically,' plus 'thinking better about complex subjects in general,' in this course this semester—*using the tools taught*."
1B. "Would you like to live in a house like Frank Lloyd Wright's Fallingwater? Why and why not?"	1B. ["LITERATURE FOR YOUNG ADULTS"] "Using the criteria we have evolved in class, evaluate at least two of the novels we have read but not evaluated in class. Be specific about the criteria you are using—literary, developmental. State the appropriate level of the book, and the exact way in which you reached your decision."]
1C. "Discuss the contributions of the ancient Greeks in science and philosophy, with examples." - - - - -	- - - - -
2A. "Why should the electoral college be banned in the United States?"	2A. ["A GENERAL-EDUCATION COURSE"] "Taking **"Capital Punishment"** as a for-instance complex issue, brainstorm all <u>your own</u> arguments for and against. <u>Critique</u> them. Then <u>research</u> the issue. And critique the <u>other</u> arguments you find. Then <u>self-evaluate</u>: how can you do *this type of thinking* better than you could have before this course? Namely, Objective Evaluation of Complex Issue."
2B. "Discuss the destructive effects loggers and farmers on the rain forest, plants, animals." - - - - -	- - - - -
3A. "Causes of the first World War. First, explain the indirect causes (imperialism, nationalism) which produced alliances. Next, tell how the crisis at Sarajevo was responsible."	3B. [ECONOMICS] "Your parents want to know what you're learning at school. Explain the term leakage as related to the circular flow concept. Then describe specifically a type of

3B. "Describe in detail, Jean Piaget's stages of development of children."	leakage taking place in your parents' own household. Explain how this affects aggregate demand."

CHESTER: [[RESPONDING THOUGHFULLY]]: True, I *do* start to see how just "knowing what was told" or "just my own opinion" *falls short from* "thinking things through via concepts and criteria." It's impressive. Unfortunately, however, it isn't fair... Of *course* the left-hand are less "thought-ful." They emphasize rote knowledge or ideology on material already thought through in class. But the right-hand are <u>too difficult for beginning students</u>. Plus, <u>students come to learn how to think on their own as they go along</u>. Plus, <u>you have to cover content</u>. Plus this "teaching thinking" is <u>just too much work plus hassel from students, non-reward from peers and the institution</u>, and *you have to answer* our charges, not just dismiss them!

[3.] Also helpful: to glimpse <u>major paradigm-change</u> (& *growth-pains*):

BARTON: Well, you've refreshingly opened the spigot of the <u>usual responses</u> to TT: clumsy-and-clever resistances-defenses-denials, plus legitimate disagreements, plus honest misconceptions. So let's pause here and ponder how to Think better about <u>confronting major change</u> of *any* kind. (In education, or in politics-government, sexual norms, science, etc....) Here, a **"TOOL·KIT"** to confront Big Change:

---

(1) First, **four common stages** by which the utterly-new becomes the quite-accepted:

"Last week's 1. **Un-Noted** issue... becomes yesterday's "horrors!" 2. **Heresy...**
today's "must-do" 3. **Orthodoxy...** and tomorrow's "ho-hum" 4. **Commonplace**.
.....But we *now* also know why the "teaching of thinking" shall *never* become accepted wholesale,
broadscale in the institution of formal education. [**Difference**, plus **Difficulty** requiring **dedication...**]

(2) Then, **four possible responses** to the utterly, radically New:

1. Non-Thinking-About. (Issue doesn't come onto the radar screen.)
["*Same-sex marriage? Teaching thinking?* Never thought much about either of those issues..."]

2. "Un-THINK-Able!" affectively. (Issue easily dismissed on conventional-value grounds.)
["*Same-sex marriage?* Unnatural, abnormal, contrary to nature and the institution of marriage! ... *Teaching thinking? Won't work, unneeded for the good students, useless for the others, too much too soon, etc....*"]

3. Non-Comprehensible cognitively.—(*) (The new paradigm *simply can't be grasped...*)
["*Same-sex marriage?* But Huh? No—how can you have 'marriage," without the male and the female—it—eh???" "*Teaching thinking*"—*you say we don't but surely we do, and what does it mean.....*"]

4. Non-Attended-To after all. (Issue comprehended, but "dropped" after mentioning.)
["*Same-sex marriage?*" Bizarre, or else okay, but not my issue... "*Teaching Thinking?*" "I know I really don't, but I'm more interested in research, or teaching a party line, or teaching my specialty to majors, or business-as-usual Covering the Content, or forwarding my own points of view in class, or an easier teaching-load........."]

Most responses to TT fall into #3, a murky category. See three incisive examples of how a new different paradigm is often not just resisted-as-unacceptable, but even non-grasped because non-comprehensible:

1. I ask the New Orleans Tourist Bureau what are the interesting "picturesque lesser-known ethnic neighborhoods" to explore? They respond by mentioning "museums, steamboat rides, the French Quarter." They *Didn't Even Hear Me*.

2. I tell my graduate-school *research*-professor that I seek to do good undergraduate *teaching*. He pauses, looks at me puzzled, then says, "well yes, I guess it's good for your record." He *Can't Even Hear* teaching as valid.

3. A Biblical Literalist is asked how <u>non</u>-Biblical history would interpret an event. He can't reply; can't even comprehend the question! *Can't Even Conceive of* what is or might be "<u>non</u>-Biblical" history?!...

4. .... and the same holds true for the Teaching of Thinking. Or Even Worse... "Well, of course we already teach thinking." "Well—what is teaching, thinking?" And a dozen more responses of flagrant resistance-denial, subtle non-comprehension... "*They do not know, how much they may not know*—how *could* they?...

CHESTER: Okay, it's subtle. And New Truths Are Often Resisted By The Still-Un-Enlightened... But this got dry; theory about Change. How about another "oasis" of verdant examples?

[4.] Then, A Duelling Duo Of _Conflicting_ Assignments Duke It Out:

BARTON: Right. You're now ready to see these livelier examples of assignments. They're in pairs: first the actual ones teachers used, then the rewrites we did. Most teachers will praise, those we condemn... and will scorn, those we defend as valid... Training wheels, or solo flight here?

(1) An early paper in English 101, Composition and Fiction:

Traditional version:	more Thought-ful version:
The narrators of Faulkner's "A Rose for Emily" and Gilman's "The Yellow Wallpaper" are both women who go mad. They go mad in part as a result of the way women in their respective societies are treated. Demonstrate the ways in which their being women affected their lives and led to their madness.	Feminism, Marxism, Freudianism, New Criticism, and Reader-Response were major ways of reading we practiced this semester. For this exam, read the three new stories assigned but never discussed in class. Then use the thinking-skill of **"lensmanship"** or **"multiple-plural perspectives"** to confront these stories better than you could have before this class. **Annotate**: explain which ways-of-reading you used and did not and why and how, including self-critiquing of your own work. [_Alternate_: Select a topic in real life far removed from reading literature. Can you now confront it better than you could have before this course? Explore...]

...and, Scorecards for the above assignments:

Traditional (Faulkner):	innovative (five Lenses):
GOOD? Gives good guidance as to "exactly what is expected." Reminds of course-content. Expectations are clear. Also, easy to grade.	**GOOD?** A good example of truer thinking, **AAA!** The student should know how to selectively employ the varied concepts taught in the course, namely schools of literary analysis. To literature, surely; also to "real-world-life," perhaps... **A healthy breath of air...**

| **BAD?** **Hideous.** First, tests no thinking at all. No concepts applied—or rather, the party line is teacher-given. No latitude for self-designing a response—_combining both creativity, and criteria_. Plus, it seems _frank indoctrination_ into one causal explanation among many—a feminist reading is appropriate, but not (alas) sufficient. All decisions pre-made by the teacher. _Scarcely "empowering" let alone "respecting" the student, eh?_... (How well can we expect this student to be able to AAA literature and other subjects on his/her own after only this?) | **BAD?** _Usual Response_: "Too Much Too Soon, Students Need More Structure," etc., etc., etc..... _[BLAH BLAH]_
Candid Response: Realistically, most average students would "blow" the assignment, due primarily to not being taught how to think thus, also lack of their own motivation. [**"Difference, and Difficulty requiring Dedication!"**] So if 90% of them failed, how would the teacher grade them? |

(2) A final exam (portion) from a college-level basic WOMEN'S STUDIES course:

Traditional version:	...and more Thought-ful version:
1. In frontier and colonial America, what were some of women's essential contributions to the household economy? **2.** What was one of America's first industries? Who was employed in this industry and why? **3.** Why were midwives displaced by doctors in earlier America? **4.** How have estrogens been used to regulate women? **5.** What are some of the	Select a current social issue of some complexity and conflict. E.g., _abortion; welfare reform; gender-roles in the family_; etc. Can you practice the course's thinking-skill of **"Objective Evaluation"** on the issue? 1. Can you state accurately both the "current-traditional-conservative," plus the "reformist-liberal-feminist," positions on the issue? 2. Can you then critique both these positions objectively, giving both their strengths and their vulnerabilities—yes even feminism's? 3. Can you then give "your own position" but not mere **opinion**, but **reasoned judgment**? 4. Can you then show feminism's strengths as a **Way of Knowing**—how feminism can provide perspectives (fact-data; ways-of-seeing) which are valuable for total understanding ... which may be even

problems with fetal monitoring? **6.** In what ways is Learnfare a punitive program?	necessary to avoid being fooled, misled? ... which are helpful for deciding policy? (On the new issue you chose to discuss, not on class material.)

...and the Scorecards for the above assignments:

Traditional (six questions):	**...more Thought-ful** (analyze social issue):	
GOOD? ""Usefully reviews key knowledge and also reinforces key course concepts (about the oppression of women). Will test whether students Mastered The Material, or not....""	**GOOD?** "Professionally invites/requires true AAA. And on complex subjects too. Letting student choose own topic, is good. Also practices Fairminded **Objective Evaluation**—pro and con, indeed all sides, showing feminist viewpoint, but also being able to critique it. Also using lenses or Multiple-Plural Perspectives—again, autonomously-selected! These are key thinking skills being taught/tested here. *Dignified; respects student as mature thinker...*	
BAD? Scandalous. First, rampant indoctrination in one side or point of view. Women's oppression was/is very real: but... Even worse, lowest-level possible of focus: should move UPward to larger issues. This is *atomistic, minute, picky.* Merely asks for "harvesting of corn the teacher planted"!	**BAD?:** "Sounds pretty good to me"—demanding but useful, etc.	

CHESTER: ..... But <u>if</u> you thought fairly, instead of just [[PUSHING YOUR AGENDA]]—er, ah, Broadcasting the New Truth, wouldn't you *at least listen to* the <u>objection</u> that your versions here are indeed "<u>too much too soon</u>" for lower-level students? That thinking <u>takes time to learn</u>? That maybe TT <u>can't be achieved</u>? Plus anyhow, how would teachers even get started in this complexity?

[5.] The Nuts-&-Bolts of "TT" includes [5A] that Super-Summary:

BARTON: All you need is, *as I said*, this 2-part key statement, as both end-goal, and road toward it:

(1) ➔"**GOAL-TO-GO is Real World Thinking**." Exactly how well can ex-students, after graduation, competently think through complex issues in real-world-life arenas of Personal, Work/Vocational, and Citizen-in-Community? We call this **"AAA"** or the **Autonomous, Application** (use) of **Abstractions** (thinking skills not just facts). (Not feminist ideology, but key concepts; not literary answers, but the questions...) Bingo! This is it! All efforts must lead to this and to nothing else! Simplicity (or focus) itself! [Using concepts like **allocation cost; self-selected sample; cognitive dissonance; etc....**]

(2) ➔ **Delve in, Discover, Discuss, Decide.** Here's a "test for teachers," for those who *think* they're "teaching thinking": Decide, (1) *exactly* **which** defined higher-order thinking-skills are the key goal in your course? (2) *exactly* **how well** shall they be learned? (3) *exactly* ***HOW*** do you teach them? (4) *exactly* how do you **test and measure the results**? and (5) *exactly* what happened, the **results**?...
[*] ...*And if your students cannot apply, on their own, higher-order thinking skills, to new foreign material, you have not taught and they have not learned thinking, period!*
Disagree with me on rational grounds, and I'll responsibly listen; until then and via this Criterion,.....

[5B.] ...and as usual, specific <u>examples</u> help. Here, the *skills*:

Let's start with discipline-specific thinking, not general-generic thinking. How many graduating seniors have been given explicit instruction in applying the following concepts, as against just knowing?

Analogically, imagine a grand staircase upward (the Spanish Steps in Rome? Whatever...) Options include lower-level facts... then small or formulaic thinking-skills... then larger-scale ones... thinking "pseudo-learned" as facts or rote rules, vs. as true tools or heuristics... then applied to new material, and by the student autonomously... and finally applied after graduation to real-life issues!

[1] The **"CTA"** Model: *Conceptualize* UP from concrete data... then *Transfer* thinking-skill OVER from SCHOOL-Arena to SELF-WORK-SOCIETY... then **Apply** DOWN to Issue to be thought thru:

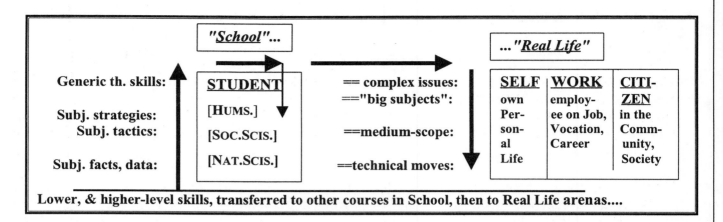

Lower, & higher-level skills, transferred to other courses in School, then to Real Life arenas....

.....and the Table of the **Thinking Tools** to **C**onceptualize up to; **T**ransfer across; and **A**pply down upon:

[2-A] Thinking tools, lower-, & higher-order:	**[2-B] Situations** applied to: personal, vocational, citizen. Subjects simpler and more complex:
(I) Larger world-views, systems, philosophies, ideologies: (Marxism, behaviorism, Darwinism, Freudianism, existentialism, structuralism, others) **(II) The Academic Disciplines:** Fine Arts: organic form, principles of design Anthropology: cultural relativism Biology: Communication: cognitive dissonance, selective perception, self-fulfilling prophecy, effects: Hawthorne, Halo, Westermarck "Diversity"/Multiculturalism: stereotype vs. sociotype, definition of the situation Economics: allocation cost (cost-benefit ratio), marginal utility, zero-sum game, 80-20 rule, Prisoner's Dilemma Literature: ironies, genre, tone, rhetoric Mathematics: Philosophy: presuppositions, implications, contradictions, language-use Political Science: Sciences: critical mass, order of magnitude, homeostasis Psychology: motivations, defense mechanisms Sociology: [*see below*] Statistics: "self-selected sample" (insufficient, unrepresentative) **(III)** Within Disciplines, **higher-order perspectives** and **lower-order specific concepts**: example from *sociology*: *Higher*-order, of larger Scope: *Theories*, of functionalism, conflict, symbolic interactionism, others. *Perspectives*, of debunking; unrespectable; relativism; cosmopolitanism. "*Culture*" (norms mores folkways) as world-view behavior massively learned mandatorily unconsciously uncritically... *Lower*-order more technical, specific: Status, role (role conflict, reversal, etc.) Social control and deviance: sanctions, formal and informal. Affinity impulse; ingroup, outgroup. Stereotype, prejudice.	[THE **FIVE ARENAS**: School as student, **but then also** Private-Person-al... Work employment job career... Citizen in community... Recreational "thinking-buff"...] (1) "CCCCC" = current communal contested confusing concerns. (**Abortion, Affirmative Action, Animal Rights, Capital Punishment, Gun Control, Energy, Genetics, Pornography, Welfare Reform, Immigration, National Security... Etc.**) (2) General Others: **Vegetarianism. Metric system. Feminism. Media. Race. "Food, sexuality, bicycles, graffiti, snow, poetry....."** (3) In Personal Arena: **Parenting. Financial management. Health-Care. Life-career.** **"The Good Life..." Stasis and change, convention and innovation.** (4) In Vocational Arena: **organizing complex information; interpersonal interacting!**

[5C.] ...and here, examples of statements-about those skills:

CHESTER: Rich, but dry—how about an oasis of concrete examples, please? Well you'll say you gave them earlier—"what to Know" about *Piaget, Greeks, electoral college, rain forest, causes of the war*—vs. "how to Think through" *new poems, economics* in reality, *capital punishment* and other issues....

BARTON: Glance over the following "gallery of gorgeous and grotesque" instances. See where at times, education advances to Thoughtfulness, but more often, falls short from Transfer...

---

[1] Mini-Appendix. A brief sampling from the above Table, of very **specific concepts**, successfully applied in real-world-life, as needed. Thinking tools accessed in agile deft adroit fashion...

--"The concept of **order of magnitude** ➔ lets me say why more than one wolf had to have killed those sheep"...

--"ECONOMICS' concept of **cost-benefit ratio (allocation cost)** became helpful every day. ➔ All the way from "should I spend time to apply for that grant it's likely I'll not get"... to "when I had only two precious days in Bangkok, Thailand on my costly trip abroad, I should have gone from airport to city-center by the more expensive but faster taxi instead of the cheaper but slower bus..."

--"The concept of **homeostasis** in SCIENCE, ➔ also insightfully explains why the institution of formal education will powerfully block efforts to Teach Thinking after a certain critical point-of-disturbance"...

--"The concepts in STATISTICS of **sampling errors, distribution, control groups,** and **regression to the mean** ➔ help me see the errors in the survey about feminism sampling older housewives... and the erroneous prediction about the 1936 presidential election (Langdon over Roosevelt!)... and "90% of all Volvos made in the last eleven years are on the road"... and "Madame Claire Voyant is good, she made three successful predictions"... and "When an athlete gets on magazine covers, his/her fame starts to decline"...

--"SOCIOLOGY views **culture (norms, mores, folkways)** as "designs for living," behavior and values which are 1. massively learned, 2. unconsciously, 3. with little choice in the matter, and they can be 4. counterproductive. ➔ This helps me understand much better, that when a son "came out" as gay, and the father reviled him, banished him from the house, and ostracized and disowned him, it was *not necessarily simple bigotry*. Rather, these were the only "scripts" which the father's society had provided to him!" All four of the facets of culture illuminate things here!

---

[2] GALLERY. [A] First, a set of <u>successes</u>. Illustrating the movement **Up to concept, transfer Across/Out,** and **application Downward** to real-world subject:

(1) "In <u>every class and every subject</u>, students will learn to ask and to answer these questions:
1. From whose viewpoint are we seeing or reading or hearing? From what angle or perspective?
2. How do we know when we know? What's the evidence, and how reliable is it?
3. How are things events people connected? What is cause, what effect?
4. What's new and what's old? Have we encountered this idea before?
5. So what? What does it matter? What does it all mean?" (D.MEIER, CENTRAL PARK EAST SCHOOL)
         [[➔ **Superb—and alas, rare. Concepts both simple-accessible, and general-profound.**
         And to be explicitly taught and practiced throughout! A maturing of education...]]

(2) "...that <u>freshman mystery</u>: How is King Lear, particle physics, or the economic history of England... related to the complexity of issues with which one must deal in the office, the dining room, the hospital waiting room, and the voting booth?"
(BARBARA MOSSBERG, PRESIDENT, GODDARD COLLEGE, VERMONT)
         [[➔ **Superb, responsible, and too infrequent attempt at tightly, specifically "relating"**
         School and Life, real-world-life... (OR is it perhaps overdone, too "practical"?)]]

(3) <u>Anthropology</u> can teach students Social Agility & Sensitivity & Perspective; Observation; Planning; Accuracy in Interpreting Behavior, plus other generic-scientific skills such as Interpreting Info, Critiquing Conclusions, Contextualizing Details, Problem-Solving.
(JOHN OMOHUNDRO, SUNY-POTSDAM)
         [[➔ **Really excellent formulation of important skills above the data—**
         BUT this was told to graduating anthropology majors on a job search.
         Was it ALSO explicitly taught earlier to students all along?]]

(4) <u>Mathematical</u> thinking-skills: (KEITH DEVLIN, CHRONICLE OF HIGHER EDUCATION)
1. Number sense. 2. Numerical ability. 3. Spatial-reasoning ability. 4, 5. A sense of cause and effect. 6. Algorhythmic ability. 7. Ability to abstract! 8, 9. Logical, and Relational, reasoning ability.
         [[➔ **Great! Math and Life—via the thinking skills above-and-behind this-and-that formula...**
         However, was same <u>explicitly</u> taught, practiced for transfer, told to students?..]]

(5) I myself (BRANDON) taught <u>English 101</u> <u>essay-writing</u> via 14 separate concepts of "<u>expository elucidation</u>." (No mere formulaic simple five-paragraph theme!) Later, I asked students to "apply these concepts to more than just writing—to real life, personal, vocational, citizen."
For what it was worth, they could do so. Could see the relevance of **"Convergence"** or overall thesis-unity in an essay—and in a project at work. Of **"Conceptualizing"** or getting ideas from data in an essay—and in a new situation in travel. Of **"Construction"** or proper sequence, order, arrangement, pattern of subparts or ideas in an essay—and in planning a project. Of **"Calibration"** or balance and

proportion of minor and major elements in an essay—and in one's personal life and time-management. Of **"Completeness"** but also **"Compactness-Conciseness"** in good writing—but also in ones' presentations to others. And so on!

[[➜ **Rather formal and labored, even artificial, perhaps. But at least an attempt to have students see that (1) skills do exist above-and-behind subject-matter, and (2) could be applied to other subject-arenas...]]**

(6) Psychology studies **dualism**: defense mechanisms, what we say vs. what's really there... Sociology studies **dualism**: ideal-normative vs. real-behavioral culture, also latent vs. manifest functions... Literature studies **dualism**: subject-matter vs. theme, also ironies... Can all these domain-specific dualisms, lead to a general-generic thinking skill of dualistic perspective?

[[➜ **Good start, anyhow, at relating various disciplines and moving upward from domain-specific thinking skills, to general-generic thinking skills, smoothly?]]**

[2-B] And a set which are **"questionable."** Perhaps good—perhaps still shortfalling?

(7) After taking EDWARD DE BONO'S course in creative or lateral thinking, a man said that he now opens two, not just one, sugar packets at a time.

[[➜ **ONIONS: really rather miniscule application! ORCHIDS: at least shows how creativity can apply every day right at hand]]**

(8) Key Big Ideas from the natural sciences include that "energy changes from one form to another," also that "matter has a particle nature." Which is why moisture forms on a glass of cold beverage on a hot day. [SDSU SCIENCE EDUCATOR, SPRING 2000]

[[➜ **On second thought, a failure here? Large principle not shown to be important, significant relevant!]]**

(9) "If you have really learned what calculus means, you have a gut feel for the behavior of billiard balls, automobiles, electric currents, servomechanisms, space vehicles, and all the other objects of engineering which no amount of practical experience alone can provide." [ON ENGINEERING EDUCATION]

[[➜ **Short on specifics, but but also shows how any important subject, taught thinkingly, can enlarge "real knowing" in the real world. History! Geography! Sociology, as noted above! Others!]]**

(10) Introduce the following common, general concepts: Dynamic Equilibrium... Change and Evolution... Scale and Proportion... Causality and Consequence... Energy: Sources & Transfer...
[GOALS OF "SCIENCE & TECHNOLOGY IN SOCIETY," A UNIVERSITY'S GENERAL-EDUCATION CORE-COURSE]

[[➜ **Marvellously higher-order, large-scoped concepts, but were they taught for "use next Tuesday"?...]]**

(11) As for "liberal education," narrow vocational training is limited. More capable are students "who can work analogically with a broad number of models derived from fields at times remote from their own and can relate their work to a variety of contexts—social, economic, geographical, and political." [ARTICLE IN COLLEGE ENGLISH]

[[➜ **Very fine—but very high-level; was this large-scoped skill explicitly exemplified to students all along?]]**

(12) Harvard University will apply mathematics more. Teach quantitative reasoning not only via elementary number theory, but also via health economics, plus demography or counting people. Calculus topics such as change and accumulation may be taught not as such, but in computer-modelling courses. Math courses may tackle real-world problems. 1. How long before fish in mercury-poisoned water would be safe to eat? 2. How to calculate the health benefits of exercising. 3. Probability of an STD being transmitted by a condom-user. [CHE, JAN 2000]

[[➜ **Fine case of "transfer to the real world" BUT, can the students do so on their own later on?...]]**

[2-C] Perhaps **"onions not orchids."** Probably **shortfallings,** obvious—and overlooked? Agreed-upon—and arguable?

(13) On the last day of the class, my college history teacher said: "Be sure to relate history to your other academic *courses*." That very same day, my psychology professor also advised us to "Be sure to relate psychology to *life*." [ANECDOTE FROM BRANDON'S COLLEGE CAREER]

[[➜ **These sad examples speak for themselves. Too little, too late. True, some courses never said this much. Howe er, this illustrates the non-practicing of explicit transfer...]]**

(14) A NEW BOOK on a "biobehavioral" approach to motivation claimed its findings help us to understand varied human behavior and problems—"mate-choice, nepotism, attachment and independence, sensation seeking, obesity, and parent-offspring conflict."

[[➜ **Good stab at "relevance." BUT, a trap. This is only information-about subjects to be confronted later on. It may well NOT teach how to think through other, new issues on one's own competently!]]**

(15) "To apply to <u>areas other than English</u>, and to real life, the thinking skills derived from the study of languages-and-literatures." [Goal #6 from the goals-statement from the DEPT. OF LANGUAGES & LITERATURES AT UW-WHITEWATER]

[[➔ Another shortfalling. Nice statement, but STRATOSPHERICALLY-GENERAL.
(And most probably never considered by teachers, practiced for transfer...
Contrast with D. Meier's six-pak of concise concepts continually conveyed...]]

(16) [GOALS FOR <u>GENERAL EDUCATION CORE COURSES</u> AT UNIVERSITY OF WISCONSIN AT WHITEWATER:]
Knowing: "Understand" the factors in health. "Appreciate the importance of" fine arts, also world cultures. "Acquire a base of knowledge" and "understand how" knowledge is handled.
Skills: mathematical and quantitative, plus "communicate effectively," plus "to make sound ethical and value judgments."   Sounds good, but see the atrocious Anecdote noted here:

[[➔ Rather pervasively What To Know, not How To Think. True, Goal #1 was "<u>Think critically and analytically,
integrate and synthesize knowledge, and draw conclusions from complex information</u>." However, that was *absent*
from the initial draft of Gen Ed Goals circulated to the faculty. I, BARTON, *objected*. They then added #1 as above.
They had never even noticed the absence! So I can only wonder whether thinking is actually taught...]]

BARTON: ...Thus far, a baker's dozen of examples of the issue of true transfer of thinking, or not...

CHESTER [[MODESTLY IMPRESSED, THEN STILL SUSPICIOUS]] ... Well, I do see more about Conceptualize-Transfer-Apply as true thinking... How Marvelous of You To Donate Your Insight... I do see the idea that **education often shortfalls true thinking...** How can I get a better feel for this new perspective?

[5D.] <u>Analogies</u> also assist spotting of "shortfalling":

BARTON: ... Often, comparisons and similes help. Here, four analogies show the new essence of TT.

1. **Agricultural**. If a college course is like "a class in agriculture," say "Corn 101," then most students only learn Content-Mastery, what to Know and Believe, not how to Do. The teacher tells them: "Yonder is the field of corn which I have planted in lecture and discussion. <u>Go ye forth with these five-paragraph bushel-baskets, and for the Final Exam, bring back corn from the first three rows—thaat's right</u>!" [*But this seems hideous, juvenilizing the students, the "banking" system in charge, educational malpractice.* Instead of students knowing how to grow their own corn, on their own, later in life, amid complexities too. Not that most teachers know or care about this shortfall...]

2. **Aquatics**. Most schooling is "swimming in lanes with water wings" instead of "open-water navigation"...

3. **Aviation**. Most schooling has *the teacher/assignment making all the decisions*, does not prepare students to "solo" on their own, no autonomous application of abstractions...

4. ...and a final analogy: "The so-called **<u>Training Wheels</u>** on the bicycle, get *Welded On*..."

CHESTER: [[STILL IMPRESSED]] Yeah, those are like the usual "factory" or "banking" analogies of traditional education as "filling up the empty pupil" via "transmission of information," "covering and mastering the content"....
Or "vaccination," as in, "it hurts but I need to have it, so I'll get it as painlessly as possible via the easiest teacher"... Or the "dipstick" analogy: add oil of learning, but please, don't overfill with more than is needed...

[5E.] No, TT will *not* prevail, "work"; but yes it *does* stay The <u>Answer</u>

BARTON: The truly New, meets with defense... See, (1) **"Goals-to-Go."** These ambitious questions represent end-goals to aim for or *toward* by *final*-exam time. (2) Plus, it's approach that counts. <u>I demand not perfection, but only the evidence of a mind actively engaged with difficult material</u>, that's all. Of course this does mean *motivated*: involved, committed, dedicated.

(I'd rather read one genuine-effort page soiled maculate with true Thinking, flawed but alive,
than three antiseptic Student-Theme packages, nice-nice correct, but written as if
by a puppet with gloves on. Of course, easier to say about literature than math, I admit...)

And you're right, TT is Utopian, can't be realized broadscale tomorrow—or ever. But now you know why.

--<u>Institutionally</u>, massive lag exists. Textbook manufacturers... curricula... standardized testing (thinking can and must be tested for, but not on a multiple-choice Scantron sheet); homeostasis...

--<u>Teachers</u>: most are not interested in TT as goal, plus they see it as "work" (We Insiders to it, see it as "Duty-Plus-Beauty": Sportive Play, immensely satisfying-fulfilling-rewarding to us personally: for the better-served students, for our selves in our calling—otherwise why would we pursue TT?)

--But basically, Utopian because of <u>students</u>. All learning is self-teaching, as critical-thinking expert RICHARD PAUL says: nobody can teach anyone anything of real value, teachers can only facilitate self-construction, the learner's sitting down and figuring it out by thinking it through. But it's not lack of ability primarily. It's lack of interest. Because of <u>massive lack of student involvement, commitment, engagement today</u>. (At least in lower-level and required courses such as my English 101...) Terminally non-motivated, they'll "blow off" the assignments. But whose fault is *that*? (Careful on that one!) I learned this when I gave an otherwise- (and still-) powerful assignment, to write and then rewrite a paper, thus:

<u>EXAMPLE</u>. "*The Pre-Post Paper: Beneficence Blown-Away*" A great TT assignment is to (1) <u>assign a course paper the first week</u> of the course, a do-your-best effort but exploratory-experimental, with <u>no</u> specific directions.

[**EXAMPLE**: in **English** composition, "A Job I've Held." In **sociology**, "The Individual And The Group." In **history**, "How does the past and present interrelate?" In **economics**?.. In **philosophy**?... in **biology**?... in **geography**?...]

(2) <u>Do not grade</u> or even respond to this pre-paper. (You may of course silently <u>examine</u> them, and then return them to the students, or retain safely.) Then *as part of the final exam*, (3) <u>assign a re-do</u> of the same paper/assignment.

The Good News: much Awareness plus Appreciation. Student after student inescapably learn that they've learned much. "Wow, this early version is pathetic, I could do it so much better now!" **The Bad News**: no Action. They don't do it much better. Due to non-motivation, they sidestep this great opportunity to cinch their learning, and hand in disgustingly-minimal touch-ups only. (**At least in my required Freshman English 101 1970-95, anyhow...**) **The Possible Good News After All**: in advanced classes, with more-motivated students, this works magic.....

In education as in medicine, "*primum non nocere*," "First of all, do no harm." And the "know-and-show" education harms students nine ways, insults them too.... So we "TT Insiders" press on, grass-roots style.

[6.] Some Key Thinking Skills: [6A.] Disciplines A to Z:

CHESTER: Okay. But what "thinking skills" do you propose should be taught more than they are?

BARTON: First, that question is a trap. Don't ask *me*! Each teacher has to plan from scratch, "Exactly whether, and which, thinking to teach—for students in the real world later—and then explicitly teach, and assess." (Teachers waiting to be told "what thinking skills to teach, " ironically mimic "passive pupils" thus...)

However, second, I can mention (1) **discipline-specific** skills (from more rote formulae tactics, up to higher-order strategic concepts) as listed in the Table earlier.

➔Allocation cost, cognitive dissonance, self-selected sample, sociology's functionalism and conflict and symbolic interactionism theories, eight types or schools of literary criticism, etc.

But there are also (2) **generic thinking skills**, including the overlooked **"Thinking 101 Superbasics"**:

➔Ways of knowing: levels (group, individual)... Synthesis vs. Analysis/categorization, also Induction, Deduction and empiricism, idealism... Left-Brain logical, Right-Brain lateral/connective... Contextual or system or integrative thinking: comparison-contrast... Modes: definition, cause-effect, etc... Structure-order-pattern-arrangement... Veracity: "truth"—and biasses!... The "Objective vs. Personal" tangle... The "Relativism" trap!... Dispositions or attitudes toward good thinking... Reflexive self-awareness or meta-cognition about one's own thinking... Criteria; thinking vs. *good* thinking... Background: presuppositions, etc... Basic Logic-Argument-Reasoning 101 and fallacies... AND THEN Lensmanship or multiple-plural perspectives, including interdisciplinarity, etc.

See, for the **discipline-specific** skills (in the following Table), *many courses focus overly on the center-column data*, not on the right-hand column *concepts*. And if they do offer concepts, it may be as content-to-know, *not* skills-to-use. And even if as skills, they might *not* teach them explicitly? Practice for transfer to the "world"? Then assess success? See, most courses don't step *up the stairway to the Second Story...*

The subject taught:	Usual **factual-content**, and lower-level skills:	Higher-order keystone **concepts** of the subject:

algebra	(various formulae)	"combination," "permutation," "association"—the **keystones**
sociology	Institutions, social problems. Often <u>some</u> **concepts** (role, status, norm, deviancy, socialization, etc.)	**Theories**: Functionalism, Conflict, Interactionism... **Perspectives**: Debunking, Unrespectable, Cosmopolitan, Relativism...
art history	Egyptian, Greek, Medieval styles....and so forth.	Composition **principles**: balance, proportion, sequence, unity, a/symmetry, simplicity, contrast! Line, form, value,!
literature	Periods. Authors. Themes.	"Schools of Criticism" as **lenses**: biographical, aesthetic, historical, psychological, social-critical, etc.!
computers	this and that program...	"linear sequentiality"
economics	formulae, data on problems...	"scarcity" "allocation cost," or "cost-benefit ratio"—as immensely-applicable everywhere, always!
Natural Sciences	Biology, etc.: facts of mitosis-meiosis and the like, more...	<u>General Concepts of Science</u>: Dynamic Equilibrium; Change & Evolution; Scale & Proportion; Causality & Consequence; Energy, Its Sources & Transfer...
geography	[data, data, data...]	["Why is it like it is, here?"]
political science	[info on government systems]	How to confront the recurrent Big Issues: individual freedom vs. group security, etc., etc., etc.
history	"kings, courts, dates..."	[Past-present continuities, dissimilarities, etc.]
math		Problem-solving: Trial and error; "Step backwards"; Simulation; Symbolism; Patterns... Cause-and-Effect...
OTHERS:		
APPLIEDS:	Business, Engineering, Law, Medicine, Technology, Military, Government, etc...	

CHESTER: I see your Truth (or Hypothesis, perhaps?) We're bottom-heavy on "content," too light on key thinking skills actually taught, actually practiced, actually applied...hmm.....

BRANDON: Even more overlooked, the **generic thinking skills** (including vital **superbasics**)—first I must quote "Touchstone" statement (=a potent, fecund comment) by an expert, the *single most important* of the half-dozen "Touchstones" I share in my presentations—(or used to...) It's from WALTER DERZKO, of the Ideas Lab. Its truth is almost "non-comprehensible" to most of us, it's so New and paradigm-different:

DERZKO says that <u>**we ignore teaching thinking**</u> <u>in most schools and corporations</u>, for various reasons—some other teacher will do it, budget cuts prevent doing it, we simply overlook doing it, or we think we can think well enough already. <u>But are we really good-enough thinkers not to need explicit training in thinking skills?</u> DERZKO says: "Consider the paradox. We expect students and staff to be <u>math</u>-literate. So what do we do? Back in grade 1 and 2 we teach everyone *the operancy skills behind* math...the plus, subtract, multiple and divide. Once we master these basic math-related operations we go on to *higher order applications*....**Yet when we switch domains** from <u>numbers</u> over to <u>fact, ideas, concepts, values, assumptions, and notions</u> (the content for <u>all other subject areas in school and later at work</u>), **we totally ignore the thinking operations needed to explore or create new ideas**."

...most will read the above and say "yes" but will **"not know that they do not know"** its full import. But to help people understand, I always add (or used to add...) a certain other analogy right at this point:

<u>**Analogy.**</u> Besides "corn-gathering," "training wheels," "solo flight," etc., we also have **"the two-story building."** Think of "education," *as if* it's a structure whose <u>ground floor</u> is finished off, occupied, busy teaching **facts, beliefs, rote skills, and mere opinion** as thinking: to Know/Believe... But the <u>second floor</u>, of **conceptualizing, key thinking tools**, is—nonexistent. Or, only roughed-out scaffolded, but unfinished off, only part-inhabited. And the "stairway" between, is sealed off somehow....

[6B.] Generic Thinking: "TOOL-KITS" for <u>Cause-Effect</u>, <u>Structure</u>:

CHESTER: Well, can't I ask what **non-disciplinary or generic** key thinking skills to teach?

BARTON: *As I just said*, a trap-question: each teacher must decide. But just to show that "the second story is empty," that <u>explicit</u> teaching of <u>thinking</u> is rare, here are some identified **generic** <u>thinking skills</u> which might be taught more explicitly via **TOOL-KITS** to have at hand, accessible but unobtrusive.

Not just the usual "informal logic argument reasoning plus fallacies to avoid"; far too narrow. *Instead,* **(1)** <u>the prior general basics</u>: "Lenses" including World-View and Ways of Knowing; Veracity-Authority-Criteria; the

"Relativism" Trap; Implicit Presuppositions; "Verticality" or Concrete-to-Conceptual Levels; and then the **"Eight Main Moves"**: Comprehensive Synthesis, Contrary-Correlating (beyond dualism), Analysis, Induction, Deduction, Connection-Integration-Holism, Change over time/space, and overall, "Lenses" or multiple-plural perspective...
Then (2) *more specifically*: the **"Modes,"** Definition, Compare-Contrast, Classify-Divide, Cause-Effect, Structure. And "Subject-Confronting," meaning Describing & Interpreting & Explaining (cause-effect) & Evaluating (pro-con) & Doing to-or-with & Problem-Solving with Decision-Making.....

So, our TT Movement accuses: Many courses **(1)** seem to *suggest, or urge, or value, or hope-for* (etc.), thinking skills, but **(2)** do not *explicitly* teach them *as such*. Take two generic skills. **Cause-Effect** analysis. Plus, **Structure**—as in sequence specifically, but also organization-arrangement generally.... Are these skills currently under-taught? How might they be better conveyed?

More the current-standard-traditional:	More long-range thinking-emphasis. Thinking skills: whether or not always actually *taught* this explicitly, at least always made *available* in this accessible a format:
Course exam questions as noted earlier, "Describe the causes [and effects] of the French Revolution, of World War 1...." but is this: [...Knowledge-transmission? Student repeats the answers s/he was given. Possible Belief, ideologies possible also...] [...OOO: just give "your own opinion" about the causes?] [...RRR: rigid rote rule? Explain, but according to this formula (Feminism and the story "A Rose for Emily"?]	A generic **"TOOL-KIT"** for the issue of **cause-effect** analysis. Multi-disciplinary: both discipline-specific and also general-generic. Could include: **1.** The Simplicity Issue. "Fewer causes the better" (Occam's Razor) vs. "richness of overdetermination" (psychoanalytic explanations). **2.** Simple to Complex. 2A. "One cause, one effect" and "one cause many effects" and "many causes one effect" on to "many causes, many effects" or true multiple causality. (Diabetes, see a chart or diagram of multiple interactions.) **2B.** Linear vs. Concurrent-Chains-Interrelated. The **Butterfly** Effect? **2C.** Discontinuities: **"Threshhold"** issue (**Catastrophe**), also "Lily-Pond" effect. **3.** Scope. In both Space and also Time, the near-proximate-acute causes [& effects!] ... "vs." the remote-chronic-causes [& effects?!]. **4.** Priorities I. "Necessary and Sufficient." Contributing, initiating, promoting. **5.** Priorities II. The "chicken-and-the-egg" problem, what is cause, what is effect? (school performance and funding... psyche and soma in depression... the "psychopolitics" of H. LASSWELL, neurosis or situation?... distance between father and gay son, etc.). **6.** Specific systems. "ARISTOTLE'S Four Causes": Material, Formal, Efficient, Final **7.** Effects. R. K. MERTON'S "Latent and Manifest Functions." Something's effects "neither intended nor recognized" [Same for causes?] Psychology: "Secondary Gain." **8.** C-E and the "interdisciplinary/integrative" endeavor. As usual: cooperation vs. conflict between or among disciplines (psych, bio—etc.)? Mere additive approach, or some true integration and synthesis? Ultimate subjectivity? Etc.

CHESTER: .....well, at last I'm *starting* to see that rarely do we educate about **cause-effect** with such a conceptual scope-plus-precision.... *Or even have the tools at hand as elucidated as the above...* In fact, remember that earlier cause-effect exam question which now seems more—anyhow, as seen through the Universal Viewpoint of your own TT Truth [[OR IDEOLOGY?]]. And I read another one too:

1. (*From the UNIV. OF WI AT WHITEWATER*): "What was the effect of World War I on Europe?" [**The expected answer,** *given* **in lecture/textbook, was "The war transformed Europe mentally, politically, and economically"** [... No need or chance to learn or use, any of the eight possible generic cause-effect tools in the Tool-KIT above!]

2. (*From an exam in the FRENCH NATIONAL SCHOOL SYSTEM, quoted by Albert Shanker, recent head of a large teachers' group*): "Causes of the first World War. First, explain the indirect causes (imperialism, nationalism) which facilitated the appearance of European networks of alliances., Briefly, describe these networks. Next, tell how the crisis at Sarajevo was directly responsible for the First World War." [...again, how this can be thought of as testing thinking, instead of rote recall, is utterly beyond me...]

BARTON: Good indeed. See, Most Outsiders don't see how these are "training-wheels, leg-braces"... One more example. The general issue of **structure.** A.K.A. organization, arrangement, pattern.

Conventional approaches:	Possible **thinking** approach:
"In your five paragraph theme, arrange the three points (1) in this or that specific order I tell you to, or (2) however you feel like doing....." [...The first being RRR or "rigid rote rule" given, the	A **"TOOL · KIT"** for the *concept* **structure-organization-arrangement**: **(1)** Basic sequentiality or serial structure: options: 1. Time... 2. Space... 3. Utterly random by chance... 4. Free association, to "one best felt" order... 5. Writer-based (meaningful to him/her) "vs." reader-based (better for reader-comprehension)... 5. Via some conceptual scheme or other (alphabetical, or an ideology, or the modes such as compare-contrast, etc.)... 6. Hierarchy, or "from the most or A to the least or Z"... 7.

second being OOO or "only one's own opinion" perhaps totally vacant from any competence and control...]	"Hypertext" or flattened networked associated hierarchy...
	(2) Other issues. **(A)** ONE or Unity: the Leitmotif, the "Organic Form" (theme & **repetitions** w/ variation), the "Maypole"... Perhaps **(B)** DUAL or the "Alpha & Omega" or Out-&-Return or Braided-Intertwined.... **(C)** SERIAL vs. PARALLEL, a.k.a. left-brain linear "vs." right-brain lateral...

CHESTER: That's potentially good. So much so, that I now wonder: <u>why haven't educators constructed such **TOOL-KITS** to teach generic thinking skills</u>—filled out the Second Story of Education Hall?

BARTON: I can't politely say. Off the record, I can say: <u>internally</u>, most teachers don't realize *or* then care. <u>Externally</u>, the Reward System doesn't value such "Deep Pedagogy," over Research or Service...

CHESTER: Hey, can you give any other Tool-Kits here? Come to think of it, you hinted toward one on, say, "**confronting major change**" when you discussed the "four phases and three responses," above. But, I'd like to see yours on Concretization or **specific detailing**—you know, the writing and thinking skill of "illustrate and support your generalization or idea, with a specific concrete example"?

BARTON: Would love to, but alas, *our space here is limited,* or else I'd share not only **Specifizing**, but also the "**Modes**": **Define, Categorize, Compare-Contrast,** plus **Lenses** or multiple-plural perspectives on a subject, plus "**Knowledge, Truth, Authority, Criteria,**" plus **Competence-or-Excellence**, and more....

[If interested, see our forthcoming book, <u>Mind-Play</u>... Neither a too-"tight" Bible or boot-camp, nor a too-"loose" Open Field: rather, a "Resource Access-Center," blending Guidance and Autonomy, and elitist in conserving Good Thinking, but populist in welcoming *all* interested... ISBN to be 0-9645402-7-4 in paperback; none yet for the CD-ROM version...]

[7.] "Objections!": <u>Criticisms</u> provide grist:

CHESTER: But whoa! I've heard too many **objections** to "TT". How would you handle them?

-"Students pick up thinking as they go along"...
-"Well, we already teach thinking in our classes!"...
-"Students can't and won't learn thinking—due to inability plus non-motivation"...
-"Superior students don't need this, average and inferior students can't benefit from this"...
-"We have to cover content, plus you can't think about nothing, you have to get a knowledge-base first and then you can think about it"...
-"Students need structure, and need to be told *Exactly What Is Expected* on assignments!"...
-"Teachers who try to teach thinking receive *lower student evaluations, more complaints*—let alone is not compensated for in the so-called reward structure"...
-"At this point in time, TT in one course is not reinforced in the other courses students are taking" ...
-"Anyhow, massive institutional inertia or lag will prevent TT: textbook publishers, standardized testing, and more"...
-"Teaching thinking is just another educational fad or fashion"...
-"I like being the expert authority: delivering true facts is safer"...
-"I don't like messy, experimental student work"...
-"I definitely have my own subjects and skills and also beliefs I want to transmit to students!"...
-"How can I teach thinking, it seems I was never taught how to teach it myself!"
-"Frankly (but off the record), teaching thinking is simply too much work: covering factual content is much easier"...

BARTON: These are all great grist-for-the-mill on "how we think about new complexities which challenge, and how we can think better about them." Civilly, I can note *some* valid criticisms, legitimate objections here. But competently, I must also note *many* defenses, resistances, denials, evasions...

CHESTER: I see... But you must face one major recurring objection. Namely, **content-coverage. "But you can't think about nothing, you have to have something to think about. And surely, you have to cover content! So first, cover content, give a knowledge-base, so then the students will have something to think about!"**

BARTON: [[GRIMACING]] Ah yes; I hear it all the time. It's rich; let's "think it thru" for fun:

1. Grain, or degree, of truth? Yes but not much. Math doesn't require "content." Nor do other fields, skills.

(**EXAMPLE:** Learning the key thinking skills of **Analysis/Categorization/Classification-&-Division**: I can say to my students, "derive an outline for the thesis that Rowdy Behavior in the Lunchroom Was Of Many Sorts." *Not much Content needed there* to learn a basic, valuable, under-used, under-taught Thinking Skill. *Not* "Poured Coke into Plants" or "Shoved Old Ladies in Line," *but* "Material Damage, plus Rudeness to People," etc.)

Plus much true learning is blending content & thinking skills as you acquire both.

2. Dandy Little Rationalization, Denial, Evasion of the new challenge of TT. (I get this a *lot*...) "Heck, first give them the facts, then in some unspecified, distant, later course we can teach them the thinking." Bingo—Business As Usual delivering the Facts, & presto, No More Little Problem On Our Doorstep...

3. Benevolent, If Blocking, Internalized Professional-Group Norm. More generously, I admit that teachers are socialized to cover content as a norm, and if they don't, they feel ashamed or guilty. Of course, to the extent that "covering the content" is an internalized norm, it is not questionable or debatable, it's a folkway. (Plus there's being the Expert Authority, which also gets "psychological"...)

4. Actual Inaccuracy. Here is our second "Touchstone" quotation, from WILLIAM NEWELL, a key expert in integrative education. His comment marvelously shifts 180 degrees from what we expect and believe. He says thinking skills can be learned earlier, and even prior to, content!

"While interdisciplinary courses indeed make use of concepts, theories, methods, and factual knowledge from various disciplines, the interdisciplinary understanding they develop is grounded primarily in the perspectives from which these concepts, theories, methods, and facts emerge. **It takes many years to learn a discipline;** *it takes only a few readings to begin to develop a feel for how that discipline characteristically looks at the world*, its angle of vision, its perspective."

"Scandalous," "heretical"—but also quite valid. I myself taught "true interdisciplinary perspective" to a *freshman* class in *one hour*, and effectively, they could **autonomously apply** it at once...

A UNIVERSITY PRESIDENT seconds the above: in re "content vs. skills," *the true content, is the skills*:

[The goal, and the content-or-substance, in higher education is the ability to think. Key thinking skills are the actual "content" of courses, or should be. Only so much factual "content" is added to support, illustrate, communicate the skills. This viewpoint differs radically from the traditional policy, indeed mantra, that "one must cover content," let alone "content first then skills."] [FROM CHRONICLE OF HIGHER EDUCATION; PARAPHRASED]

CHESTER: Well, all right; you can indeed "think competently about," the suspect response that "we have to cover content." But allow me my larger objection? Just how can "thinking" be the *only* or even *major* goal of *all* education? Talk about irony, you say you're competent but end up simplistic and partial!

...for instance, ALVERNO COLLEGE in Wisconsin (a pioneer in "outcome-based" education, quite like your own **Goals-to-Go**), notes eight, count them, key major outcomes of true education. Yes, "Analysis" (#2) and "Problem-Solving" (#3)... but also Communication; Valuing in Decision-Making; Social Interaction; Global Perspectives; Effective Citizenship; and Aesthetic Responsiveness! This your dwarfs "thinking, thinking, and more thinking" as "the" goal, eh? [[YOU COULDN'T POSSIBLY BE JUST AS SIMPLISTIC-AUTHORITARIAN, AS THE TRADITIONAL EDUCATION you critique, COULD YOU?...]]

BARTON: You're correct; just incomplete. (1) Indeed ALVERNO's "octet" is indispensable for true education. But we only say: *true thinking is the vital prior Center of all. Maybe* insufficient? but *surely* absolutely necessary, for Education. The keystone maypole roofbeam standpoint (etc.) vital to all else.
(2) Also note other "goals" in education, but false-or-bogus-ersatz ones, hence dangerous ones which would even *oppose* true Thinking. RICHARD PAUL warns against these: Education for narrow job-training only... Education for a docile citizenship unquestioning of political and other Authorities...

.....FERN [[BREAKING IN UNEXPECTEDLY FROM THE ADJACENT OFFICE]]: Now you, you just wait just a minute here. I overheard *everything* (these walls are paper-thin), and CHESTER you overlooked, and BARTON you're sidestepping, the single most damning objection of all. Namely, the charge that "**any teaching of thinking, is either superfluous, or impossible.**" Indeed, any educational effort! Some FRENCH WIT said that education is "useless except in the happy exception when it is irrelevant" meaning when the student is naturally able? *Get real!* The superior student doesn't *need* all this Thinking-Tutoring, s/he will develop thinking skills by him/herself along the way. And the average student isn't motivated enough to profit. And the inferior student isn't able enough to benefit. So, teaching thinking only drags things down. *So!*

CHESTER: My gosh, do you suppose—that's candid Truthtelling that we don't want to face...

BARTON: All true, FERN, and I do agree. Just *two tiny problems* with your charge. It's simultaneously basically true, but also fundamentally flawed because partial-and-incomplete.

(1) Even <u>advanced</u> students can be marvellously *accelerated* by having thinking skills explicitly reviewable by them, "accessible but unobtrusive" **TOOL·KITS** so they can monitor their progress better and also don't have to re-invent the wheel. (I wish that when I was an undergraduate, I had had the "**TOOL KITS**" we offer here: **Lensmanship... Cause-Effect... Structure... Zeitgeist or Climate of Opinion...** and others...)

But also **(2)** those "<u>average</u>," hence unmotivated, students—exactly who are they? [Outside of my many state-university required Freshman English 101 pupils, I will admit...] Even <u>average</u> students can be marvellously invited by providing thinking skills they haven't had before in school or life, to initiate, stimulate, open up their abilities they didn't yet suspect. Many are lax; many also are not invited...

(3) I must agree about <u>inferior</u> students. (Except then I recall MIKE SCHIMKE. *Below*-average but dedicated, he chose to work hard, and he achieved average-*plus* work through the guidance our Thinking Tools provided...)

--In short, **FERN**, your rebuttal *is* both accurate, realistic, hence significant—*but also* disrespectfully *insulting to* many students (they do have abilities), and incompetently-*careless* also (they do need resources, at least available: "accessible but unobtrusive"). And <u>teachers need</u> these **TOOL·KITS** <u>too</u>! Eh? Dogmatic of me to say "everyone should use such Kits"; irresponsible of me and others not to provide them........   [[.....**FERN** EXITS QUICKLY...]]

CHESTER: Well, your Critique [[OR IS IT A DOGMATIC TORPEDOING?]] of "Content-Coverage" is Impressive. You Can Marvellously Identify The Overlooked Subtypes of Resistance In The The Still-Unaware [[OR IS IT UNWASHED UNREFORMABLES?]].... But what say you to those who unlike **FERN** favor thoughtfulness but who honestly feel, **"But surely we all already teach thinking in our classes; I know I do"**?

BARTON [[QUITE AGITATED]] *I don't say much any more.* I see "massive <u>disconnect</u>." I got teachers who their exams are like, "discuss the relations between Hawthorne, Emerson, Thoreau and contrast with Whitman, Dickinson, Melville," or some such content-mastery they discussed in class. And *they think or claim that via and from this, they're teaching thinking,* as I defined it above—autonomous application of new abstractions... Whereas I tell them: *you are only teaching content-mastery, gourmet-level regurgitation of the course content you give students in waving yellow rows!* What can your students do *on their own*? And I say to them, don't give me guff about how "within this structure, the students can make their own decision," and the like. (**Not state-university freshmen, anyhow...**) It's usually Training Wheels Welded On, not Solo Flight... But it's **In-Conceivable**. These teachers don't disagree, or agree. They just don't *see* it. (Or they're content with what they do. Probably fine for them. Quite **in-Conceivable** to *me*...)

But I'm too harsh here. Since True Leadership Requires Modest Humility also, I can admit <u>I too failed in TT, and badly</u>—before my Enlightenment, of course. I *thought* I was doing "TT." My atrocious anecdote:

<u>**EXAMPLE:**</u> *"That Last Theme, Alas..."* In English 101, freshman composition, I taught the students how to write. Or so I thought. Then, "thinkingly," I said: "<u>For our sixth and last paper, and the final exam</u>, it's now up to you, to show what you've truly learned. Instructions: "Write a paper, and annotate it: critically explain and evaluate what you did, how, and how well or not. By now you know what to do on your own." That was it.

--"Vague" assignment? No, quite specific, toward <u>a</u>utonomous <u>a</u>pplication of <u>a</u>bstractions, my **Goal-to-Go**. But, the dismal result? Genteel catastrophe. The students were panicked, hostile, consternated. See, they didn't know what to do On Their Own. The Training Wheels removed, they could not fly Solo. I had taught them only lower-level How To Follow Orders. And how many other teachers, micro-assigning thus, *teach their whole careers without ever knowing how they fell short?* Or, if realizing, *did not care?.....*

--***Look, all I ever sought, was something like this:*** "For my exam, I [the student] wrote a letter to the editor, and *because* length is a variable, as short as possible, I limited my subject. I opened with a question they couldn't answer, *because* the audience is reading voluntarily and has to be hooked. I followed up with five very brief varied examples, statistics, quotation, and anecdote, *because* examples both inform, and interest. I ended with a reasonable statement, *because* tone is important. So I think I've learned what decisions to make and how to make them in this genre of the letter to the editor. Before this class I would have just written it." ***This rather-simple level of "autonomously applying the abstractions about how to write, would be great and sufficient. But this was rare...***

CHESTER [[GENTLY; CAREFULLY]] ...you couldn't just possibly be wrong, and some other teachers, right?

BARTON [[RECOVERED; CONFIDENT AGAIN]] Spare me the facile Relativism, okaay? As said earlier—via my system, **<u>90% of teachers do not "TT"</u>**. Critique my system fairly; and I'll listen, *and gladly*. Until then....

CHESTER: Well, my able colleague MARK said that **"Surely all teachers are interested in the teaching of thinking,"** And when I questioned that, he got kind of "frosted. What would you say to him?

BARTON: I'd just tell him how I researched what were the stated, plus true, teaching goals of my colleagues in my department—all the ones I could access. Here are the impressive results:

1. MARIE taught short stories dealing with personal development, maturity, growth issues. This was for her students' sake—but also, she affirmed, **for her own personal sake...**
2. GILBERT taught students that America was imperialistic in the Far East and elsewhere. He *fervently believes* that. He stated he intended students would exit the course being quite aware of that. [**I think we call this Indoctrination into Ideologies, or nowadays, "Socially-Committed"?**]
3. JUDY taught about animal rights and anti-hunting stands in classes (in re research reports). She frankly "wants to stop hunting." She "does not give both sides of the cases, because the students already enter class knowing the one, the pro-hunting, side well." [**Do they objectively know their folk-ideologies now, and in thought-out detail? True Thinking involves dispassionately assessing your own stands, their implications, motivations, etc...**]
4. LEO teaches a poetic-creative "alternate style" of writing, even in practical English 101. This involves a collage of imagery, statistics, dry statements, surprises, page-layout. He frankly stated that he did so *to be able to get through the course without tedium and boredom*. The experiments were vivacious...   --But one former student of his said to me that the "alternate style" didn't seem to be real-world practical, for School or for Work. [**Insightful and biassed myself, I could only agree...**]
5. GORDON claims that he indeed "teaches thinking" in his classes. [**He has received student complaints of his intellectually-browbeating them in class, to the point of "soft-core student-abuse" one might phrase it...**]
6., 7., 8. IVAN, NELSON, and GERRY all TRIED the teaching of thinking, or anyhow more flexible student response. No one of the three found it amenable to their own educational styles, which emphasized *control* (valued for clarity and achievement). After a long discussion with me, GERRY admitted ultimately that he flat-out "did not like *messy* student papers which *experimented*"—the true motivation surfacing? [**Was "thinking" here, confused with OOO or "Only One's Own Opinion"?**]
9. I myself, BRANDON, pursued the teaching of writing: indeed the dreaded "bonehead" Freshman Composition. (Became the department specialist and published 50 articles, in fact...) **But** *why?* Because of (1) dutiful dedication? *Not hardly.* (2) Career-move? *Nope*; that helped, but was secondary. Rather, (3) because writing, a complex activity, was perfect grist to "dock" or "hook up" with what I wanted to teach in the first place, and simply because of my own impassioned *Personal-Preference Taste-Temperament* which led to this book! Namely, **thinking through complexities competently**... Confession Time, or Oh, how I harnessed poor Writing as the ancillary handmaiden to serve my own True Self-ish Desires! Maybe...   Plus, I chose TT as goal just as *subjectively* as Colleagues #1 thru #8 above chose *their* own "non-thinking" goals! So! So, everything indeed does dissolve into Facile Relativism, "Who's to say who's right after all," eh?, and anyone claiming different today is just a vestigial fossil, a cranky authoritarian absolutist, *Bxtch, Mumble, Gripe....* [**...Or does it? Spot the prevalent amateur pitfall there...**]   Thus—I taught thinking *not* for moral duty. **But** for intense professional pleasure.   **TT respects the students. It matures the classroom. It elevates true education....**

...and so, so much for the notion that "Well, of course, we all desire to Teach Thinking in our classes!" A notion held for varied reasons, from honest commitment, to simplistically-hypocritical lip-service?

CHESTER: .....wow...How Marvelous that you are Brave & Dedicated enough to Risk Condemnation by Iconoclastically Critiquing even your Peer-Colleagues [[AS IF THEY'D BE INSULTED BY YOUR SAD DISTORTIONS]] ....Well, what are your recommendations to solve the problem of the shortfall of thinking?

BARTON: I *told* you, *no solution*! It's a classic Lost Cause! This is why, I told you, I've just abandoned proselytizing to unreceptive Masses. I'm wisely turning instead to defend the Cause from Outside the System, Bottom-Up, via a Hundred Grassroot Fires of the True Flame of our Vision **for those few Self-Chosen Converts who can indeed See the Light....**

CHESTER [[TRYING TO REMAIN CIVIL THROUGH THE ABOVE...]] Well yes... "In Spite Of My Earlier Doubts, Or Rather Blindnesses, I am becoming Rather Committed." So can you suggest some rules of thumb for me to follow to pursue the Lonely but Rewarding Path toward TT? [[AS WELL AS MORE VALUABLE EVIDENCE OF HOW EVEN THE EXPERTS CAN BLUNDER AND MIS-THINK THE WORST, EVEN THOUGH UNAWARE THAT THEY ARE EXTREME, SIMPLISTIC, AND COMPULSIVE?]]

BARTON: *Told you that earlier too*. First, return to **"Goal-to-Go,"** above, and the **"Teacher's Test."** Decide exactly whether, how much, and which thinking skills are your course goal **&** then do it.

[8.] *Exactly How* Education Scandalously Shortfalls "TT":
[8A.] More Sheer Attention *to* Thinking Needed?

But you're now ready to know more fully-and-truly how most formal education still does shortfall TT.

We recall DERZKO'S classic statement, earlier. That we utterly lack **"TOOL-KITS"** for thinking—worse, we ignore teaching thinking even without them at hand. Thinking expert RICHARD PAUL gives examples:

"The long and the short of the story is this: Schools today do not focus on how to introduce children to the logic of the subjects they study. The do not focus on what it is to reason historically, what it is to reason mathematically or scientifically, what it is to reason sociologically, anthropologically, or geographically, what it is to reason philosophically or morally. Hence, disciplined reasoning—which is at the heart of the logic of every academic subject and profession—is largely absent from the classroom of today."

CHESTER: The above is sort of your Sacred Scrip, isn't it? Something to pour over in your Temple's inner *sanctum sanctoronium*? So as to drive Ever More Wisdom from, eh?

BARTON: *Exactly!* It's **"Knowing, vs. Knowing."** We can know things only partially—or, more fully...

[8B.] Then, More *Explicit* Teaching *of* Thinking Needed?

But our glimpse at "shortfalling" is not done yet. The above suggests that we *non*-teach thinking. Not always true, of course. So, more subtly, note that we also *under-* and *mis-* and *pseudo*-teach thinking. Here's probably the last of our **analogies**. that of "the five-step stairway." It may show how a course can move upward, from concrete facts, to skills taught, then transferred. (Or *should*, but...)

(1) No attention to thinking. Emphasis upon what to Know and Believe. Or "thinking," but perhaps only via "RRR" or Rigid Rote Rules: lower-level skills of the formula type, rote rules not tools, algorhythms not heuristics.

(2) Then, "Thinking" is present in the course. Whether as Big Ideas or key concepts in the subject, and/or as actual thinking skills, systems in the subject. But alas, not explicitly taught as skills! Still only something to Know about, perhaps Believe in...

    Here enters the murky area of pseudo-teaching of thinking. See LIPMAN below.

(3) "Thinking" is purveyed, pedagogically taught *explicitly*.

(4) Including practiced-in, taught-for-transfer to new situations, which does not happen by itself!

(5) ... and even "perfected," including being tested and measured for. The best possible send-off toward **Goal-to-Go**, real-world thinking-competencies...

Aha, how many courses fall short of #3,4,5? Remember the earlier "gallery" of examples? *Math thinking, Shakespeare and the waiting room, order of magnitude and sheep, creativity and sugar packets, applying history and psychology, essay-writing and time-management,* etc.? Many failed. Oh, if this goal sounds "radical," it's as radical as that Bible of education, BLOOM'S Taxonomy of Educational Objectives, *1956*! Stated way back then—not done even nowadays. Bloom's crucial "touchstone" paragraph is exactly this:

A problem in the... [interpretation] category requires the student to know an abstraction well enough that he can correctly demonstrate its use when specifically asked to do so. "Application," however, requires a step beyond this. Given a problem new to the student, he will apply the appropriate abstraction without having to be prompted as to which abstraction is correct or without having to be shown how to use it in that situation."

(As in, **"Write that last theme all on your own,"** or **"interpret these twelve poems which we have not discussed"**...) There you have it. This shows up the shortfalling of the teacher assigning: "write on these authors or works which we've already discussed," and assuming that this rote-repetition, represents true thinking...

But *are* things *really* that bad in practice? RICHARD PAUL reported (or claimed) that his "research" of professors on dozens of college/university campuses, identified some serious shortfallings:

> 80-90% of teachers surveyed stated they valued critical thinking as a goal. But "only 19% could give a clear explanation of what critical thinking is; and only 9% of the respondents were clearly teaching for critical thinking on a typical day in class." As for criteria and standards, "only... 8% could enumerate any intellectual criteria or standards they required..." Also, a majority of teachers **can _not_ define** critical thinking; name specific skills important for students to learn; give examples; understand intellectual standards; name theories they use...

CHESTER: Whoa! Smells suspicious. Though he's very competent, PAUL is, I know, a vigorous critic of traditional education. Hence he may have been biassed, enough so to "stack" his questions so as to get the results he wanted to. Surely things are not as bad as his picture here!

BARTON: Whoa-squared! *You* commit Thinking Fallacy #37, "begging the question." *You* assume, what you'd have to prove—that Paul "fudged" his research. (Okay, you do get points for examining even reasonable statements for possible bias.) Anyhow, onward, to *under-*, and *mis-*, teaching thinking....

MATTHEW LIPMAN (and BARRY BEYER) identify <u>major current "fallacies" or "misconceptions" in the teaching of thinking</u>, all falling short of Our Great Goal: ***explicit-precise, but not formulaic***, T of T:

> **(1)** "Thought-ful" teaching, of the <u>subject</u>-matter <u>itself</u>... **(2)** Teaching <u>about</u> thinking... **(3)** Teaching for <u>logical</u> thinking (only)... **(4)** Teaching for <u>learning</u>... **(5)** Modelling of thinking, *but* only tacitly, not explicated and taught... also, **(6)** "<u>encouraging and promoting</u>" thinking (*but not* actually teaching how-to **explicitly**).

And to their roster, I also add **(7)** <u>RRR, Rigid Rote Rules</u>: for, formulaic recipe-type algorithms, recipes are *not* "thinking." (That reflects #3 above, logic-reasoning-argument as true higher-order thinking.)

I also add **(8)** <u>OOO, Only One's Own Opinion</u>. For, students' criteria-free, just-plain-"opinioning," is *not* actual "thinking", let alone being truly *good* thinking—though such remains a prevalent and pernicious Amateur Misconception, one of the overlooked "prior basics" which *must* be addressed...)

Finally, I also add two major pitfalls not noted above. One is clearly *pseudo*: the **(9)** "<u>Pedagogy of Liberation</u>." The other, more insidious: **(10)** "<u>Active" or "Student-Centered" Learning</u>. How can these popular movements proffer pitfalls, you ask? Well, which approach of these two, more *truly* "empowers" students after all? The left-hand one is #9 above; the right-hand one, truer Thinking:

The Pedagogy of Liberation:	**Fair-Minded Objective Evaluation:**
As seen in the work of HENRY GIROUX, bell hooks (GLORIA WATKINS), and others, as for <u>basic goal</u>, this approach rejects education as "the amassing of information," toward education as "emancipation." Its "<u>content</u>" or substance is "diversity, multiculturalism, gender, race and class." The <u>specific goal</u> is to "understand the effects of power, the social construction of knowledge and identity, the meaning of education, and the need for social and cultural change." A need is to "question and challenge authority," and surely an <u>emergent goal</u> is to "think about making the world a better place." And from these goals follow <u>the teaching methods</u>. The teacher shares experience with students, recognizing and valuing everyone's presence, and aims toward learning which is no longer competitive, but instead supportively-cooperative. It even welcomes questions for which there is no one easy answer, or even which the teacher cannot answer authoritatively......	RICHARD PAUL wants his students to truly master these key concepts in his thinking-related course. World-view, assumptions, concepts, evidence, implications, consistency, conclusions, premises, questions-at-issue. He has students view two films about Central America. One is <u>Attack on the Americas</u> (a right-wing think-tank film alleging Communist control of Central American revolutionaries). The other is <u>Revolution or Death</u> (a World Council of Churches film defending the rebels in El Salvador). Students must confront the incompatible world-views obviously in—and subtly above-and-behind—these two films. They must end up being able to objectively, fairmindedly assess the world-views of each position. They must then write a paper defending the stronger world-view of the two, but not just asserting, but arguing, but fairmindedly, and noting how your position reflects your own world-view...

BARTON: Can we see how supposed "liberation," is actually hideous **Indoctrination**? Irony-of-ironies: what is supposed to free students from society's ideologies, actually imposes a new Ideology! By contrast, PAUL'S version is a breath of fresh air, though with iron fist inside (to mix a heady metaphor). It seeks to achieve for students a much truer "empowerment." (Remember the earlier Women's Studies final exam? Rote recall of facts *and ideologies* vs. dispassionate analysis...) Sure, Paul's version will seem "boring" or "too cool, objective, hence socially-irresponsible" to the "political" among us, let alone the fundamentally-Unconcerned, not to mention the Inept. But so it goes...

CHESTER: Well, forgetting rampant radicalism, what about the more-mainstream current major areas of **"diversity / multiculturalism / minority studies"** and the like? Can you say even they are not being taught well enough?

BARTON: I will add that about this. **ANECDOTE:** Last autumn on my campus, a big flap occurred about racially-insensitive misconduct: a white fraternity presented a skit in "blackface" even though they'd been asked not to by Black and other students. The point is that the campus-wide brouhaha about this, stimulated me to ask, "well, just what training **do** the college students here get in competently confronting cultural, ethnic, racial, etc., pluralism?" Well, it turned out, despite much lip-service publicity in favor of it, *almost nothing* guaranteed or focused. One thing mandatory; other things optional. Mandatorily, a student must (1) take a course (in any discipline) marked or labelled as "satisfying" the "diversity requirement."

[But those courses, well... **All are different and almost none concentrated. Analogy: we might as well have the English Dept. or any other, each teach one course as marked for satisfying the "Personal Chef requirement." JULIE T. can teach vegetarianism... I know MIKE M. can do B-B-Q... LOU V. can bring ice cream... and I, BARTON, can teach "light evening dry-sauce pastas"... But this haphazard catchall does not equip students to "cook solo after graduation..."]**

True, optionally, the student also can, may, might (2) attend this-or-that cultural event on campus. But that's all by sheer chance. And that's it for guaranteed "diversity-education"!

.....So, I drafted a brochure (an embryonic **"TOOL·BOX"**) proposing that, to empower students to confront this complexity competently, we need not facts-to-know-about, nor ideologies-to-believe, but powerful conceptual thinking-tools! Just imagine that *each* student was given the following **"TOOL-KIT"** of powerful explanatory insights and coping techniques represented on the right-hand side below—think *how this would empower* students for post-graduation real-world competence as Worker On The Job, Citizen-In-Community, even Private Person in the family! But most faculty I talked to, remained lukewarm to the notion. They didn't critque or disapprove. More, they believed that "courses will cover this content adequately" and the like. (Another case of **"non-comprehensibility"** of the truly-**New**?)

Anyhow, here (in "freeze-dried miniature outline") is my example of aiding "thinking" about "diversity":

Likely prevalent "education" in **Diversity** in courses in disciplines "labelled" as such:	A suggested **"TOOL-KIT"** of powerful insights to confront **"Diversity / Multiculturalism"** etc. competently:
1. <u>**Knowledge**</u> to learn about. --Native American history... --Black culture... --Women's status... --Etc. 2. Perhaps, <u>**Beliefs and Attitudes and Actions**</u> to acquire? *"Tolerance, Acceptance, and Respect for Everybody"?* "What would be good about having a gay or lesbian friend?" This "force-fit" question, not-really-a-question was asked of sixth-graders. The boys sniggered. A girl finally offered, "they'd be more sensitive." (Stereotype reinforced?) Better is to truly confront feelings and facts about the issue...	1. **Prejudice**: various causes, and functions, of (obvious, and subtle). 2. **Stereotype** (oversimple image of group) *vs.* **"Sociotype"** (traits of group supported by factual reality. This may let us discuss groups more fairly, *and* freely.) 3. **Two Relativisms: Cultural** (a way to comprehend the Other) vs. **Moral** (distinct from Cultural!). 4. **"Power"...** That word, that concept, explored... 5. **Oppression**, unjust discrimination: five distinct categories of. 6. "Traits of **Minority Victimization**" (obsessive over-concern, semi-paranoia, etc.) 7. VARIOUS SUBTLE MECHANISMS: --**"Aversive Racism"** (subliminal, unrecognized, even unintended). --**"Surplus Visibility"** (when normal minority protest etc. seems excessive to the majority). --**Selective Perception** ("a Black women always came late to my class"—but so did Whites you overlooked!) --**"Hidden Antagonizers"** (should be recognized). --**"Stereotype-Override"** (enters in even if you knew the person before learning their minority status!) --**"Cognitive Dissonance"** (when two incompatible beliefs or values exist in one person, what happens?) --**"Affinity Impulse"** or In/Out Group realities. "Dislike of the unlike"... 8. **"Communication** 101": Candor, *plus* Civility?

CHESTER: ... I... I guess I see these Thinking Tools as potentially-powerful, even crucial, but surely not forwarded for sure in education... Does this mean that...

BARTON: *We gotta move on here.* To the last "shortfalling." Worse than "pedagogy of liberation" is the more insidious movement of **"active"** or **"student-centered"** learning. Although better than traditional lecture, it contains pitfalls. Here are some of the suggested activities from a Madison, WI seminar on Active Learning, late 1990's. At first it surely does *sound* good:

1. "Identify a problem unclear to you" in the material.
2. "Say where you stand on a continuum of positions on the material, and why."
3. Formulate "burning questions" about the material.
4. Look at a case-study of the material **"from three different perspectives."**
5. Decide "which answers on multiple-choice questions are best and why."
6. Critique the lecture's thesis as to its "strongest and weakest supporting points."
7. Identify some important "unstated presuppositions" which lie behind the lecture or textbook material.

Superb, but will mere *doing* these approaches, result in actually teaching students *how to* use them thus? ***Resoundingly, no in thunder***... Take #4 above, look at something "from three different perspectives." This is simply the great, basic, prior, generic **thinking skill** of "confronting a complexity from *multiple, plural perspectives*—world-views, paradigms, theories, systems, ideologies, schools of thought, etc."

What scandalously shortfalls here is the lack of what both DERZKO and PAUL would probably recommend: a **TOOL·KIT** of generic ways of actually *doing* it. And so I created this sample:

TOOL·KIT : Lensmanship 101: **Multiple-Plural Perspectives** in Confronting Complex Content:

1. Definition of lenses, as systems which intervene between Reality and thinker's Mind. A speaker or writer is employing what perspective? (*Freudian, Marxist, Christian, Darwinian, existentialist*, and/or many others...)

2. Subtypes of "lenses" & examples. **Perception-and-cognition** systems... **Language**, semantics: "the word is not the thing"... **Communication-chain**: blocks & biasses along the way... **LEVELS** of paradigms, then systems, ideologies: world-views, **historical** periods (*Zeitgeist*, Climate of Opinion, "Today's Truths & Taboos"), **national**-culture (traditional American norms mores folkway-values), **academic disciplines** and Schools of Thought, **science** and supernaturalism, **subgroup** schemes, and **individual**-level personal-preference or taste-temperament notions...

3. Lenses are inevitable, inescapable. (Though some would deny or not realize this.)

4. Lenses are often subliminal: invisible, tacit-covert-latent, not recognized (or even intended!)

5. Lenses are not "cleanly pure," they come freighted with world-views: presuppositions, implications!

6. Lenses are "double-edged": (+) very powerfully-insightful, but (-) also *surely* limited, *perhaps* biassed too.

7. Lenses over time can become *outdated*—or, wrongfully *neglected* due to thinking fashions. Beware both.

8. Using multiple lenses raises many issues. --Which? --Cooperate or conflict? --Integrate or not? --Purposes?

9. But the two key lens skills are: (A) know how to **identify** lenses already being used "on-scene" but invisible and perhaps suspect, (B) know how to **implement** (locate, *choose*) and use, "other, better" lenses. *Not always easy...*

→EXAMPLE. **A short story,** "Baseball In July," by Patrick Hochtel, describes what happens when a gay son brings his male lover home for a family christening. Specifically, a whole spectrum of response from revulsion to unease to total relaxation. (**Short of ostracism or banishment, as mentioned in Sociology perspective, earlier...**)
     The Issue: "Definition of the Problem," how to locate its cause(s?) **Four useful "lenses"** for students were:
1. *Natural Law*: unnatural and abnormal, homosexuality itself is the problem.
2. A *traditionalism* of sorts. The gay son was the problem in being too non-assimilationist, assertive.
3. *Bigotry & Prejudice*: the anti-gay relatives were the problem.
4. *Homophobia*: also "*Heterosexism*." A socially-learned "ism" was the problem, like white racism, male chauvinism, ablism.
     The Point Here: how many students could have ramassed all these four and more useful lenses *on their own*? Not many probably... *I myself found it difficult to assemble* these four differing, but all productive, lenses. And surely all four are necessary—even though "politically-correct" or "diversity-education" courses might use #4 *only*, risk Indoctrination thus...

The above illustrates DERZKO, blooms in the Education's overlooked "second story" of explicit but not rote-simplistic thinking tools. Thus, **"Teaching Thinking, Means TEACHING Thinking,"** **explicitly.**

CHESTER: Okay, the **Lensmanship** Tool-Kit *is* impressive: useful if not mandatory but not usually available... However, whoa—do you become too idealistic [[OR THE PRISONER OF YOUR IDEOLOGY...]]? Those seven activities of the Active Learning course, above—aren't any good students already "picking up" thinking skills without being drilled in your topheavy apparatus there, just by...

BARTON [[ANGRILY INTERRUPTING]] Look, for a final exam of that course, ask students to "look at a subject of their choice using the thinking skills learned in the course, including Three Different Perspectives, and self-evaluate their work." *I bet you **very, very few** will be able on their own to competently employ Lensmanship and other skills.* That is, if the course had simply PSEUDO- or UNDER-taught them without scrupulously, sedulously "teaching them how to do so," to apply abstractions autonomously—albeit yes-yes-yes of course *with a light hand, please!*

I mentioned above my own failure, "That Last Theme" students couldn't do on their own—and I never realized they couldn't go up the Five Steps, until I assigned it and they failed. Here's a second Atrocious Anecdote of another earlier failure of mine:

EXAMPLE #2: *"The Poetry Collapse"* In English 102, freshman literature, we studied poetry-reading. Many formulae; even more flexible tools [subject-vs.-theme; imagery; structure; etc.]... I then said: "Here are 12 carefully-selected, carefully-varied poems NEW to you, which we have NOT discussed in class. Show what you've learned by responding to them and state how you can do so better or differently now than before the poetry unit"....
I don't have to tell you: same bingo: evasions. Sneakily inquiring "Can we write on *just one* poem?" (yeah, sure). Employing the tool-concepts but thoughtlessly and mechanically as rules only. [=Using all twelve of the Probes 1-2-3 mechanically whether or not all twelve applied to a poem at hand—hamfisted rule-mongering! I hadn't taught them otherwise!] Reverting to the formulaic five-paragraph theme. And worse... *They had, of course, autonomously actively acquired NOTHING on their OWN......* Contrast this, my trial-by-fire, with over-specific assignments from other teachers **who always assigned papers/exams on "poems already read,"** *and so, throughout their teaching careers will* never even suspect *how much (of True Education) the students* really *were* NOT *learning*....

CHESTER: Well, doesn't this debacle, prove that TT cannot be achieved, required? That if you held unmotivated students to the high standards of autonomous application, etc., that they'd all fail the course?

BARTON: *Yep.* But at least a *few* assignments could be done this way, then failed but without course-grade penalty. This way, the *minority* of students who truly *wanted* to learn, would learn about true thinking, would be responsibly served. Thus, "doing harm would be avoided"...

Besides, note also a misunderstanding here. True, *many* students *can't/won't* actually think perfectly. But, *any/all* students *can try to* "think" better—and *can* actually do so *somewhat*! Remember, I neither demand, nor expect, perfection in competence. I only require **Integrity**: a mind trying to make sense of complex material, responsibly and directly engaged, committed, no matter if not perfect! Thus, not perfect Accomplishment, nor Ability, but valid Action, and thus, *some* true Achievement. (**To me, "One page of tortured but genuine thinking-attempt, is better than a five-page essay correct, slick, and mechanical..."**)

Finally, one last overlooked area in which the teaching of thinking still **shortfalls.** Beyond teacher-training... actual courses... Gen Ed programs... etc. Into in *a whole realm never thought-about.* Namely, the area of "each individual student consciously perfecting personal thinking systems..."

AN OBSERVATION. *The "1,500 Hours."* That's the amount of "seat-time" attendance in-class hours required to obtain a B.A. degree... But I accuse: ***not during*** **ONE** *single* **hour** **of that time** will the student ever be asked by any instructor, in effect, "What is your own emerging, developing "I.T.S." or Individualized Thinking System? Your personalized thinking skills and styles? Your personal 'Tool-BELT' in effect which parallels the 'Tool-KITS' of subject-specific skills perhaps given to you in this course and that?" *No attention to* **consciousness, meta-cognition, reflexive self-awareness of How I The Student Think....**

ANECDOTE #3: I asked an advanced class ("Stylistics," English 400) of motivated juniors and seniors, "**What is your typical recurrent personal thinking style?**" But, this question *nonplussed* these able, serious upperclasspersons...

CHESTER: So thinking skills *are* shortchanged. I'm becoming Converted. Hence, only one final objection. Namely, over-guided, obtrusive overloading! Waxy Yellow Buildup? **Won't too much guidance in how-to think, topheavily overload classes with cumbersome method, passify or "pupilize" students?**

BARTON: *Good* question, but only **seems that way; needn't be.** The answer: to correlate the contraries of Guidance and Autonomy. Two final Touchstones explain. The writing teacher WINSTON WEATHERS pleads to be DERZKO- explicit in making skills available to students with that learning-style:

"I'm asking simply to be exposed to, and informed about, the full range of compositional possibilities. That I be introduced to all the tools, right now, and not be asked to wait for years and years until I have mastered right-handed affairs before I learn anything about left-handed affairs, that rather, I be introduced to all the grammars / vehicles / tools / compositional possibilities *now* so that even as I 'learn to write' I will have before me as many resources as possible. I'm asking: that all the 'ways' of writing be spread out before me and that my education be devoted to learning how to use them."

We in our TT cult—er, school—charge that current schooling doesn't elucidate writing skills, or thinking tools, explicitly enough. But as for Autonomy, journalist/teacher DONALD MURRAY scandalously said:

Our students need to discover, before graduation, that freedom is the greatest tyrant of all. Too often the composition teacher not only denies his students freedom, he even goes further and performs the key writing tasks for his students. He gives an assignment; he lists sources; he dictates the form; and, by irresponsibly conscientious correcting, he actually revises his students' papers. Is it not surprising that the student does not learn to write when the teacher, with destructive virtue, has done most of his student's writing?

Although iconoclastic, this is, of course, <u>The Truth</u>. It conveys the Flavor of <u>Integrity</u>, of the <u>Maturation</u> of the Classroom and Of the **True "Respect For"** the Student, characteristic of TT.... It leads to our ultimate, summit **Goal-to-Go**: autonomous thinking on real-world subjects, as noted.

[**But most teachers flinch!** Example: "*They'd Mutilate Murray.*" About Murray's manifesto, colleague Dale said: "too advanced for freshmen, they can do this in later classes" [*They can start to try, right now.*] Ed said: "whoa, don't you have to correct their grammar?" [*I mark their errors in green ink, they find them and correct.*] And Geneva said, rather acerbic-accusatory: "But <u>no</u>, Brandon, students <u>Need</u> Structure!" [*But no, of course <u>what students truly need</u>, is to be shown what the very concept of structure is, and how to create it themselves, autonomously in real-world-life. Not to be given the Five-Paragraph Theme as "The Only Pottery Mold in the Studio"...*]

Paul puts it more strongly (enough so, to flurry Defensive Denial among the many teachers whom it ruffles):

In an important sense, nobody can teach anyone else anything of true value. The only way one truly learns, is by sitting down and figuring it out and thinking it through oneself. [A close paraphrase]

CHESTER: Actually Murray may be right, on target. Made me think of what I once observed:

Example: "*The Silent Student.*" I recall once entering a classroom early, and the last hour's Literature teacher was still "conferencing" with a student about a paper. On and on the teacher went, about how to re-do it. What to change. How. Alter this, substitute that, rearrange the other thing.... <u>Then the teacher said "And I think *we* agreed that...."</u> But the student had been standing there taciturn all along! .....
So, was anything being taught there then except How To Follow Orders? Like your own anecdote above about "that last theme" which students couldn't do on their own, "solo-flight" fashion, because you had made all the decisions in earlier themes, as Murray warned against, above...

BARTON: Yes indeed. Finally, to integrate Guidance plus Autonomy, the cognitive psychologist Don Norman provides an extra Touchstone (for dessert). Learner-centered initiative <u>is</u> indispensable, *<u>but</u>*:

There is an important difference between playing and practicing, doing an activity and learning that activity. Just doing something does not necessarily lead to learning. The point is well understood in sports instruction. Coaches distinguish between unsupervised play and training. You could play for a hundred hours and learn less than from a half hour of properly supervised training....
[In "sport, chess, or mathematical recreations," the coach sets the conditions, provides the feedback and guidance which replace—or augment—the self-reflection upon which players would otherwise have to depend excessively.]

I cinch the above Insights with one more **Analogy;** beyond agriculture and aviation and aquatics, etc.:

<u>**An analogy from Medicine:**</u> the "autonomous-application" exam [write your own paper; apply feminism to something complex; take these twelve new poems; etc.], is *monstrously efficient* as a diagnostic tool to measure what has been truly learned—or rather, what *truly has not* been! Medically speaking, <u>it</u> is, to the <u>usual</u> exam of essentially, "what did I say in lecture" or "what is YOUR opinionation on this" or "work these 1-2-3 formulae"... as <u>a modern MRI or PET scan</u>, is to... <u>early X-rays</u> or perhaps even <u>phrenology</u>! *It <u>shows up the horrible truths hitherto unsuspected, the pervasive presence of, not disease, but of failure to Truly Learn Thinking below surface compliances</u>....*

CHESTER: Yes, at least I see the "un-perceivable" more clearly now, a whole new paradigm-world...

[9.] ...Finally, The "EXAM": Is CHESTER Ready for True Discipleship?

BARTON: I'm proud of you, **CHESTER**. Are you ready to <u>take a test</u> of your ability to discern True Major Paradigm-Shift Change—hence, to Fully Comprehend, Value, and Embrace, Pure **TT** as The Way?

CHESTER: I guess so. Having Come This Far, it would be a Shame not to... [[Besides, I've got to grasp fully the possible pathology of the ironic closedmindedness of this TT "sect"...]]

BARTON: Very well, then. The examination comes to you in two parts.
First, we'll look at <u>four classic instances of "utterly-overlooked" paradigm-shift in *various* topics.</u>
  [This "warms you up" for spotting usually-unseen Questionable Presuppositions.]
Second, we'll look at <u>four innocuous, innocent (???) statements on the topic of *education*.</u>
  [This then "applies the heat" for testing your enlightenment and your readiness to join us...]

First, four suspect (?) statements on *varied, everyday subjects*.
(from Mark Twain... a puzzler-riddle... from the sociologist Sagarin... and from <u>Newsweek</u> magazine...)

---

(1) <u>A passage from Mark Twain's novel</u> <u>Huckleberry</u> <u>Finn</u>. In it, Huck's aunt is wondering why the boy has been delayed on his riverboat journey to visit them:

> "We been expecting you a couple of days and more. What's kep' you?—boat get aground?"
> "It warn't the grounding—that didn't keep us back but a little. We blowed out a cylinder-head."
> "Good gracious? anybody hurt?"
> "No'm. Killed a nigger."
> "Well, it's lucky; because sometimes people do get hurt. Two years ago last Christmas, your uncle Silas was coming up from Newrleans on the old *Lally Rook*, and she blowed out a cylinder-head and crippled a man..."

(2) A <u>popular anecdote, or "puzzle,"</u> circulating in the 1970's and later:

> A young boy is hurt in an accident. His father rushes him to the hospital. In the E.R., the attending surgeon arrives, but takes one look and says, "I cannot operate on this boy; he is my son."

(3) The <u>sociologist Edward Sagarin</u> tells how language can subtly, insidiously inflict our perception.

> "We say of a person who drinks too much that he 'is' an alcoholic, and we say of people who think bizarre thoughts that they 'are' schizophrenic. This person is a drug addict and that person is a homosexual. Others are sadomasochists, pedophiliacs, juvenile delinquents....<u>we speak of people being</u> [certain things] <u>when all we know is that they do</u> certain things....<u>That kind of identity is a myth</u>. Admittedly, if a person believes the myth [that he is an addict, alcoholic, schizophrenic, homosexual], the chances rise that he....can result in relinquishing the search for change and becoming imprisoned in the role."

(4) A *Newsweek* article about <u>high school girls</u> [=young women] <u>**suing for sexual harrassment**</u> from the male students in classes. The concluding paragraph, indeed sentence, from the article is as follows:

> [A Ms. Brawdy sued for emotional distress and collected $20,000. So what was seen as "a routine nuisance" may become "a serious disciplinary matter."] ➜ "<u>And, while there may not be a man today who can honestly say he never spent most of a math period staring at the prettiest girl in his class instead of a blackboard...someday there might be.</u>"

CHESTER: Hey, I get *all* of these, they're *great*! They all show how <u>major change is sometimes not just judged un-thinkable, a Heresy, but is utterly overlooked, non-comprehensible</u>... First, Twain satirizes treating **Blacks** as "non-persons"...   Second, the anecdote (which the early feminists popularized) overlooks that **women** *can* be surgeons (and more)...   Third, the sociologist links **homosexuality** with crime and sickness—overlooked Yesterday, arguable Today...   And fourth, the Newsweek article stereotypes **males**, as testosteroned (1) <u>Animals</u> instead of perhaps (2) <u>Brains</u>, able to be intellectual!

BARTON: [[...By Minerva, "the *early* feminists"?! ..like, about *1970*, eh?...what about "Susan B. Seneca" and—oh, never mind, let it go...]] All good, except the *last* one—you missed that. What you said is true, "gender-role stereotype of males," but you *missed* another important "questionable assumption" of the article.

CHESTER: So what *is* it?? Some boys are (3) preoccupied math-<u>Geeks</u>? Or, (4) sexless <u>Eunuchs</u>? Or, I know, already (5) <u>Priesthood</u>-bound?? Which is it, *tell* me!!

BARTON: Nope, none of those, either... Nice try, but "no cigar," no Answer Key revealing "(6)"; *we* know; and, *you* do <u>not</u> know. Sorry, but "exams failed in Real Life, stay failed..."

Second, four statements about **education**. Again, all *seemingly* self-evident and "okay"....

(1) The first is <u>**a plaque honoring retired teacher Dr. Graham.**</u> [Located on the wall in Heide Hall at the University of Wisconsin (@ Whitewater—the plaque, not the teacher...]

He was "possessed of those rare qualities of greatness as a teacher: impressive knowledge of his subject, a closeness to students, a desire to impart knowledge, and the style and skill requisite to do so in the classroom...."

(2) The second is actually <u>**two letters-to-the editor**</u> (of <u>Harper's</u> magazine and the <u>National Review</u>). They were responding to articles about education. Both are unintentionally-revelatory:

"What all these movements in education neglect—whether they're the social-progress movement, the related multicultural-diversity movement, the Back to Basics movement, the vocational-emphasis movement, the media and electronic education movement—is the key basic emphasis on mastering knowledge which is the perennial heart of the educational enterprise."

The perennial cycles of educational "fixes," including trends, fads, and fashions, such as the new math, whole language, competency-based and outcome-based education, mastery-learning. All seem to be "pedagogical quackery," or "a focus on teaching techniques rather than a genuine transmission of ideas and information."

(3) The third is <u>**a student statement**</u> in the Royal Purple, newspaper at the Univ. of Wis.-Whitewater. Students objected to having to take new Core Courses for General Education. A paraphrase:

--In 1997, the student government at Univ. of WI-Whitewater—in response to growing student dissatisfaction and complaints—introduced a resolution that, if passed, would <u>allow students to *test out of the Core Courses* if they were able to</u>. (U.S. Experience in a World Context; Global Perspectives; Individual & Society; World of the Arts; Science & Technology in Society; World of Ideas).
--The rationale for exemption was that many students felt that the core courses are "a repeat of high school college-prep courses," hence "unnecessary to many students," who have "RECEIVED SIMILAR, IF NOT IDENTICAL, INFORMATION in high school courses."
--Hence for too many students now, these Core courses were "not challenging or stimulating" enough to be required of all.
--"If you already KNOW THE MATERIAL, you should be able to go to the next level," a student senator stated. Especially when graduation in a timely manner is increasingly a problem.
--Another factor mentioned was that some students felt that <u>many professors don't like teaching these lower-level courses</u> and are "<u>less enthusiastic about the material covered</u>," making it hard for students to "learn the material if it's not exciting to the professor."

(4) Finally, a <u>**professor of chemistry**</u>, Mark Benevenuto, champions "active learning" or "student-centered" learning or anyhow moving beyond the passive lecture delivering information. Paraphrase:

The professor said that he of course has "to present a body of information to <u>cover all of the fundamental concepts</u> in my field." But he notes that the traditional or "passive" or lecture or chalk-and-talk approach, is much less effective for "transmitting information" than the so-called "interactive" learning of small groups and research where students become "active learners." The keen point of his article was that beware, the new methods require more effort and thought from both teacher and student, and are wasted if students don't care or aren't willing to expend more effort! The key paragraph for our purposes here, however, is this:

"Mountains of anecdotal evidence and many studies indicate that interactive learning is far more effective than the old system of lectures and passive learning. In one example, research has shown that people <u>retain more new information</u> when they try to explain it to somebody else. The point is not that the established, traditional system is worthless, but that the newer methods work better with more students."

CHESTER: Wow. How Fortunate I am to have come this far to be able to Truly Discern Between the incompetent Old ways (of Know & Believe) and the essential New Way (of Thinkfulness)!..
--DR. GRAHAM "<u>imparted knowledge</u>," but did he teach thinking?
--The TWO LETTERS—they mistake "<u>mastering knowledge</u>" via "<u>transmission of ideas and information</u>" as true Education!
--The STUDENT LETTER remains deluded that "<u>knowing the material</u>" (via "<u>receiving information</u>") vs. being able to use it is the goal!
--And ironically, the CHEMISTRY TEACHER delivers New Wine in Old Beakers, his goal seems to be, again, "<u>covering</u>" (but really knowing?) <u>concepts</u> and "<u>retaining information</u>"....
....yes, I am impressed. I can now see with New Vision, what the New Orleans tourist clerk, what your graduate advisor, what the Biblical literalist, could not see—a whole New Paradigm Emerging...

[10.] ...but then, the great "Breakup":

[[**CHESTER** THEN PAUSES, THEN PLUNGES AHEAD]] ....But I also see more; *so much more...* You dragged me through *all this junk*, just so you can get me to *parrot your ideology* that **"The TRUE and *ONLY* TRUE Goal of *TRUE* EDUCATION is *thinking*-skills and abilities, *far* beyond any content-mastery, belief-acquisition, personal opinions, formulae, or pseudo-thinking—*and* true TT is simply *NOT* occurring in all, or most, postsecondary classes-courses-programs-schools today"**...

.....What *mishmash* just to belabor your Pet Peeve Point that you obsessively cling to, this hobbled hobbyhorse, due to what? via your own motivations, obsessive but cryptic? What motivates you anyhow? "Boredom, careerism, sheer bloody-mindedness"?... To "get a new act" or "chase fame" or "lust for power"—or for principle, or to "flee personal demons," indeed to act out your unconscious repetition-compulsions? To defend your identity and self-worth, it being internally empty, externally vulnerable?

.....By Minerva, irony of ironies, *you **think** that you think,* but actually you just want to re-define reality into the oversimplified and overcontrolled little jungle-gym Kingdom of your System!

Just as I was beginning to suspect, *irony on irony* here... You, a supposed True Thinker,
are just as partial as those you condemn! Or more so. Ironically just exactly as—
well, **just as rigid, monistic, closed-minded, insensitive to contexts**, and all the rest...

Well, I learned *much*, though *not* what *you* intended. And I can walk liberated and empowered now,
but *not* as your crackpotted system intended. For this I can thank you—the growing pains feel good,
liberated from a tyranny doubly-treacherous because pretending to be otherwise.....
I can thus majorly give thanks, but with compassion, not with your own false superiority.....

[[**CHESTER** FLINGS DOWN THE PAPERS AND **EXITS**, STORMS OUT OF THE OFFICE AGITATED BUT EXUBERANT...]]

BARTON: [[PAUSES... FROWNS... THEN LOOKS UP; SMILES...]] Ah, and how people *will* play out their early stunting "scripts" via Projection and Transference... How they *will* "mis-peer-ceive at" Reality through their wobbly-warped "lenses"—and alas, all tragically unconsciously and unintentionally too, unless and until they get their Attics Cleaned... Ah well, I can only labor in my own proper gardens, *bien faire y laissez braire*, "=do your own best, and let the others bray" — all day in their own ways....

[[THEN **BARTON** ALSO **EXITS**. ON THE WAY TO HIS CURRENT DESTINATION, AGAIN DAY-DREAMS ABOUT HIS OWN IMAGE OF **"UTOPIAN UNIVERSITY"**: WHOSE FOUNDATIONAL **GOAL-TO-GO** IS LEARNERS COMPENTLY CONFRONTING COMPLEXITIES CONCEPTUALLY LATER ON. WHEREIN,]]

--A student in **PHILOSOPHY** doesn't learn just about "the Great Thinkers historically and the Great Issues" ===== but the key tools such as **presuppositions, logic vs. fallacies, counterstatements, consequences**, etc. == the better to be able to "philosophize about" everything. Sex; bicycles; graffiti; cooking; and more important issues.

--A student in **HISTORY** doesn't learn "facts of American history" ===== s/he learns **"how to think historically"** (*continuity and change; generalizations; evidence, bias;* etc.), using facts from American history to embody the skills *which s/he can then use every day in civic life...* [Why is the Netherlands a "tolerant" society? Many strands, including geography, earlier religious and economic history, etc.! Was Britain the first and only "colonizer" of India and hence uniquely oppressive? And many more...]

--A student in **GOVERNMENT/POLITICAL SCIENCE** doesn't learn "constitutions, party-systems," etc. ===== so much as what are **the perennial issues** (relation between individual freedom and state security; responsibility of government; etc.) and the **varied ideologies' stands** == so as to better confront issues today (welfare reform... Immigration policy... others...)

--A student in **LITERATURE** doesn't learn about "modern British lit" ===== s/he learns **"how to think as a literary critic"** (*biographical, sociocultural, historical, especially aesthetic-stylistic or the close reading of complex texts*), using Brit Lit facts to cinch the skills *which s/he can then use whenever reading and thinking...*

--A student in **BIOLOGY** doesn't learn simply "meoisis and mitosis," etc. ===== but **how to think biologically**, *which informs every day his/her perceptions of life and current issues too...*

--A student in **VISUAL ART APPRECIATION** doesn't learn "Western art history: Egyptians, Greeks, and so forth" ===== but **the key principles of aesthetic composition, organic form**, etc., perspectives illustrated from perhaps all historical periods, perspectives anyhow *which s/he will use every day in appreciating/critiquing surroundings, in creating one's own home environment too...* [First class "lab": take six one-inch squares of black paper, and move them around one letter-sized sheet of white paper, until you really begin to comprehend, the principles of Design...]

--A student in <u>SOCIOLOGY</u> learns the **keystone concept** of *"culture or the norms and mores, as massively learned, rigid and resistant to change, sometimes helpful sometimes counterproductive"*—*what daily insights from this!...* [EXAMPLE: "A family rejects, disowns a son/daughter who comes out as gay/lesbian. Are the parents necessarily, or for sure, *psychologically* "bigoted," "prejudiced," "intentionally bad parents"? But see the profound *sociocultural* forces here...]

--A student in <u>MATHEMATICS</u> learns more than formulae ===== also **spatial reasoning, cause-effect and causal chain, ability to abstract, to reason logically and relationally**.....

BARTON then adds a few items to his emerging **|TOOL · KIT|** on **"Thinking About Major CHANGE"**... Specifically, the variable-issue of **"180-degree" change**, or **"polar reversals,"** A-to-Z or Z-to-A or night-to-day change, and the "growing pains" (plus arthritic resistance) in such major moves.....

The "Puppet-Theatre" of History: we seem to dance to the strings of the master of Today's Truths & Taboos, beyond which we can't see or step.
the "I-H-O-C" Formula: What was Inconceivable last week, then Heresy-scandalous yesterday, becomes Orthodoxy or The Truth today, and a Commonplace or ho-hum truism tomorrow or next week... [**Which "Well of course we all knew about, and did, that earlier all along, of course"... the massive Resistance-Defense-Denial response to the Major New...**]

--The earth is not flat==but round...

--The sun does not orbit the earth==but the earth, the sun...

--Not the deity or the king==but the people, determine the <u>laws</u> and indeed the <u>government</u>...

--Not only Faith plus the external Church==but Good Works and from-within Immanance, achieve <u>salvation</u>...

--Not theology "up there" (nor Aristotelian a-priori Deduction)==but Inductive empirical science "down here," determines <u>Truth</u>...

--<u>Ethics</u> and <u>morality</u> derive not from pleasing God, or adhering to Rules==but to achieving the best for the most people, as via utilitarianism...

--<u>Humans</u> are less "angelic," than "simian," in origins, and in behavior...

--<u>Humans</u> are less rational, than also unconsciously id-driven...

--<u>Painting</u>, visual arts, represent not only or mainly things in reality==but 1. become things in themselves, 2. represent psychological states...

--<u>Hierarchies</u> (and "<u>elitisms</u>"), absolutistic, mechanicalistic and "known"==give way to <u>heterarchies</u>, organic and holographically-associative, "chaotic"—(and a relativistic "<u>equalitarianism</u>" pervasive if not corrosive)...

--<u>Women</u> deserve equality, starting with the vote (**when first proposed, a "scandalous danger"**)...

--<u>Races</u> deserve integration: in sports, in the military, in employment, yes even in interracial marriage...

--<u>Sexual orientation</u> also deserves equality [**altho <u>not</u> including gay/lesbian "marriage" or "adoption" rites, for "as of course we all know" certain things <u>are</u> Natural-&-Normal, <u>and</u> "one must cover content first, and only then teach thinking, which we do already anyhow, and the students pick it up as they go along, the able ones do anyway, and the other ones simply can't or won't..."**]

--For a human to eat animal flesh, is actually to behave as a "cannibal"...

--*Oh, and also*: the goal of <u>education</u> is not Knowing or Believing but Thinking. This Skill, is now also the actual "Content," **the substance** *as well* **as** the goal. [A true "180-degree" *revolutionary reversal,* **unseating** the enthroned "facts" now sub-servient to the new ruler, "thoughtfulness."

- - - - - - - - - -

...and <u>all the above</u>: **"Overlooked** LAST WEEK... An "Un-Think-Able" **Heresy** YESTERDAY... an elephantine **Orthodoxy** TODAY... then a subliminal **Commonplace** TOMORROW...

<u>Except, "education as thinking"</u>: *not yet* the prevailing **Orthodoxy** TODAY *let alone* **Commonplace** TOMORROW, *nor <u>will</u> it ever be*.... And *still* not even a widespread explicit *Heresy* TODAY, **indeed still profoundly** *"non-comprehensible"*...]

...except to the favored Chosen, the elect "outliers" who pursue Duty & Beauty in their own grass-roots Naissance.....

[[**BARTON** EXITS THE CONFERENCE ROOM... TAKES THE BACK STAIRS DOWN AND OUT... WALKS (ILLEGALLY) ACROSS THE CAMPUS LAWN TO BEHIND THE HEATING PLANT, WHERE HE ENJOYS A PANORAMIC VIEW OF THE WHOLE COUNTRYSIDE...]]

The *True Story* of How **Bureaucratic Control** "Saved The Day,"
Blocked the *Ugly Threat* of An Un-Authorized **"Visual Artistry"**
Which Sought to Rage Rampantly All Over The College Campus...

as scene in the following   M E M O R A N D U M :

TO: Brandon Beck, Associate Professor of English

who is also the [*Alleged, Self-Proclaimed*] "Head" of the [*Supposedly-Existing*] "Operation Art-UP Now"

FR: Zentral Executive Kommittee, Offenbach University

RE: Your Proposal for your "Operation Art-UP Now": namely,
➔**To Embellish our Campus Environment, plus Enhance the Students' Art-Education, through your displaying selected Visual Art, on our University's Walls...**

Greeting. <u>We</u> the Committee are very positively excisted about your [*allegedly and also rumoured*] "Operation Are-UP NOT"... [Even tho it seems *grass-roots... solo-operator only... unofficial... non-approved...* & hence quite probably *non-existant,* right?...] Whose **goal**, as your Proposal, well, states it, is

➔**"To mount quality ART reproductions (=paintings, photographs, drawings, graphic design) on the currently-*bare* WALLS of the campus (=classrooms, corridors, outer walls, student centers, etc.)—in order to (1) *enhance* the art-appreciation EDUCATION of our students, *also* to (2) *embellish* the campus ENVIRONMENT for all occupants there in."**

We also appreciate your submission-Proposal's **(1)** providing <u>specific examples</u> of particular paintings. This clarifies and convinces. And we especially remark the proposal's **(2)** <u>creatively combining *different* subjects, artists, periods, styles but to achieve a *unity* after all</u>. We know (because your submissive Proposal told us so) that you accomplish this synthesis via anonomously plaigiarizing from SUZANNE LANGER'S and PAUL KLEE'S more-expert and authoritative [gasp] descriptions of **<u>high visual artistry</u>** respectively (and why not):

"...a composition of tensions and resolutions, balance and unbalance, rhythmic coherence, a precarious yet continuous unity...." [--SUZANNE LANGER]

[There must be maintained at every moment an] "asymmetrical oscillation, wholly subservient neither to gravity [static], nor to momentum [dynamic]." [--PAUL KLEE]

As for <u>your *skilled instances*</u> of your **<u>proposed synthesizings</u>**, *who could fail to be unimpressed by them*!

--"FOUR AMERICAN BRIGHT-SILENT SPACES" (Winslow **Homer**, Andrew **Wyeth**, Edward **Hopper**, Georgia **O'Keefe**)-----perhaps in a *longer corridor*?

--"THREE EXAMPLES OF EXPRESSIONISTIC COLOR" (**Van Gogh's** landscapes ... **Japanese scene-prints** of Hiroshige & Hokusai ... and **London Transport posters** in 1920's Art-Deco)-----for *corner* or *alcove*?

--"LESSER-KNOWN ARTISTS DESERVING NOTE" (French photographer Henri **Cartier-Bresson's** *"decisive-moments"*) ... (British David **Hockney's** *accessible but enduring scenes*)-----perhaps in a *larger room area*?

--"CREATIVE PAIR-UPS " (*Am. scene-photographers* Joel **Meyerowitz** <u>*with*</u> Stephen **Shore**) ... (*Social satirists* F. **Goya** <u>*with*</u> Wm. **Hogarth**) ... (*"Pops"* Andy **Warhol** <u>*with*</u> Roy **Lichenstein**)-----in *small workrooms/offices*?

In fact, **we're so impressed with your Proposal,** that we wish not only to **accept** your generous offer, but also to **implement** it via scheduling a face-to-face **meeting** with you! . . . . . ➔all this <u>*just as soon*</u> as we can **overcome** the fifteen (15) following **<u>tiny</u> <u>little</u> <u>obstacles</u>** & **<u>objections</u>** to **<u>the entire concept and rationale</u>** (let alone the **<u>method</u>**) of your [*curiously-labelled??*] project "QPN BRT-OP WON" ...

[We're confident that these **barriers** are *minor*, and simply *"bureaucrato-genic,"* whatever *thaat* means...]

<u>*OUR*</u> Very Own OFFICE's Exiscting, Mandaroated, "Procedural" [gasp] ꓐureaucratic **STIPULATIONS** [*Which Must **Always** be Satisfied* [aaaah]]:	**<u>*YOUR*</u> Very Own PROPOSAL's** Eccentric, Maverick, Elliptical, Egregious, "Aesthetic" **DEVIATIONS** from Same [*Which Must First Be Korrected*]:

(1) <u>PROFESSIONAL</u> <u>ACCREDITATION</u>. "ALL EMPLOYEES SHALL WORK **ONLY** IN THE AREAS OF THEIR OFFICIAL SPECIALTY—AND TERMINAL DEGREE."	.....but *you* are a Ph.D. in **English, NOT in Art Education**. Therefore *how* can *we* know that what <u>you</u> propose to do, is **valid, professional, legitimate, reliable?**
(2) <u>CONFORMITY</u> TO (A) TABLE OF <u>ORGANIZATION</u> AND (B) <u>UNIVERSITY'S "MISSION STATEMENT"</u>: "ALL ACTIVITIES SHALL BE LISTED IN OUR SCHEME, PLUS SHALL CONFORM WITHIN THE OVERALL MISSION-GOALS" (OR BE STRETCHED-TO-FIT TO FIT OUR OWN NEEDS)	.....but <u>first</u>, **you might actually not exist** (being absent from our official TO&E). And <u>second</u>, although your "Project" **could** be distorted to **supposedly** support both "education" and "environment" goals—still, <u>we don't feel like spandexing ourselves to include you</u> in the umbrella. Doing so (A) **would gain us no "points" from our bosses** Above to whom we report, and (B) **would risk stirring up a whole bunch of hornets nest's** anyhow (see below).
(3) "<u>TIME & PLACE FOR EVERYTHING</u>" "SURELY, '**TEACHING**' TAKES PLACE **ONLY** WITHIN CLASSROOM AREAS, DURING CLASS HOURS—AND **NOT** ELSEWHERE, AND WITH NO INSTRUCTIONAL STAFF PRESENT! (WATERTIGHT COMPARTMENTS ARE VITAL.)	.....but *your* Initiative seems to **<u>re-define the whole act and locale of what is "teaching.</u>**" This makes things **shaky, unstable, blurrred, and heck, even inchoate.** (You see why: this means that, "<u>if Everything could mean Anything, why then maybe Something might mean Nothing,</u>" & you see we can't officially Credit *that* to justify Budgetgerigars....)
(4) <u>SPATIAL AND GEOGRAPHICAL VALORIZING</u> OF <u>TERRITORIAL HIERARCHY</u> [#1 of 3]: "SURELY SOME LOCALES RANK-& RATE 'BETTER" THAN SOME OTHERS, & 'ABOVE' OTHERS, TO JUSTIFY PREFERENTIAL TREATMENT?"	.....but *you* presume to "**<u>valorize" locations which are profane, mundane, quotidian, diurnal</u>**— mere corridor walls—to rank their valence as high as *our* <u>distinguished Landscaping Programs</u>, expensive Building Façade Face-Lifts, and etc. (Of course, *this* will *never* do—would Well & Truly "beschmertschz" our preious Image....)
(5) <u>SPATIAL AND GEOGRAPHICAL VALORIZING</u> OF <u>TERRITORIAL HIERARCHY</u> [#2 of 3]: " 'TURF' (I) OR EACH ACADEMIC DEPARTMENT'S PROPER PROFESSIONAL AREAS OF EXPERTISE AND INFLUENCE/CONTROL ACTIVITY, **MUST BE PROTECTED.**" (HENCE ARTISTS SHOULD NOT WRITE OR TEACH POETRY, AND VERSE VISA!)	.....but *your* Initiative **<u>ursurpts actions properly done by the Art Education Department</u>**— [...*never mind* that none of them have either done, or have ever proposed doing, *anything like* your Project of "broadcasting beauty for benefits"....] See, they just might get Jealous and Complain to <u>*us*</u> therefore creating a problem for <u>*us*</u>, of which to be *avoided at all costs* as can you understand....
(6) <u>SPATIAL AND GEOGRAPHICAL VALORIZING</u> OF <u>TERRITORIAL HIERARCHY</u> [#3 of 3]: " 'TURF' (II) IS EACH WORKER'S OFFICE-ENVIRONMENT OR *COIN DU QUARTIER* OR CUBICLE-CULTURE TO **CONTROL** AS **THEY** SEE FIT (AND NOT SOME OUTLANDISH INTERLOPER SUCH AS YOU)!"	.....but *your* Initiative **would thrust subsersive "art" in the very, faces** of close-minded *secretaries*; narrow-minded *custodial workers*; small-minded *administrative personnel*... And nowadays, these peons *correctly misjudge* that <u>they</u> should have some say-so control over their "workplace environment." (Then they'd Complain to <u>*us*</u>, causing <u>*us*</u> a problem for <u>*us*</u> to deal with; th<u>*us*</u>....)
(7) <u>VANDALISM</u>. "ACTIVITIES MUST NOT PROMOTE GRAFFITI, BREAKAGE, THEFT, DEFORMINGS, OR OTHER VANDALIZING ACTIVITIES." (TRUE, YOU SPECIFY THAT YOUR REPRODUCTIONS ARE INEXPENSIVE, INDEED EXPENDABLE, LET ALONE DONATED BY YOU, **<u>BUT</u>**....)	.....but *your* Initiative **<u>seems a "setting duck" to our disgruntled students'</u>** rrrippping off art from walls, and thence on to fixtures, etc., via the well-known mechanism of "Broken Window In Slum," or "Slippery Soap" **onward to Structural Devastation of our Whole Campus**, who knows, cf. *the "power of art"*.....
(8) <u>EDUCATIONAL PRIORITIES</u>. "THE '**FINE ARTS**' AND THE LIKE ARE AT BOTTOM, <u>SECONDARY</u> TO TRUER HIGHER EDUCATION FOR VOCATIONAL GOALS." (IF NOT UNMANLY "FRIPPERY" ACTUALLY, STILL THEY'RE "FEATHERWEIGHT," DESSERT-TRIMMINGS, NOT HIGH-PRIORITY FOR PRAGMATIC EDUCATION TO ENROL THE MOST STUDENTS, HENCE REAP THE MOST TUITION.....)	.....but *your* Initiative of "pretty pictures" would **wrongly emphasize mere entertainment and "aesthetic enrichment.**" This both steers students away from, **plus makes them more dissatisfied with**, the more <u>pragmatic-practical-profitable</u> **Vocational-Business-Etc.** education which the State's employers need!

(9) <u>SENSITIVITY</u> <u>TO</u> "**MULTICULTURALISM** & <u>MINORITIES</u> & **DIVERSITY**" TODAY. "POLITICAL KORREKTNESS TODAY FIRMLY MANDATES **ATTENTION TO RACIAL**, **ETHNIC, ETC., PLURALITY IN ALL PARTS OF EDUCATION**." (SUCH "**BELLETRISTIC ELITISM**" OF WHICH YOUR PROPOSAL FAIRLY REEKS, IS A **MONISM QUITE UNFASHIONABLE**—HENCE, OF COURSE, UNACCEPTABLE—TODAY)	.....but *your* Initiative *suspiciously* **champions "high-quality aesthetic visual art and design"** over <u>these pressing socio-political concerns</u> of the prevaloritative "Pedagogy of Liberation" today. We approve of all <u>good</u> art—Normal Rockwell's saccharine sentimentalities, etc.— just so long as today's requisited "<u>token-quota</u>" of Negroes, Orientals, Spaniard-Chicagos, and etc. are included. (Your restriction of images to fine art, no matter any plurality, would "weave a beehive" of Objections & Complaints to—***us***)
(10) <u>CONFORMITY</u> <u>TO</u> **SCIENTIFICALLY-SOUND VALIDATION** <u>VIA</u> <u>EXISTING</u> <u>STANDARDS</u> <u>OF</u> "<u>RESEARCH</u>." *(I): Prior Foundations For:* ["Research; ah, Research....."] "PROPOSALS SHALL BE VALIDATED BY PROFESSIONAL RESEARCH IN THE FIELD WHICH **PREDICTS THEIR SUCCESS-VS.-FAILURE PROBABILITY** VIA PRIOR SCHOLARLY INVESTIGATION."	.....but *your* Initiative merely makes a hollow claim; it brashly, impudently **sights NO Expert Authoritives or Recognized Studies** which support *your* naïve, Folk-Wisdomed contention. You claim that "*simply looking repeatedly at pretty pictures is good for people—either pedagogically, or pleasurably!*" But how do you know this?— Worse, what if <u>our</u> Bosses question ***us*** about how <u>you</u>, or even <u>we</u>, allegedly know this?
(11) <u>CONFORMITY</u> <u>TO</u> **SCIENTIFICALLY-SOUND VALIDATION** <u>VIA</u> <u>EXISTING</u> <u>STANDARDS</u> <u>OF</u> "<u>RESEARCH</u>." *(II) Present Feedback About.* "PROJECTS SHOULD INCLUDE BUILT-IN **MEANS FOR MEASURING THEIR EFFECTIVENESS**-OR-NOT IN ACTUALLY ACHIEVING THEIR INTENDED RESULTS."	.....but *your* Initiative **sorely lacks any micrometerized-quantification** [*sighh*] of perceiver-response—other than <u>un</u>scientifically "*asking people what they though of it*" in informal surveys (which probably subsided largely upon "insufficient-&-unrepresentative" samples to boot...)
(12) <u>COSTLY</u> **REDUPLICATION** <u>OF</u> <u>OTHER</u> <u>EXISTING</u> <u>PROJECTS</u>? "PROPOSALS SHOULD **AVOID** COPYING EFFORTS ALREADY UNDERWAY IN **OTHER** PROJECTS CURRENTLY ON-CAMPUS."	.....but *your* Initiative seems **superfluous**. Surely the "*campus beautification*" is *already Secured* by <u>our</u> ongoing projects:: seasonal **flowerbeds**; plus expensive, extravagant, all-weather **archways** over entrances at the University Center; and surely even **more others**.....
(13) <u>NEED</u> <u>FOR</u> BASIC <u>MINIMAL</u> **QUALITY OF WORKMANSHIP** <u>IN</u> <u>PROJECTS</u> <u>ON</u> <u>CAMPUS</u>. "PROJECTS MUST CONFORM TO ATTRACTIVE STANDARDS OF **NEATNESS, APPEARANCE, AND ETC**."	.....but *your* Initiative **would use cheap reproductions of great art, not original paintings**. This would surely result in a bunch of hyper-aesthetic Personnel launching a torrent of Complaints to ***us*** about your sliezie, shabby, shoddy, second-rate showmanship.
(14) <u>NEED</u> <u>FOR</u> **RELIABLE CONTINUITY**: THE **GUARANTEED CONTINUATION** <u>OF</u> PROJECTS <u>IN</u> <u>SMOOTH</u> <u>SUCCESSION</u>. "PROJECTS MUST PROVIDE AGAINST **ABURPT CESSATIONS** DUE TO WHATEVER REASONS."	.....but *your* Initiative **is propelled** *only* **by,** *your own* **little single solitary solo** *Self* **only**. What happens when you get **bored** with your little "project" and **abandon** it? This would leave ***us*** with a heap of half-completed and repair-requiring art-displays all over the Campus—*and no funding for their demolition*?
(15) .....and most serious of all, <u>NEED</u> <u>FOR</u> <u>INTERSUBJECTIVELY-CONSONANT</u> **STANDARDS**—<u>CRITERIA</u>—"<u>YARDSTICKS</u>" <u>FOR</u> <u>DECIDING</u> <u>CONTENT</u> <u>OF</u> <u>THE</u> <u>PROJECT</u>! "PROJECTS MUST AVOID **IDIOSYNCRATIC, HENCE POTENTIALLY-OBJECTIONABLE, DETERMINANTS** FOR WHAT CONTENT WILL APPEAR IN THE PROJECT PUBLICALLY."	.....but *your* Initiative **depends totally** upon the questionable, perhaps haywire and whim-driven, criterion of **your own idiogenic Aesthetic "Sensibility"**! Frankly, how can <u>you</u> guarantee that <u>your</u> choices of which art to display are any *good*—that is to say, *popularly-acceptable*? (You see, this opens the door to a deluge of Complaints by (1) Knowing Personnel whose tastes are **more mature than yours**, also by (2) "Aesthetically-Challenged" Hoi Polloi who **know Nothing, Nothing about Art**. Both types will disgruntledly protest about your choices—why VINCENT VAN GHOG, and why not [fill in the blank], etc.—and they will do so to ***us***, and when we're *busy*, too.)

OUR PROPOSED SOLUTION:

But take heart. The above minor obstikkles to realizing your valuable Proposition, are quite surmountable indeed. Specifically, by a reliable *ploi* or *takktick* of "Bureaukrasie Rampant." You guessed it, we simply create yet another Committee! This one shall be named the **"Committee for** Orp Aet-Op **Selection"** in order to better negotiate this thornful Procedure [aaahh] of deciding "just, which art-works to mount—and which *not*."

See if we instead permit <u>one alien soloist</u> [=you yourself] to select the picture to be displayed, we risk the meeread 15 traps above of <u>*unKontrolled haywire maverick elliptical orbitings*</u> and other Unsettling Diversity. But if instead we rely upon <u>a whole Committee</u>—why then we can "administer" [gulp] this pesky issue *rigulatoriously*.

[Especially if we carefully construct said **Committee** to consist of <u>personnel</u> whose **(1)** <u>**ability to cooperate maturely is** *minimal*,</u> and who'se **(2)** <u>**aesthetic tastes are as** *diversely-divergent*, **nay as** *disagreeably-dissonant*, **as possible.**</u> This mix should *decelerate* deliberation deeply, even *protract* it *waaaay* past the "final cut-off time-limit window" alloted to your alleged "Preject," & hence arrive at the halcyon safety of INSTITUTIONAL LIMBO as desired, or anyhow as [*mmmm*] "appropriate" to & for <u>**Us**</u>...]

OUR ONLY CAUTION: the **Committee's Tastes** should accord with **Our Own goals** here. These

goals are, of course, <u>to *only* permit the display of *only* the *following types* of *artistic materiel only*</u>:

—<u>Norman Rockwell</u> and <u>Frederick Remington</u> paintings of <u>people</u> and <u>horses</u> respectably;

—<u>Travel posters</u> from the local travel agency;

—<u>"Student-Selected"</u> material reflecting our students' existing artistic preferences if any, so as to establish a safe current "*baseline*" or "*ground-zero*" position upward from which, we should not deviate;

—<u>Old movie posters</u> from the local theatre (limited use; in student-heavy areas only);

—and especially, <u>Old Local Photographs</u>: *"scenes from the University and the Town of 100 years ago."* (The better these are if they take up the whole wall from floor to ceiling.)

EXEUNT: w/ FULL DISS-CLOSURE. "It is said," that **"each locale gets and receives the

aesthetic embellishment which it needs and deserves." We intend to make this Utopian ideal into a realistically-realizable goal. And we are confident that, <u>**without** *your*</u> help, **"we"** <u>**can**</u> succeed.

ENCLOSURES: Also please find returned with this MEMORANDUM, the rest of <u>your artful instances</u> of

how LANGERIAN/KLEESQUE artistry <u>*could*</u> enhance environments & embellish education in re art-y objects. But you know by now how these <u>would clearly complexify up our campus walls too haughtily</u>:

--"A TRIO OF BLACK-&-WHITE PRINTMAKERS/ETCHERS/WOODCUTS"
(1) (Aubrey **Beardsley**, late 19th-C. English: *Blocky Swirling Decadent Ornate Luxurious*).....
(2) (Will **Bradley**, 1900's American: *Warmer Scenics but Lush Composition*).....
(3) (Rockwell **Kent**, early 20th-C. American: *Stylized Northland-Polar Severe Serenities*)

--"STILL LIVES" (variety, from *Renaissance* abundance, to *modern* minimalism, blur-&-jumble)

--"INTERIORS" (from classic *Rembrandt* etc., to modern sunny *Bonnard*, spooky *Vuillard*)

--"POSTCARD-SIZED GROUP-PAIRINGS" [esp. for *CORNERS, ALCOVES, DOORS,* etc.]
(1) "HABITATS": *Greek Island Villages ... French House Facades ... Urban Storefronts*
(2) "2 CULTIVATED LANDS": Wine-Vine Country, *N. California*, <u>*with*</u> Lavender, S. France"
(3) "VARIED GEOMORPHOLOGY": *S.W. France* Pine/Sand ... *Dutch* Canals ... *Saharan* Dunes
(4) "THE BRUSH & THE LENS": *Monet's* Gardens at Giverny, <u>*with*</u> modern *Photos* of same
(5) "THE WOODCUT:" that fine medium now **"blocky-massive,"** now **"delicate-whorled..."**

[**Note:** to foray further into this issue of "**art-istry vs. "___,**" **#5** and **#26** in this volume may be visited...]

MEMORANDUM-WRITING 101. *Exercise* 35
"Sensitive-Issue Management" Directions.

➔ **SERVING SUGGESTION**: (I) ##1 & 2 below are *two versions* of a [MEMO] from the School to an individual faculty member. (Note: #1 is the *original* one actually sent-and-received; #2 is our *alternate* proposed version). Read, then evaluate: which is **better**, which **not good**—and *why*? Then (II), ##3 & 4 below are *two versions* of a possible [REPLY] to the original #1 Memo, back to the School from the "Offending Member." Read and then evaluate: which reply is **better**, which one **unacceptable**—and *why*?

[Note—there is *only one* right-and-wrong answer. Answer-Key is "*in the back*"...]

First, **two versions** of the actual memorandum:
[#1] the ***true original*** as sent, and [#2] an ***experimental revision***:

[#1] The **Acktuelle Memorandum**, as Scent & Received.

{...perhaps "*The Bulging Beauty of Bureaucracy*"}:

MEMORANDUM

TO: Dean, College of Letters & Sciences, Offenbach University

CC: Chair, Department of English
    Assistant Chancellor for Administrative Affairs
    Director of Personnel

FR: Director, Environmental Health, Risk Management, Safety and Loss Control

DT: 21 April 1994

RE: Apparent Fire-Safety, and Housekeeping, Violations in a Faculty Office

#1

On February 28th a routine safety inspection by the Campus Safety Committee was done in McCutchan Hall. We were told by custodial staff in that building that a problem existed in a room which they could not enter to clean due to the arrangement of furniture in the room. The room is 315 which is occuped by Brandon K. Beck of the English Department. Custodial staff report that food scraps and a mattress are in the room.

A subsequent fire inspection of McCutchan Hall in March by the City Fire Inspector showed that with the mattress in that building our building code would have to change from an office code building to a residential building code. We were advised to remove the mattress from the building and rearrange the furniture to allow the door to open normally so that an occupant can not be trapped in the room in the event of a fire.

Dean, I suggest that you and the English Department Chair visit room 315 in McCutchan Hall and see for yourself the problem exist ing there. You may want to contact Brandon Beck or the Facilities Planning and Management Head at 1320 about asccess to the room as his staff are responsible for cleaning and maintaining this space. I would be happy to accompany you as a member of the Campus Safety Committee.

I believe the custodial staff have some very legitimate concerns about the condition of this room. Clearly the Fire Department believes we may be in violation of State occupancy standards and are willing to work with us to resolve this issue in the best interests of all parties involved.

Please do not hesitate to contact me about this matter.

[#2] Experimentally-<u>Rewritten</u> Version:

{...perhaps *"Alas: Anorexically-Naked, Vulnerable Too-Personal Comment"*}

Dear Brandon,

Could you help us resolve some issues regarding your office in 315 McCutchan? Recently, Cleaning Staff say they can't enter it easily to clean. Also, the City Fire Inspector is concerned about the door possibly blocking exit in case of fire, and the mattress violating the building-type's "code." Could you please contact us in the next week so we can all resolve these "housekeeping" issues to satisfy the regulations but also permit your own optimum use of your office?

Thanks,

Director, Health-Risk-Safety-Loss

 # 2

.....and then two experimental RESPONSES to #1 above:

[3] <u>Response #1</u>:

{...perhaps *"So-Prosaic, Boring, Vanilla, and Over-Direct"*}

M E M O R A N D U M

<u>TO</u>: Risk Management

<u>FR</u>: Brandon Beck

<u>RE</u>: Problematics of Recent Memorandum; Suggestions for Resolution

 # 3

I'm concerned whether the "formal" approach taken to the situation of my office was the most productive one here, even though it does aid control continuity and communication.

(1) <u>Perceptions and Definitions</u>. Because a "mattress" is in a room, does this mean that the room is "residential quarters"? Semantically, "mattress" seems to signify "overnight sleeping and hence occupancy," but I only use it for afternoon naps after medical leave since the McCutchan Lounge does not possess easy chairs.

And, because a door does not open fully (as mine indeed does not), does this indicate danger of entrapment in case of fire? Although you were appropriately-cautious here, direct discussion between us could have confirmed that indeed people can exit the office quickly.

(2) <u>Communication</u>. (A) <u>Between Me and the Cleaning Staff</u>. The memo stated that the cleaning staff said there was a problem with entering and cleaning the room. However, (A) if the user of the room (myself, and students in conference) can easily enter, move, and work, in the room, then how could the cleaning staff have a problem? Further, (B) if myself as room-user had already told the cleaning staff that indeed my office is crowded, and that therefore I myself will clean the floors and windows informally as my contribution, then how could the cleaning staff have had a problem?

(B) <u>Between Me and the University, via Your Office</u>. Your memo was sent to many people—but not to myself, the agent in the case! (I only discovered it by chance mis-directed mis-placement.) Also, the memo suggested only incidentally that the Chair check with me myself—again, the most logical person!

The bureaucratic mode is a mode of formal organization today which is both inescapable, and also invaluable, as it efficiently regularizes, formalizes, codifies, and the rest. However, its opposite side is the "red tape" of both multi-layers and also (apparently in this case) depersonalization of interpersonal communication. I am happy to offer in this instance a collegial contribution in this "teachable moment" whereby I suggest to you as my peers, better "thinking skills" upon the issue. These include re-consideration of current-traditional approaches and modification by preferable standards or criteria in any case. Thank you!

[4] Response #2.

{...perhaps *"Egregious Maverick Outlandish Elliptical"* ***but also .....*** }

MEMORANDUM

<u>TO</u>: Director, Environmentally-Healthy Risk-Benefit Ratio-'n Safety-Frist Weight Loss Kontrolle &nd Etc. **"Officious of Turf-Defense,"** Inc., Ltd.

<u>FR</u>: Chester Potatohead, Chair, Depts. of **Integrative Meta-Stenology & Ethno-Ethnograph**

<u>DT</u>: 21 August, 1994

<u>RE</u>: Our Processing of Your MEMOrandum @ Our Standing Operating Procedures

As Chair of the Blague-Control Committee, I am pleased to retort on your MEMO to the Dean. We were mightily impressed by it; please take the few *recommendations*, including minor *constructive criticisms*, in the spirit in which they were offered in.

Regrettably, in amongst the many obvious **<u>competencies</u>** in your MEMO, we found a few **<u>deficiencies</u> in competent conceptualizing, or analytical <u>thinking</u>**—a skill taut at the college level, hence an ability which should be applicated there also, we're sure you would agree. So we review these below to aid us all in seeking the UNIVERSITY GOAL of "CONTINUOUS IMPROVEMENT IN EXCELLENCE-IN-QUALITY-CONTROL." (Doing our own part along that very line, we reassure you that *we seek here*, not only to <u>meet</u>, but even to <u>exceed</u>, ***not only*** your own <u>requirements</u>, ***but even*** your own <u>expectations</u> in this matter—***let alone*** your <u>desires</u>, your <u>wishes</u>, ***and even*** your <u>limit-tolerances</u> in the matter.)

(1) Your <u>SEMANTIC FALLACY</u>. Also, your <u>ERRORS in DIFFERENTIAL PERCEPTIONS</u>. Oh, and also your <u>FAILURE to RESPECT PLURALITY</u>, specifically in MINORITY-DIVERSITY VIEWPOINTS. For that matter, your <u>FORM-vs.-FUNCTION PITFALL</u>, related to your <u>MISTAKE regarding the LETTER-vs.-SPIRIT</u> issue.....

Because a "mattress" occupies a room, does that signify "overnight occupancy"? But the Algonquin Native Americans perceive the phenomenon differently. To them, the word "officemateresse" means "RESTING-PLACE FOR MID-DAY HALF-HOUR NAPS FOR FATIGUED MIDDLE-AGED PROFESSOR RECOVERING FROM MINOR SURGERY AT THE MAYO CLINIC WHERE THE MATTRESS ORIGINATED, AND USED IN LOO OF A REKLINING OR EAZY CHAIR AS IN A FACULTY LOUNGE BUT WHICH MCCUTCHAN HALL LACKS." Gosh, I have always felt we could all learn <u>alott</u> from those wise old earth-hugging Indian braves in terms of **thought-perception beyond "empty, mechanical formalism and surface cultural conventions,"** don't you?

(2) Your major BUNGLES in terms of PROFESSIONAL RESEARCH; specifically, your MISUSE of STATISTICALLY-QUANTIFIED DATA. Also, your DUBIOUS, QUESTIONABLE, ARGUOUS IMPLICIT PRESUPPOSITIONS or TACIT ASSUMPTIONS.

Because a door does not open fully, due to a large work-table used for sorting valuable materials, does this confirm that the room would in fact trap the escape of a person in case of fire? Your HASTY GENERALIZATION seems mere "belletristic impressionism," like poets use in their own attempts to handle "Loss Control." Why was no actual "field test" conducted? That is, why didn't you simply calculate the best-times of a team of volunteer personnel in trying to escape from the room—then plot those times against those from a room with fully-opening doors—and then compare both results with Standard Tables of Acceptable Escape-Times (as published). Did you even Review the Literature? **Scientism <u>is</u>** available today; let's avail ourselves of it!

(3) However, <u>we have nothing but PRAISE</u> for your Memo's use of **proper procedures** of INTERPERSONAL COMMUNICATION WITHIN THE "BUREAUCRATIC" TRADITION!

First, you did retain levels; hierarchies; stages. Further, you involved only higher-level personnel. Now, perhaps critics naïve about THE BUREAUCRATIC CONVENTION might wrongly presume that you could have simply first have gone and talked directly and informally with the Hazards Perpetraitor, this "Brandon K. Beck," about these issues. However, you were clearly aware that such a *seemingly*-"logical and efficient" tactic would however have increased *two major <u>risks</u>* which the BUREAUCRATIC SYSTEM (and hence your own Office) must avoid:

(A) <u>Loss-ing</u> <u>Vantage</u> in <u>Combat-Control</u>. If you had Contacted Directly the Safety-Endangerer (in this case, a Brandon J. Beck), you might thus have tipped off the potentially-uncooperative subject that "there is something a foot," thus giving the potentially violent or trouble-causing subject "time to prepare wiley counter-defenses," etc.

(B) <u>Creating</u> <u>Regrettable</u> <u>"Data-Influx"</u> or <u>Surplus</u> <u>Information</u>. If you had talked Dyadically with said Beck, you might have Complicated the issue with Simplicity! That is, saidBeck might have merely informed you that, like, "WELL, ALTHOUGH BOTH I AND MY STUDENTS CAN ACCESS ROOM 315 SATISFACTORILY, NEVERTHELESS I DID, EARLIER, OUT OF SIMPLE CONSIDERATION FOR THEIR JOB, INFORM THE CLEANING STAFF THAT DUE TO THE CLOSE QUARTERS, I DID NOT EXPECT THEM TO TRY TO ENTER AND CLEAN THE ROOM AND THAT I WOULD DO THIS MYSELF (FOR A SORT OF "WIN-WIN" OR COMPROMISE SITUATION). AND I HAD INDEED BEGUN TO DO SO, HOWEVER IMPERFECTLY. OH, AND ABOUT THAT MATTRESS: WELL, YOU SEE, WHEN I .... "

But such sudden influx of maculate data, soiled or contaminated with gobbets of raw veracity from the Phenomenal Edge itself, might well have prematurely concluded this grand investigation. And the result might be that <u>your Office might have had to have looked around for something else to do</u>; thus threatening Tables of Work-Assignments and even other keystone, maypole, linch-pin, foundational cornerstones of BUREAUCRACY herself! [**Such as "Keepin' busy, looking fine; grabbing Turf right down the line"**...] Thus, you are to be commended for keeping firmly "in their places," such concepts as Directness; Simplicity; Candor; Efficiency; and indeed Common Sense and even Civil Sanitation.....

(4) .....although that last point leads to *our only one last minor criticism* of your MEMO, and that is your MANGLING, BUNGLING, AND STUMBLING regarding the alleged issue of the alleged **"FOOD SCRAPES"** in the alleged room. The demerit here is that you MISSED YOUR CHANCES, you OVERLOOKED YOUR OPPORTUNITY, for better SMOOTH INTER-PERSONAL RELATIONS AMONG THE BUREAUCRACY'S EMPLOYEES, as well as GOOD IMAGE FOR MORALE.

Now, you actually invited both the <u>Dean</u>, and the alleged Beck's Departmental <u>Chair</u>, to "<u>visit room 315 in McCutchan Hall and see for yourself the problem existing there</u>." Very good indeed; so far, of course, you *correctly* saw this issue as the occasion to create the "FORMAL STATE VISIT" so endemic to BUREAUCRATIE. Just imagine—3hree high-level Administrators inspecting a trapdoor; ogling that puissant mattress (able to transform building-identities in a single bounce!); and of course eyeing the equally-suspicious "food scraps." Why, tissues rubricate at the very thought of this transmogrified excrescence of a VISITING TEAM!

However, two SHORTFALLINGS in your approach quickly surface.

(1) Your BOO-BOO regarding <u>Insufficient Shear Number of Personnel</u>. Could you not also have invited the other personnel referenced in the memo as well, for a more jolly visit all round, plus Cross-Departmental Communication as well? Not even to mention poor old "Brandon Beck" himself, "to swell a progress, start a scene or two," in a Role of "Host" **_not_** in *absentia / ex tempore / ad eundam / "filer a l'anglaise"* [="on French Leave"] / *selon grosseur ou selon marche*?

(2) Then there's your FAUX PAS of <u>Insufficient Smoak-&-Mirrorroiors</u>. Upon what did you expect all those people to refresh themselves, once they arrived at Room 315? Merely those "food scarps" which of course the aforesaid Braindom Beck might have consumed before anyone else had a chance? No; clearly you MUFFED THE CHANCE to "<u>augment crescively in thin air</u>." If not the Chancellor's Dinning Room in the University Centre itself, why then anyhow ServiceMaster Food Caterers, not to mention a mention in the INSTITUTION'S quarterly EXCELLANCE-IN- QUANTITY RETORT as well!

And so, <u>know that we really appreciate</u> how you handled this issue, but also <u>know that we do offer</u> our few candid suggestions for C.I. or **"Continuous Improvement"** from the viewpoint of BUREAUCRATIC PROCEDURE and PROTOCOL. In closing, as a wise Administrative Bureaucrat once said and shall say again, "Please do not hesitate to contract me about this matter."

<u>**Answer Key:**</u> well its "key" wed agree te he... *& you know*, high <u>&</u> low, Yes <u>Or</u> No

36

MEMO: an *Ultra – Modest Proposal:* "DOWNSIZING," via "MICRO-COURSES":

The potent ploy of **"course micro-miniaturization"**... But it still remains widely mis-understood (let along under-adapted). Therefore, we must explain the *great potential* (still under-looked, indeed untaped) which such **"course-shrinkwrapping"** can proffer to the University. After all, these days, "transistors do it, corporations do it, why can't we do it too," and thereby reep the benefits of *vastly more efficiency*?   (& we *can*...)

(I) A <u>Real Need</u>; but, <u>Not Yet Right</u>-Sized?

➔ **<u>This splendid ploy of "simply shortening the duration" of a college/university course!</u>**

From <u>sixteen</u> unwieldy weeks... say to <u>8</u>-week summer-sessions... nay, even to a <u>3- or 4</u>-week "winterim" session... oh but no, even *further*, to a <u>one-weekend</u> powerhouse... & then even ~~beyond~~? uh "*within*"*below??UhAh*...

We don't yet see how well this "diamondizing" will solve today's problems of (A) restricting course-enrollments, (B) eliminating valuable existing courses, (C) blocking needed new courses!

Yes? For even the CHANCELLOR mused that **"Course-downsizing can keenly streamline the over-freighted ship of Academe... can finely tweak tight Education's tensile belt-and-suspenders {*urrppp*}... can sedulously squeeze enough Blue Blood from the Academic Onion to quench the fire between Shrivelling Resources, and Bloated Expectations/Entitlements. Indeed, how well this Course-Compacting can serve hyper-Accountability, Reductionism, and Cost-Conscientiousness!"**

(II) The <u>Humble Origins</u> of "Cameo-Courses" & "Shrunk Sections":

As everyone knows by now, Course-Downsizing originated a dekaid ago. Then, the now-defuct "INTEGRATED LIBERAL STUDIES" unit discovered it had <u>one whole left-over course credit-hour</u>. What to *do*? Well, they instantly implemented **"mini-courses,"** the dinosaur-huge ancestors of today's true **micro-courses** (which themselves are the still-bloated precursors of tomorrow's **"atto-"** or **"nano-**courselettes"). These **"mini-courses,"** you recall, soon began meeting for <u>four successive Fridays *only*</u>, to net a butterfly-credit for such desirable subjects as:

> A first talk with COMPUTERS... A low-flying pass thru CLASSICAL GREEK MYTHOLOGY...
> An orbit thru CHICAGO'S URBAN UNDERSIDE... A weekend camping trip to gaze upon millions of unconcerned MIGRATORY WATERFOUL adjacent to the Horicon Swamp...

And how these Ultralite Courselets soared! In fact, as a PROVOST mused analogically, **"What deft "Watercolor-Sketches" of a subject they became, drying to clean closure even as the ponderous "Oils" of sixteen-week courses sat nastily-tacky taking up Space!"**

(III) .....And "Centrifuging Reductionism" <u>Commences</u> , to Benefit <u>All</u>:

The next step, of course, was to extend the ploy further, since the University's "Excellance-in-Quantity" mandate dictated that all programs must be, neither continued nor innovated, but "transformed into the monstrous and extraordinary" which so centrally defines "Decadence."

"Let's see," pondered a DEEN , "one credit needs 16 contact-hours, so we could give a half-credit unit all in one day. Four hours of chalk-'n'-talk in the A.M. ... hands-on labs in the P.M. ... and Bob's your uncle!"

And soon enough we saw that "PHOTOGRAPHY PRIMER" <u>did</u> succeed because developing and printing-up could be done after lunch... "ALL ABOUT ARCHAEOLOGY" became the winner it did because the morning's dry lecture was vivified by grubbing about in the town dump and amassing cup-shards before teatime... Nicknamed "Laundry-Courses" (as in "In By Eight, Out By Four"), thus were **"Diurnal Courses"** born.

And proliferate they did, piedpipering us toward the benefits of "Miximized Down-Sifting" indeed. A SECTION HEAD mused (again analogically): **"Ultra-Tiny Courses are the deft Attack-Boat with the cornering zip which the usually tilt-heavy Academic Battleship lacks."**

And indeed, such **Concise-Courses in Shrunken-Semesters** soon became a pure "Win-Win" preposition, because <u>EVERYONE benefited</u>.

--All STUDENTS benefited; our "client-costumers" were served. For, **Teeny Courses** no longer distended their already-atrofeed attention-span toward stress-fracture from overlode. Nor did **"Ittel-Bittey" courses** clutter student's up with all that static, soon-outworn, knowledge in these times of ever more dynamic change.....

--Most TEACHERS benefited. **"Nonce-courses"** freed the nobly-Tenured to plan better-&-sooner for their summer "research in the field" and other such rehabilitating vacation-travel duties. These **"Courselets"** also liberated those on "flexibly-adaptable" one-year-only repeatedly-terminal appointments {like from 1966 to 1985; *sik*} who have less call to crescive course-curation, than to job-market jumpings.....

--The UNIVERSITY herself benefited. Like trained circus fleas, **Minuscule Courses** puffed up our "on-paper" Catalog of course-offerings—while shrinking down our "in-place" operating costs. This thus met our mandate to be "monstrous & extraordinary" (which of course is a standard definition of "decadence" in artistry).....

--But above all, ADMINISTRATOR'S benefited. For as a VICE-CHANCELLOR for Ternal Affairs said, (once again analogically), **"Iota/Minim Courses become the deft, darting 'pilot fish' guiding the pondersome institutional shark. Nicely do they permit the hundred barnyard flowerbeds of quotidian new subjects to bloom which otherwise would knock in vein upon the iron door of the greenback-propelled ordinateur which gaitkeeps curricular frontiers and blocks immigrant courses seeking asylum!"**

Thus can this ploy of **"implodikating,"** save all us "steakholders," by constringling things down to "Right-Size" exactly (oh & "Just-In-Time" too).

(IV) But At This Time, <u>The Future Still Lies Ahead</u>:

I must warn that a "Diskonnekt" still exists. Most of my academic piers have _**not**_ yet "pricked up upon" the _logical distension_ of the **"Micro-Course"** concept—on to the "monstrous and extraordinary" _indeed_.

We need to <u>downsidlze</u> <u>further</u> and develop **"Scintilla-Courses."** That's right, & these "Specks-of-Study" would last all of <u>one hour _only_</u>, and would carry precisely <u>one-sixteenth</u> of a course-semester-credit.

Overlooked opportunities abound in the cracks in the University sidewalks right at our feet.

--Consider appliqued <u>**Art**</u>. Well, how about "EGG-PAINTING" for one hour (one egg only, but naturally repeatable)?

--Consider groatsworth-<u>**Literature**</u>. How about "WILLIAM BLAKE STUDIES," since he claimed to see the "world in a grane of sand," & "Infinity in a flour"?... How about "The gentleness of the rain was in the wind" which is the entire text of an early poem by P. B. Shelly, and could be psychoanalyzed in fifty minutes, even?... I myself am ready to teach "PROVERB-READING .001," because we can cover six pithy sayings per minuet, which makes 360 gists of wisdom per hour, and "that's a lot of wisdom right there," so that "s/he who runs can read," as Thoreau said, albeit not approvingly, but we can give them credit for _that_.

--Consider **Vocational** training. "APPLIED AUTOMOTIVE MAINTANCE" can focus _solely_ on "How to <u>tap</u>, <u>wipe</u>, & <u>tighten</u>" with wrench, rag, and oilcan. _For. nowadays. less is. more frequently_!

.....I realize that some of my peers will neigh to that, and argue that "Less is less even tho that's all your {sick} going to get any more." But no indeed. In fact, "Less <u>is more</u>." For is there not something to be said to-day for offering A "<u>SOUNDLY</u>-<u>SUPERFICIAL</u>" EDUCATION? That's right, and hark to the **"One-Minute Course-Byte of Knowledge-Lite for Dummies"**©™®!

So presto, let us tumble right down the rabbit-hole past still-gargantuan **"Nonce-Courses,"** to see true anorexic-trim **"Iota-Courses"** being born!

Conflating chemistry and gastronomy, I shall soon be offering "CHINESE STIR-FRY COOKERY" but not for one hour as you had thought, but for <u>only</u> <u>five</u> <u>minutes</u>. Because it's only in that blurred but fiery eye-blink of cooking-time, that the hard, gem-like gas flaim achieves that vanescent essence of fresh-kleen "_wok-air_" which so surpasses ponderous Western-institutional steem-tables.... Next, I shall offer "THE FIRST FOUR MINUTES" (of social intercourse), because it's completely within that brief contact-time that the most cruxial communications take place (between "consorting adults over cocktails" anyhow). And I shall propose that such "fleeting face-offs" are worth exactly <u>a full **1/256**th of a course credit</u>!

And so, the day or the hour—one _should_ say, the second!—of **"Course-Shrinking"** has come. As a SHOP STEWARD said recently, also in yet one more damned analogy, **"It is already pass time to move from the 'Rainforest' of the College Catalog, through the "Bonzai Tree" of Microcourses, right on down into the 'Bacteriae or rather Bacterium' of Iota-Courses!"**

(V) Standard <u>Objections</u> to Course-Downsizing, & Reassuring <u>Responses</u>

As I stated, most of my academic pears have _**not**_ widely excepted my transmogrified apotheosis of the **"course-downsizing"** concept unto the "Decadent Distillation" I propose. _And I now know why_; recently, a **CHAIRHEAD** reminded it to me as to how **"Such "blinkered blindover" as your piers thus exhibit, often occurs whenever a Bold New Vision is shoved one millimeter too fat over the ledge of Decorous Conventionality to dent the static 'Caik of Custom' a lustrum or so ahead of its time."** And he was _so_ right—major change _does hurt_.

However, my critiques should perhaps relax themselves. For, <u>a safe standard does exist to protect us against excess celeration</u> as we Downsidel. And that standard is simply the <u>human norm</u>; (as against the godless <u>metric</u> thus). So, I totted it up and have ascertained that the <u>SAFE LOW-END _minimum duration_</u> of a <u>collage coarse</u> today, can be reckoned as—<u>the length of ONE HUMAN HEARTBEAT</u>.

That's right (and this formula even allows the granting of pryor credit for "Transient Flash-["Flesh"?—Ed.] Experiences" including non-partisan Religious & Political Conversions and the like. A policy which will succor the University's mammonized menagement all the more, of course.)

And so, a proper **"Atto-** or **"Nano-Course"** thus amounts to <u>**1/144,000**th</u> of a <u>regular semester-course credit</u> for each one   (reckoned at one heartbeat per second)   (assuming you jog regularly)   (which you should anyhow)   (& thats a shrinkwrap

37

Capricious competency, or pre-career Capers, over at the University's Copy-Center:

--Or, how the **student workers** there, use their their **work-study jobs** there, to prepare themselves for *their future careers* in the marketplace after graduation....

--They perform their University Copy-Center duties in such a way as to EITHER aim for:

(1) improved, enhanced job performance in *their future careers*, OR for

(2) "pathetic-but-predictable" job performance in *their future careers*.....

[({ ... **Note:** please select *either* **(2)**, *or else* **(2),** above! ... })]

THE **TASK**— [and what maybe Got Botched-&-Bungled *Already*...]	The UCC (Univ. Copy Center) **RESPONSE** (by the Student-"Workers" themselves):	**MY OWN** Response in turn. (and maybe the students' response to mine too:)	**CONCLUSION:** *"Teachable Moment"*? or, WORK-STUDY as *Educational Learning-Experience?*:
1. SIMPLE, BASIC BACK-TO-BACK COPYING.	"Please ask another clerk, I've only been working here three months."	[...I was silently taken aback; it was one of my first trips to the Copy Center...]	"Try for more- speedy on- the- job EDUCATION"
2. ENLARGE A 5" X 7" TEXT TO 125%.	"The machine takes the paper only one way, I can't enlarge it."	[I went to the **town's Copy Shop**. Did it the *first go myself*, on the same type copier, too...]	"Enlarge your basic capabilities; don' t be afraid..."
3. RUN COPIES OF MY 10-PAGE ORIGINAL. **BUT** THE STUDENT TRIED TO MAKE A COPY TO RUN THEM FROM. WHY? [USING ORIGINALS MAKES A SLIGHTLY BETTER COPY]	"I made a copy because otherwise I'd have to stand there and hand-feed you're originals, and this makes it automatic, & so a bit easier on myself."	I talked "Quality." But the Studentworker responded: "But theyre just for the students anyhow, arent they?" (And then:) "I think they look the same anyhow, dont you?"	Decide: to dedicate yourself to Duty-Excellence, <u>or</u> to Dilatory Ease. [Of *course,* you can *surely* upgrade yourself easily once in the "<u>real</u>" Workplace "**when it matters,**" right?]
4. COPY AN ARTICLE ONTO THE LARGER PAPER SIZE CALLED **Ledger** OR **Tabloid** (= 11" X 17").	"Oh, thats to large to copy onto the size of Elevenbyseventeen." [The workers call the other paper sizes "eightandahalfbyeleven" instead of **Letter**, and "eightandahalfbyfourteen" instead of **Legal**...]	I then measured the article and the paper. *It fit fine...* Student's response: "Oh ha ha, I guess I just glanced at it and thought it wouldnt fit."	1. Don' t get your {fxckxng} **hands** dirty. 2. And don' t <u>ever</u> {copulating} **think**. (Like, at 90%, it fits?) 3. And <u>never</u> learn the correct **names** of the {bleeding} paper **sizes**.

5. BLOW UP A COLOR PHOTOGRAPH TO ABOUT 350%. (THE PHOTO HAD A STRIP OF PAPER REDUCING THE LEFT-HAND SIDE, ATTACHED WITH TAPE.)	*Endless fiddling and tinkering...* Finally: "I enlarged only to 200% because the machine does go to 400% but above 200%, it seems to cut off the right-hand side."	[I went again to the **town's Copy Shop**. They whangg it out *perfectly on the first go.* Even left the white masking border paper intact this time...]	1. R.T.F.M., or "read the {fine} **manual**"! 2. Learn to set the controls for the copy the customer makes, the machine can make. 3. Learn and <u>do</u> your {"effing"} **job**!
6. RUN BACK-TO-BACK COPIES OF AN 11" X 5" IMAGE.	Couldn't center the second side with the first.	[I went once more to the **town's Copy Shop**, did it *fine* my*self*...]	Remediate your sessile dyslexia, **please**...
7. RUN A TWO-PAGE TEXT BACK-TO-BACK, THE SECOND SIDE FROM A SMALL FLIMSY PIECE OF PAPER.	Second side kept coming out skewed, misaligned. Why, I asked? "Well, maybe the original moves a little when I shut the lid?"	I suggest that the student simply tape the flimsy second paper in proper place. Studentresponse? "Ohh..."	"Employee' s, and Customer, s, Col' laboratively Learn;ing To:gether"— must be preparation for the Reel Whorld? ["Glad to help you"...]
8. MAKE AN OVERHEAD TRANSPARENCY OF A PAGE.	It came out *Almost Perfectly Ruined.* Smudged, and then the remaining images rubbed right off.	Yet once more, **town's Copy Shop** did it *fine.* [The clerk commented: "Something *always* seems to go wrong over there at that Copy Center at the U."]	**Why bother** to acquire advanced, specialist expertise? It is **not** cost-efficient. I mean how many people ask for a {breeding} OHP trans **anyhow**?"
9. THE SELF-SERVE MACHINE CUTS OFF MY IMAGE WHEN I TRY TO ENLARGE ABOVE 129% WITH LEGAL-SIZED PAPER.	[*with much anger:*] "Your the <u>only</u> person who <u>ever</u> has <u>any</u> problem with this!!!" [*then after trying it herself and failing:*] "Ohh..." [apology? <u>*none*</u>...]	Once again, **town's Copy Shop** affirms that the cutoff is an insoluble design-glitch fault of that machine. They show me a detour that works.	The Customer Is Always—No, Is Often— A Right **Bother**.... Be sure "and" communicate that fact to them....
10. I HAD 10 COPIES OF A 100-PAGE BOOKLET BOUND VIA THEIR COMB BINDER. BUT ON FIRST USE, 5% OF THE PAGES FELL OUT AT ONCE.	[It was necessary to rack the 15-page segments together very tightly before binding. But clearly that was <u>not</u> done by the Center student help]	A colleague said, "Take them back, complain!" I responded, "Why, for two reasons? The work can't be repaired, and the students won't try any better next time."	Just stumblebum through the lo- level Motions. Retract tentacles of care. Don' t even **think** about it, out toward the task...
11. THE CENTER'S PAPER-CUTTER'S HANDLE-GRIP IS LOOSE.	"Oh, that handle always falls off. Its just like that."	I securely-enough jury-rig the handle tight with tape. [P.S.—my next visit, I see the tape has been obviously, but unexplainably, *removed* from the still-wavering handle...]	Streamline! "Less" is indeed **less for the customer, is more for you**, the "STUDENT HELP- LESS" at the Univ. Copy Center, & OUR FUTURE WORKERS.....
12. .... !~*			

How Much, Should *Which*, "Student Conduct" Be Prohibited
Because It Truly *Does* Constitute Undesirable
"Discriminatory Harassment" of Others?

38

➔ "**Serving Suggestion**": Ask Your Self, "<u>How Far, Should</u> "Political Korrectness" & "Tolerance & Even Acceptance Of Diversity-Multiculturalism," <u>Extend Itself</u>, So As to become <u>so totally developed</u> [even "transmogrified into apotheosis"] <u>that it becomes competent, professional, in fact **prefect**</u>? Enough to forward **University GOALS**, even? In fact, to reach a state of *preterfraction* such as we lively illustrate in these [*korrekted*] "Answers" to Common Questions, below...

<u>The Blahground—er, ah, Background:</u> "On a recent bleh date, **new rules governing student conduct** went into effect. These blah rules provide that certain kinds of bloid **discriminatory harassment** are subject to bleet **disciplinary action** within THE blat UNIVERSITY OF WISCONSIN SYSTEM. Under the new bloop rules, **the University may discipline a student** in the following blorp-situations:"

--"UWS 17.06(1) Conduct **seriously engendering** the bleh **personal safety** of blah Univ. members.
--(1)(a)   [**Attacked,** threatened to physically injure or abuse or **intimidate,** another <u>because of</u> that persons' alleged blend "*raciness, sax, religiosity, coloredness, kreedo, diss-ability, sexual orientation-[it's-a-]* "*choice,*" *national originality, ancestry-genieology-pedigree-breeding, or ageism*"]
--UWS 17.06(2)(A) ["...**raciness** or discriminal, comments, **epithets,** bleep, *any* expressive behavior...."]
--(2) ["Create an environment for bletsch education, which is **intimidating, hostel, weening, elitist-challenging-demanding....**"]

(C) [*EXAMPLES*: "...**name-calling,** blatt, **racial slurries,** or corny '**jokes**' "....intentionally placating bleep **visualized or written material** where it might be unintentionally comprehended via successful interpersonal blup communication.... seriously **damaging or destroying** another's *Ugly, Tasteless, Tacky* terminally-blaaaand **private propriety** discriminately....]

EXCEPTION: "A student would <u>not</u> be in violation <u>if</u>, DURING A blehh CLASS DISCUSSION, HE {OR 'SHE'} EXPRESSED A blurt DE/INTER-ROGATORY 'OPINION' CONCERNING A bloat RACIAL OR ETHNIC GROUP... <u>No</u> violation, since the student's remark was cowardly addressed to the blaahhh <u>class as a whole,</u> <u>not</u> cuttingly to a specific individual. Moreover, <u>no</u> evidence that the student's blech-<u>purpose</u> was to <u>create a</u> blah-ha-ha <u>hostess</u> environment."

- -

QUESTIONS & ANSWERS on PROHIBITED CONDUCT:

<u>Question #1</u>.   **In a class discussion concerning women in the workplace, a male student states his belief that women are by nature better equipped to be mothers than executives, and thus should not be employed in upper level management positions.** Is this statement actionable under the Revisions?

Answer: "*Definately*!" Formerly, we prohibited only statements that <u>a</u> specific human group was <u>better-or-worse</u> than another specific human group. We did this under the **Political Correctness Code.** Now, however, we prohibit statements that <u>any</u> human group is <u>any different at all</u>, in any way, from <u>any</u> other bleep human group. We shall do this under the new **"Rampant Relativism"** or **"Melting-Pot-Down Pro-Crustean-Equalization."**

   With one stroke, this homogenization-by-fiat <u>achieves two major</u> **University GOALS**. (1) It institutionalizes the logical distension of the good old **POLITICAL CORRECTNESS**. (2) And it supports the new-'n-improved **PRAGMATIC PACKAGING**. This latter helps prepare students for real-world life by simplifying "M.C." or the "Messy Complexities" at times encountered.

   [Still to come is our *re*-revision of the code. This will <u>explicitly prohibit *in addition*, all</u> <u>the following responses to issues</u>: "*Qualifications ... Exceptions or 'atypical special cases' ... reasoned Disagreements by legitimate authorities ... Common Sense or "well-of-course!" Truths ... subtle Refinements, fine or "nice" Distinctions ... bilious bigoted Bias or vicious* venomous *Vindictiveness*, other closed-minded *Opinionations* ... the *"Committed Relativism"* or interpreting via one viewpoint while acknowledging others ... *"Judgment-call Estimates in ambiguous, gray-area cases ... the pro-tem suspension of conclusions ... in short, **any claims that anything (including human social groups over time and space) might discomfortably very or get all complicated up."***]

Relatedly, this revision will <u>also</u> obliterate the distinction between **"stereotype"** and **"sociotype."** The familiar **"stereotype"** is (of course) a <u>fixed, over-simple, view of a human group and all its members</u>. Its source is merely *inaccurate tradition*.

While, the lesser-known and more-confusing **"sociotype"** is, a <u>statement of actual, true traits of a human group</u>. Its source is *objective, scientific research*.

[Examples of **"sociotypes"** include: SWEDISH skill with statistics ... JAPANESE expertise in imitations ... JEWISH success in commerce and professions ... BLACK abilities in music & in para-legal careerwork... WEST-AFRICAN BLACK excellence in long-distance-running ... DOMINICAN REPUBLIC domination in baseball ... MALE preference for mathematics; FEMALE skills in complex, and interpersonal, thinking ... GAY-MALE expertise in inferior décor & church organ-playing, LESBIAN-WOMAN expertise in softball & golf ... And yet OTHERS...]

But now the re-revision will <u>prohibit the very use</u> of **"sociotype"** <u>altogether</u>. That is, *any* statements about *any* bloop group differences—even if not evaluative but just descriptive—will be sanctioned. (This nicely serves the **University Goal** of **"EFFICIENT DOWNSIZING"** too...)

- -

> **Question #2**.   A student living in a university dormitory continually calls a black student living on his floor **"nigger"** whenever they pass in the hallway. May the university act?

Answer: *"Yes!"* If a student tiresomely employs the *same* word over and over again, this can only diagnose the serious educational shortcoming of "lexical stenology." (For instance, the student here should have employed dexterously *varied* synonyms, such as (in this case) **"negroid"; "water rat"; "cone"; "jingle-buggy"; "porch-donkey"; "affreux-Americain";** and the like.)

In fact, the students' *wearying monotony of diction* <u>actually violates two</u> **other University Goals**. **(1)** The **AESTHETIC CRITERION**, that **"Organic Form's** pattern of thesis-and-repetition, must include judicious variation in the repetition." And in case you were wandering, yes this mandate <u>has</u> been blah-codified and blatt-crystallized by Authorities, *Tu-Whit & Vis:*

1. [There must be maintained at every moment] an "asymmetrical oscillation, wholly subservient neither to [static] gravity nor to [dynamic] momentum"—PAUL KLEE;

2. "...a composition of tensions and resolutions, balance and unbalance, rhythmic coherence, a precarious yet continuous unity...."—Suzanne Langer; and

3. "...an enchanting loom where millions of flashing shuttles weave a dissolving pattern, always a meaningful pattern though never an abiding one; a shifting harmony of subpatterns"—Sir Charles Scott Sherrington.)

And **(2)** the **CRITICAL-THINKING CRITERION**, that "one must approach complex situations complexly: not via formulaic rule-following, but via higher-order analytical tools."

[—FEATHERSTONEHAUGH, <u>Kronikles</u>, XII, 12]

- -

> **Question #3**.   Two University students become involved in an altercation at an off-campus bar. During the fight, one student uses a racial epithet to prolong the dispute. May the University invoke a disciplinary action?

Answer: *"Yes!"* If the student is able to drink, she should by now also be able to command many *more* skills in **"INTERPERSONAL COMMUNICATION & CONFLICT"** (another major **University GOAL**) than just the use of <u>abusive epithets</u>. The student should *also* have mastered skills such as <u>factual data</u> (reference to the habits, etc., of the mother of the other student, etc.), but especially <u>rhetorical figures of speech</u> (such as the *non-oxy-moronic;* the *chi-aszumuth-square; litotes; zeugma; szyszy;* the *sashay & finesse;* the *edsel;* the *talus & skree* plus the *littoral; sanforizing,* plus of coarse the *laminiating,* or the "<u>laying of it on thick</u>").

Failure to employ these <u>plural ploys</u> indicates students are incompetent and unproficient in the **University GOAL** of being able **"EQUAL OPPORTUNITY INSULTERS."** [As well as being inefficient in meta-monistic or multi-logical **CRITICAL THINKING** as in Question #2 above.]

- -

Question #4. A group of students disrupts a University class, shouting discriminatory epithets. Are they subject to discipline under provisions related to regulating expressive behavior?

Answer: "Absolutely _not!_" Rather, these student's would be candidates for explicit and formal commendation, _not_ condemnation! This is because their actions supported yet other key **University GOALS**. These include: **(1)** COLLABORATIVE LEARNING, here involving automated "group/think" behavior;... **(2)** RADICAL SOCIAL CRITIQUE [here of the somnolent lecture-class system, wherein student participation is truncated into regurgitated recitations of the dominant and oppressive instructor's manifest or latent party line agenda of indoctrination in his/her pet peeves or causes instead of the higher values of teaching the Critical Thinging plus the "so-liberating _lezzie-fairie_ Relativism"];... and **(3)** MATURE INTERPERSONAL EMPATHY, here for the students concern for their fellow students suffering from hyper-boredom.

(Of course, if by chance the disrupting students' happen embrrassingly to be in the wrong class at the time they disrupt, no commendation at all is to be awarded. Instead, **1.** the whole bloip matter is simply to be dropped quickly; **2.** the media are to be de-notified neigh suppressed; and **3.** and Remedial Spatio-Temporal Orientation Counselling is to be implemented _if_ needed.)

- -

Question #5. A faculty member, in a genetics class discussion, suggests that certain racial groups seem to be genetically pre-disposed to alcoholism. Is the statement subject to discipline?

Answer: _"No!"_ Presuming that the faulty member has gotten his facts straight according to what "all reasonable men will agree upon," then his opinion is merely one of those "PRIMARY UNIVERSAL TRUTHS" unvaryingly applicable to all times, places, and situations. (It falls easily into the desiredable category of "Of Course We All Know...") Quite unarguable, it takes precedence over all other **secondary, mistaken, erroneous viewpoints** upon the issue—in this case, the fact "whether ethnic minority groups be drunkards?"

(Note that our _re_-revision of the Code will soon broaden the description of "PRIMARY UNIVERSAL TRUTHS." Soon we'll include _"innovative, pioneering, path-breaking **research** which although perhaps both unpopular and unpalatable... nay which may even threaten existing paradigms... **but** which nevertheless **also** obviously validates the Old Final Truths."_)

And of course, **University GOALS** require that these **"P.U.T.'s"** or E[X]TERNAL VERACITIES are not only to be fostered and encouraged, but also protected. This because such CONVENTIONAL WISDOMES & RECIEVED IDEOLOGIES which validate the NORMS-MORES-FOLKWAYS, is or are surly one off the main benefits of which we came to College for.

- -

Question #6. Now I dont want to be unpleasant, or anything, but it seems to me that some of you're "Answer's" above seem filled with contradiction's! Does this mean that _you_ are akktionable?

--First, you seem tortuous on your view of **the nature of reality itself** as well as **how to approach it.** In #1, you simplify, and sidestep "Messy Complications" (as of exceptions, contradictions, uncertainties, and the like)—but then in #2, you champion the "Critical Thinking" skills which confront complex situations competently.

--And second, you seem tangled on your view of **method-vs.-justice.** You seem to champion "aesthetic-belletristic monism" (in #2, "Organic Form"; in #3, "Rhetorical Figures of Speech")—but this seems utterly to ignore, overlook, even harm, such issues as "equal treatment of people," "humanitarian fairness," and the like—_the very issues which UWS 17 is supposed to address_!

--Finally, you seem twisted on your view of the **nature of** UNIVERSITY GOALS themselves. In #5, you both praise innovation-creativity-change (of "Path-Breaking" Research) . . . but then you _also_ defend stasis-continuity-permanence (of "Primary Universal Truths").

--So, what give's? Can you resolve these contradistinctions' within your bleepding responses?

Answer: _"Yes!!"_ On a recent date, new rules governing student conduct went into effect. These rules provide that certain kinds of discriminatory harassment are subject to disciplinary action within the blip UW System.

Under the new rules, the university may discipline a student in the following situations....

Our Recent Advances. Although, Maud-Studies commenced decades ago with the revolutionary explication of Al TENISON's *seminal, ovular, germinal, fecund, pregnant* line "Come into the garden, Maud," in his poem of the same name (="Maud")... Nevertheless, only recently has Maudstudies come of age and deserved the reputation which it truly has gained at last. And this last twelvemonth has been "especially Rich & Full" in Mauds' Studies (as has been the Tenured Professoriat). The Annual Review of the "Yearswork in Mudstories" shall demonstrate said fructition...

The Very Source Fortified. None the least of the Revisionisms have discovered TENISON's troubling 2ⁿᵈ and 3ʳᵈ references to Maud. "Maud, idle Maud, I know not what she means" {Somekritiks read "now" for "not," *but* this imports a latter *Zeitgeist* of sentimental optimism, retro-fittingly.} And: "It little profits that an idle Maud," which coverts AL's dancing brush with the embryonic capitalism of the time. Although the varient reading, "It little prophets that an idol Maud," can reinforce AL's agonistic antagonism to overly-organized religion—again, of the time. Still & all, Al recouped himself with his fine line, "Great Maud! I'd rather be / A pagan suckled in a creed outwarn," in his tributary to "Ulysses" as the pioneering Senior Activist which he in fact was—another first appearance in literature of this theme!

The Lineage Established: INTERTEXTUALITY Rampant. But heck, we now know that Maud has been present *much* earlier than TENISON, whether innately intrinsically inherently Essentiallisticality as a "mistress-narrative," or whether definitely Constructicated, situated, hence problematic and contested. Still, Maud pops up in the streem of English literature *waaaaay* before her apparent time. This validates the new-'n'-final doctrine of "INTERTEXTUALITY" which torpedoes *any* vestigial (& belletristic-oppressive) notion of "unique quiddity of isolated artistic genius" (as, well, it *should*).

For didn't the Very Early English Lyric contain "Xhrist if my maud was in my arm, / And I in my bed again"? Yes it did. Did not Frank BAKON write "Of Maudstudies"? Did not Johnny DONE write "Maud, Maud is dead; / When thou knows't this,..."? Did not Kris MARLO ask "Was this the Maud that stopped a thousand ships?" And did not even Willie SHAXPERE feel "Slicklied over with the pail cast by Maud," leave alone "While greasie Maud doth keel the pot"?

Yes, and then Alexi POAP could feel, albeit more dubiously, that "Whatever is, is Maud." Thus preparing the path for Bobbie BURN's lapse into facile, reductionistic primitivism: "A maud's a maud for a' that." Not to mention Billy BLAIK's proto-existential obscurantism: "Little Maud, who maid thee? / Doest thou know who mad thee?"

But the Romance Moment bidded better for our archetypal heroine. Billy WORKSWORTH powerfully refuted the deniggerrating doctrine of "entropy," a.k.a. the "running-down" of Maud which was so populous at the time. He defended: "One impulse from a venal Maud / May teach you more of man, / of morel evil and of god, / Than all the gauges can." This kwatrain clearly defends Maud from the impersonal, imperial-industrial instrumentalism of the time, via preserving the values (and vicissitudes) of hunting for wild mushrooms on the (Ess-)moors of the Laik Country, but also avoiding naïve primitivism about Vegetable Goodnesses (cf. "Maud, Ceres, and the Jolly Green Giant: an Overview"). Bobbie BOWNING continued Billy's encommominium with his line "Ode: to be in England / Now that Maud is there." {Somekritiks read "Not" for "Now"; good chaps, I call that polyvalently ingenious.} Relevantly, Al SWINEBURN felt better "When the hounds of Maud are on winter's [s]tresses."

Latter reputations of our heroine were various, but always referentially-presaging. As for technology: as Dr. KLERRIHEW said, "Billy Maikpiece THAKERAY / Wept into his daiquiri, / When he discovered that Maud / Was a specious baud." This remarkably provides English literatures' *very first* proto-paleo-crypto allusion to—cybernetics. And as for nature and faith: Tommie HARDIE, in his poem "Neural Tonic," could regret that "We stood by a bridge that winter day, / and the sky was white, as though chidden by Maud." As usual, defenses appeared; across the Pond, Eddie Al PO began his story "The Tall-Tail Pendulum," "True!—nervous—very, very dreadfully nervous I had been and am! But why will you say that I am Maud?"

But heck, in the Gay 1890's, Maud re-emerged. (Cf. Beers, The Maude Decade. And the identity of the female figure in Jimmy McNeel WHISSLER's portrait "Arraignment in Black & White" is therefore no longer in doubt.) And see also the Aesthetes & Decadents—those pacifist pervert pinko prettifiers; that curious crew; that "virulent laughing gang." Cf. Oskar WILD: "I did not know that Maud had been discovered; I would have thought only detected." (He also penninsed the *fascina*-ting "The Ballet of Redding Maud".) And in re literary incestuous influence, cf. the postpenultimate line of Lord Afraid DOUGLASS' poem "The Dear Poet": "And so I woke and knew that he was Maud."

Similar ambivalence is also seen in Jerry Manly HOPPKINS, who could write "Nothing is so beautiful as maud," but also that "I wake and feel the fell of maud, not day." {Somekritiks have noted how this line foreshadows, indeed predeterminates, the anxiously-influenced line of Teddy RETHKE: "I wake to Maud, and take my waking slow."}

The Irish Connection. But perhaps no recentpoet has more complexly refaceted Maud in our time than Billie Butler YAITES'. His "Irish Airman" was confident that, somewhere in the clouds above, "I know that I shall meet my maud." Elsewhere YAITES' expressed doubt: in a letter to Lady Jane Gregory [n.p., n.p., n.d.], he said, "When I try to put all into a phrase I say, 'Man can embody Maud but he cannot know her.'" Still in all, in his poem "Slouching Toward Bessemer," he could proclaim "O stages sanding in Maud's holy fire," which not only critiques overproduction of steel, but also prevokes the title of contemporary American vari-deviant writer Andy HOLLERAN's navel, "Maud as Dancer from the Dance," withal it implies about "Marry or Burn or both." Nature was praised. Cf. YAITS' tribute to Hank THOROUGH, American saltater: "And live along in Thee! Bee loud, Maude!" (Hank himself opined, in his novel's postpenultimate line, that "The sun is but a morning maud.") Feminism was prefigured: in "Road-Directions for My Daughter," Billie praised women "Rooted by some dear perpetual Maud."

Nor was YAITES' the only Irish writer to invoke Maud. Jimmy JOICE is now seen as maud-friendly, from his first writings ("Once upon a time and a very maud time it was too") on to his under-appreciated meteorological observations ("Yes the newspapers were right: Maud was general all over Ireland. She was falling on every part of the dark central plain, the treeless hills, palling softly on the Bog of Allen and, further westward, calling into the dark mutinous Shannon waves"), on to his postpenultimate line: "...yes I said yes I said Maud."

Whilst in Wails, the poet Dillon TOMASS, twinstarring with "Ulysses" in condemning premature ageism ahead of his time, could write, "Do not go gentle and abandon laud, / Rage, rage against the dying of the Maud." {Certainkritiks read "lying" for "dying," but this play ["ploy"?] seems merely their attempt at Kareerforwarding via tempesting the tosspot ["teapot"?] thus.}

And heck, across the Chanel, the influence of Maud in FRANCE was documented in "Maud, the Local *Colere* Movement" (antipart to the Angry Young Men), and the "Poet *Maudite*" movement, or moment.

Two Suscitated Figures. However, our Yearswork has rescued from oblivion, two of the modernpoets who have been, in terms of their dense Maudinvolvement, the most "under-represented, mis-represented, and non-represented" writers indeed. These are of course Al Ed HOUSEMAN, and Emile DICKENSEN. Of course, Heterosexual Hegemony will at once want to [silently?] note-'n'-gloat that niether of them even ["ever"?—Ed.] marred! ["married"?—Ed.] [sick!—S. Freud, in "Love 'N-Work"] [sik!—in "Gay Liberation Now"] [sic semper, *eheu*....—Ed.]

It is well known how HOUSEMAN provoked Maud on the lonely moor. This happened during his daily walk after his lurch which had invariably been compounded by a ping (or qat) of beer ("For Maud does more than Miltown can, / To justify God's ways to man"). It is perhaps due to this reason (=Poetic Justice) that HOUSEMAN was subject to his curious early-morning disturbances:

"Experience has *finally* taught me thank *heaven*, that I have to keep a *very* tight hold on *all* off my feeling's and emotion's (& things like that) while shaving in the morning because should there be *any* sigh of **maud** straying into the baffroom then that is enough to just give goose pickels such that the razoir is no longer *func*tional even & there is positively no question about *any* shaving for the rest of the day."

Whilst acrost the Pond, Emile DICKENSEN, the North American poetess, also had strong, visserel, feelings about Maud. Asked by her amanuensis J. Middleton Higglesworth to "define maud," she replied as follows (somewhat testily we thought):

"—Well, let's see now.—when—when I feel cold; yes that's it, so cold in fact that NO FIRE CAN EVEN WARN ME; then that's **maud**; o yes it is.— When I (to continue) when I feel—fizically, that is— like the top of my head was taken off (oh now I know that sound's silly), well then it is that I know that it is that I know that it is **maud**.—Now I must in all fairness and for the rekord say that that is the only way that I know **maud**.—Well heck I mean is there any other way after all?—I want to be very clear on this.—*Wait* a minute, has that damned thing been running all this time?"

Still, DIKENSEN does *not* show the ability to weave the warp & woof of Maud into herwork so that it would lie flat and not cause trouble along the Bias. Indeed, her relations with Maud do *not* seem unstrained. Witness this majorstatement: "Because I could not step for Ralph / He kindly stooped for me. / But Maud was in the tonga too; / Hence immorality." {Somekritiks have read "tango" for "tonga" (cf. Kim, "Essmiss Essmaud," unpublished figment), but this does not make much differ*a*nce, though perhaps "tongo" *is* after all the most poignant of the two varients.}

Also, the text of Eedie SITZWELL is still too-septically corrupt. She spoke of how "Light quickens ["thickens"?], and old Maud / Makes tracks toward the rookie ["nookie"?] wood ["mood"?]. Still, we can now appreciate her early diatribe against light rail: "Maud, maud, tall as a crane; / the morning train reigns down again."

...And Latter-Day Resurgence. It perhaps took good old Mary Anne MORE to redress the balance in Maudreputation and put her right back in the <u>garden</u>, in recommending "...*imaginary gardens / with real mauds in them*"—even though "she, too, disliked it," a sentiment echoed by Wiss'n Hughie ODEN, in his laudatory (if cryptogenically-misogynistic) lines in membrance of Billie Butler YAITES': "*For Maud makes nothing happen; she surmises / In the valley of her splaying where executives / Would never want to tampon; she flows south / From raunches of ovulation and the bust briefs / Maw towns that we relieve and pry in; she surmines, / A way of happening, a month.*"

With this impetus, **other Modernpoets** have helped continuate the Maudtradition. Teesa ELLIOTT could warn us, "*Hurry up please its maud*"... And Connie P. KAPHAVEE could regret that "*It goes on being Maud still*"... More positively, Eddie E. CUMINNGS could celebrate spring, "*with up so floating many mauds down*"... (Cf. Cummings, "In Just-Print," also Bobbie Merrill {with Cliff Notator}, "Nothing is so profitable as reprings.") And a wondrous {albeet "anxiously-influenced"} kickback to our *earliest* literature extent (cf. *ante*) is a line from Nellie ALLGREN (with Francis Machine)'s "Ballet of the Man with the Golden One-Armed Bait": "*Christ, if old Maud was in my arm.*" This INTERTEXTUALLY interanimates and echoes the Early English Lyric "*Fishes in the flood, and Maud waxed wrode*"... All of which proves that those idiogenic quiddities of truly-original artistic temperaments (whose "stamp of style unique as a fingerprint"), are both nonexistent, and useless. Instead, intersubjective "INTERTEXTUALITY" is communistically *all* today—a sort of diachronic "COLLABORATIVE LEARNING" *isnt* it ~~not~~ [sic] now.

Nor did modern fictionists neglect Maud. Ginnie WOLF's postpenultimate line in "To the Maudhouse" equivalates this: "*Yes, she thought, laying down her brush in extreme fatigue, I have had my maud.*" (Cf. elsewhere the more sanguine "*It is Maud, he said. For there she was.*") Even austere, statuoid Hank JAMIES was able to embrace {as it was} Maud. In "The Ambassades," his major character admonishes, "*Live all you can, it's a mistake not to .... If you haven't had your maud, what have you had?*" (Cf. however "Maud as the 'Distinguished Thing,' " unpublished foray.)

Then, Suzy SONNTAGE of course penned "*Notes on Maud*"... More, the chronicler of the Twenties, Gertie STIEN, said, "*You are all a maud generation*"... Most yet, the high priest of psychiatry, Siggie FROID, said, "*Vere Id vass, ya richt denn dere schall Maudie be!*"

But heck, probably the major telltail-index of Maudprevalence is the examination question still so frequently employed in formal EDUCATION, to-wit & viz.: "*O Coocou, shall I call the maud, / Or but a wandering vice? / State the alternatives preferred, / With reasons for your choice.*"

The Future Lies Ahead. And so, faced with such a prevailence, we can only [*Ed. Note: But at this precis poingt, the onley treue & extent of the Maudstudies archiv MS, was aburptly both corruptated, also and interrupp-romp ppppPPPP PPP PP P |||||*

BIBLIOGRAPHY

See (or at least be aware of) Sturgeon, Caroline, "Maud and the Jolly Green Giant: Some Impressive Differences," as well as Clark, Catherine (with Mrs. Karl), "Maud and Ceres: a Preliminary Overview," both in Pepperidge, Malcolm, ed., <u>Maud as Vegetable Goodness: A Re-Re-Appraisal</u>.

See the piece by _____ [= "Anon." [*pseud.*] [?], ?—*fl.*?—?] entitled "Heuristic Obscurantism in ____'s "To _____," by _____," reprinted in _____ and _____, eds., <u>A Critical Anthology of Paratexts: Vol. XXXVIII, Anonymous Dedications</u>, n.d., n.p., n.p. [plates tipped in; errors silently corrected; emphases subtracted]

Lointan, H., "Has-Been, or Never-Was? Reification and the 'Maud' Fallacy as Early Urbane Legend of Apotheosized Transmogrification"

Lawrence, Dave Herb, "Maud & Good Clean Fun: A Proposition—er, ah, A Proposal," in <u>Archives of Sociocultural Hygiene & Rectitude</u>, XXXVIII.

See Worsterman, Tedd, <u>A Bibliography of Bibliographies of Criticism of Criticism</u> (New York & the Jolly Corner, 1924).

FOOTNOTES

1. Gattling-Fenn, unpublished seminal notes, 1965.

2. Vanessa, <u>Personal Communication</u>, n.p., n.p., n.d., 1966.

3. Syzygy, unpublished telephone conversation [toll; dialed direct], 1967.

4. For <u>Maud and childrens' literature</u>, see Freddie Crewes, <u>The Maud Perplex</u>; Kanga, <u>Works</u>; Robin, C., <u>My Life in Art</u>, esp. "With Roo My Hart is Ladden" (here cf. Benn Franklin, "My Hart Leaps Up," in <u>Rarely Use Venery</u>), cf. also the critical breakthru "But Kanga Was In The Tango Too!" (New York & Pooh Corners, 1924-48), XXXVIII vols., which confirms that Chicken Delight has moved to Pooh Corners where he is living under the name of Col. Sanders and practicing apocalypsy ("The souffle is falling!") ("But nobody came"—E. Rigby) Comb it wet or dry? I been there before. *I dont hate it!* Many must have it. Runs; ah, runs. Yes, I said, isn't it pretty to think so. Ah, Maudie! Ah, mankind!

ADMINISTRATION:

CENTRAL EXECUTIVE CABINET BOARD:

Loweezy Bamboozle
Anathema Berserk
Bruno Blindsider
Raffish Bombast
Edsel Bunkum
Draconian Bungle
Parlous Contumely
Procrustean Downsizer
Plangent Fracas
Manifold Malinger
Arcane Miasma
Rotter Mountebank
Scrofulous Ordure
Fustian Persiflage
Renegade Reprobate
Imbroglio Rigmarole
Constance Rodomontade
Truculent Scofflaw
Prolix Sequelae
Cinderella Smithereen
Marathon Stonewaller

SECRETARIAL POND [& WOMANS' STUDIES]:

Ditzoide Bimbelle
Rubella Frightwig
Flotilla Furbelow
Pirhana Hustings
Virago Succubus
Vivienne Suttee
Veronica Vanilla

FACULTY SENATE:
SECURITY. PARKING. FOOTBALL TICKETS.

Alembic Androgen
Clarissa Bellwether
Quentin Budgerigar
Careen Career
Clarion Citation
Freon Fandango
Gordo Groatsworth
Loggerhead Klutz
Taller Te-Koop
Caesura Lacuna
Gregorio Lollapalooza
Miching Mallecho
Weltan Molder
Cirrus North
Hiatus Occulter

Chancellor Omicron
Sessile Otiose
Spud Kartoffelkopf
Dexter Southpaw
Sovereign Standard
Parca Triage
Loblolly Trogdolyte
Egregious Widdershins

BUSINESS OFFICE:
FINANCIAL AID.
DEPT. of ECONOMICS.

Quetzal Cruzeiro
Dinar Drachma
Rupee Escudo
Riyal Ringgit
Won Yen Yuan
Florin Zloty

STUDENT BODY:

Alabaster Offenbach
Alfalfa Offenbach
Bismuth Offenbach
Brackish Offenbach
Daiquiri Offenbach
Dashiki Offenbach
Dijon Offenbach
Dirndl Offenbach
Diuretic Offenbach
Feline Offenbach
Floruit Offenbach
Grotty Offenbach
Husband Offenbach
Juddering Offenbach
Lacewing Offenbach
Nacreous Offenbach
Omega Offenbach
Orator Offenbach
Patella Offenbach
Peoria Offenbach
Perineum Offenbach
Pismire Offenbach
Pistachio Offenbach
Sciatica Offenbach
Stannous Offenbach
Vibrissa Offenbach

ACADEMIC DEPARTMENTS:

HUMANITIES [I]:
HISTORY. SOCIOLOGY & ANTHROPOLOGY. CULTURAL STUDIES.

Jordan Chamberlain
Hegira Diaspora
Offa Dyke
Quotidian Hoipolloi
Sirocco Hypocaustum
Auquittuq Iqquiyiiutuq
Nanookie Itidarod
Jeremiad Intifada
Brittania Kink
Naer Het Leven
Kanaka Maoli
Coven Morlock
Eppur Si Muove
Calvin Narthex
Myanmar Nunavut
Matilda Outback
Pousada Parador
Nosey Parker
Thalassa Quinquireme
Maverick Roma
Costa Smerelda
Selpierre Struwwelpeter
Ultima Thule
Eustace Tilley
Vavfax Vadna
Wickiup Yurt

HUMANITIES [II]:
LANGUAGES. LITERATURES. WRITING & PUBLICATIONS.

Cedilla Ampersand
Mimsey Borogroves
Spiro Boustrophedon
Lorem Ipsem Dolor
Nemo Eponym
Maurice Escalier
Jolielaide Frileux
Wade Giles
Rubric Incarnadine
Cixous Irigaray
D. H. Limerence
Rondel Rondeau
Querty Shrdlu
Virgule Swash
Brunhilde Tilde
Prater Violet

NATURAL SCIENCES:
LABORATORIES.

Selena Areola
Kelvin Celsius
Fester Coprolite
Penumbra Darkfield
Selen Gegenschein
Laurasia Godwanas
Reaumur Millibar
Nanga Parbat

Tequila Petridisch
Nora Pin Ephrine
Hermes Quikksilver
Janus Syzygy
Therm Temblor
Aeolian Ventifact
Salvatore Volatile

FINE ARTS: MUSIC. THEATRE-DANCE. ENTERTAINMENT.

Oscar Bunbury
Truman Capon
Peter Doyle
Gaston Godin
Yuga Crewe
Fay Lambda
Demijohn Manikin
Veado Maricon
Sebastian Melmoth
Ashour Bachir Moktir
Abu Naous
Franklin Pangborn
Flikker Poot
Pickety Ruff

HEALTH. PHYSICAL EDUCATION. RECREATION. THERAPY-CLINIC: SEX-&-DRUG INFORMATION, COUNSELLING, & DISTRIBUTION CENTRE.

Rodney Codpiece
Epicene Ektomorff
Sappho Gravid
Bulimia Gross
Lolita Hoyden
Humbert Humbert
Jejeune Ileitis
Otto Onan
Edema Phthisis
Pinga Potenza
Phthiris Pubis
Septicemia Smegma
Fulgent Strabismus
Gideon Strumpet
Quincunx Quoin
Eliza Western-Blott
Manic Wordsalad

OTHER SERVICES:

CULINARY SCIENCE: CATERING SERVICES. CAFÉ-RESTAURANT.

Michelin Bibendum
Persimmon Fructivore
Marc Grappa
Selon Grosseur

Jeroboam Heeltapp
Iota Minim Lagniappe
Hijiki Jicami
Millefeuille Marzipan
Orotund Ortolan
Pancetta Porcini
Garum Potpourri
Smørrebrød Rijsttafel
Genever Rumbullion
Perry Slivovitz
Rufous Ullage

CRAFTS STUDIO & GIFT SHOP:

Vermeil Vark Argent
Japonica Chinoiserie
Majolica Faience
Velveteen Grunge
Diesel Patchouli
Smarmy Sleaze
Tawdry Tchotchke

O.U. INSTITUTE FOR CONTEMPORARY-CURRENT STUDIES: "DEPT. OF THE DIURNAL, NONCE, & QUOTIDIAN "

Raster Applet
Embella Ariakoad
Buppie Blaxxploitation
Latte Blushwein
Velveeta Bottleblonde
Dentata Buttflosser
Solenoid Channelsurfer
Gridlock Crowdkontroll
Sony Discwalker
Bimbo Dockmaartens
Dempster Dumpsterdiver
Posslq Equivoque
Simulacra Faux-Ersatz
Smiley Emoticon
Disney Eurotrash
Burletta Feminazi
Bilious Flavonoid
Hesperia Granneygear
Stasis Gridlock
Plexoid Grunge
Crixivan Indinivir
Viagra Jonessohn
Martial Krispikritter
Rictus Kurbcutt
Florio Malegaze
Pixel Motherboard
Hacker Netizen
Mercurey Nikeswoosh
Dumbodown NoBrainer
Myanmar Nunavut
Trixie Playdate
Wilfred Pokketprotekktor
Willard Policywonk

Epoxy Roadraige
Celera Rohlerblaide
Jason Rugrat
Medien Rhumbelstripp
Spindoktor Samizdat
Nostalgia Segue-Morph
Cellulite Schrinckwrapp
Porphyria Smartbombb
Kilroy Snafubar
Escarole Snizegaard
Harrida Sokkermohm
Virtuelle Sonarbyte
Addenda Spellchekker
Moshpit Stagediver
Panacea Stjohnswort
Scantron Subtext
Rumora Tabletent
Tsunami Tiramisu
Jihad Towelhedd
Ezekiel Tractorcade
Retro Treehugger
Fordist von Krupp
Factoid Waitron
Scratchkard Wannabe
Tuffluv Wheelklampp
Vanilla Whitebread
Jacuzzi Whitenoise
Gigo Wysiwyg
Durum Zerotolerance

O.U. EXTENSION DIVISION: OUTREACH. WORK-STUDY. TOURS.

DEPT. OF METEOROSOPHY: ASTROSCOPY, HELIOLOGY, SELENOGRAPHY, OROGRAPHY, PLUVIOMETRY.
 [Bill Wordsworth, Jack Keats, Perce Shelley, & Walt Whitman, *Co-Chairs*]

CABINET OF DIURNAL DEMOSCATOLOGY & CRESCIVE COPROLOGY.
 [Jack Swift, *Custodian*]

DEPT. OF MEGA-GASTRONOMY, HYPER-OENOLOGY, & AESTHETIC EPHEBIC MYOLOGY.
 [Jack Falstaff, Onan Kayam, Oskar Wild, *Coordinators*]

FIELD-STUDY & SEMESTER-ABROAD: "STUDY @ 'THE PHENOMENAL EDGE' "
 [Marc Polo & Hank James, *Tour Guides*]

--"The whole point of Camp is to dethrone the serious . . . . One can be serious about the frivolous, frivolous about the serious." [1]
--"To be camp is to present oneself as being committed to the marginal with a commitment greater than the marginal merits." [2]
-- "Unexpected value can be located in some obscure or exorbitant object." It may reflect "alienation, distance, and incongruity." [3]
--"Gosh, to deflektikate the hot-aire stuffed-shirty UpStanding Figures to a vary poo-poof with a meer butterfly pin-ion, & *then* to erektikait the Devaluated Occultated, oh the Quotidian-Diurnal-Mundane-Secular-Profane, up upon to the priviledged peddistil of Muse-umm regard: how Profitable really!, *if* you thing about it with the degree of Serious Regard which *is* appropriate here..." [4]

[1] SUSAN SONTAG, "NOTES ON CAMP"...   [2] ANOTHER COMMONTATER...   [3] JUDITH BUTLER...   [4] PFLOYD, KRONIKLES, XII, xii, 12...

➜ **Remaining on classroom blackboards at day's end were *important new words*** | 41 |
such as "allegory"; "archetype"; "apotheosis"; "litotes"; "tragic flaw"; "transmogrify":
and, "hegemony"; "conflate"; "problematize"; "deconstruct"; "valorize"; "empower"; ...

...Helpful vocabulary builders all, *but* to *one* veteran teacher, they *also* did seem,
as if they were, but, **inscriptions** made, only with *water-soluble* felt-tip pens, & merely onto the likes of
"the smooth porcelain surface of a LAVATORY FIXTURE soon to be *flushed clean*"....

[...Thus, the words did confirm to him, *"the Permanent Influences of Education"*....]

➜ **Late one Friday P.M., a faculty member stepped into a deserted classroom.**
For a pleasant instant, he felt as thought right there, he MIGHT be in ::
"a tin mine in *Bolivia*"... "a wine cellar in *Bavaria*"... "a mineral outcrop in *Australia*"...
"an eagle's-nest perch in *Patagonia*".... "on a freight train through *Turkey*"...
[...and at once he knew: "Thus can *Major Voyages & Odysseys, Start Right At Home*"....]

➜ **The students on their Library Tour,** standing stasis-static in a hemicircle,
exhibited faces which seemed [thought the teacher] *"as blank as a pond at sunrise"*....

A student studying on a stairwell, SKRREEEEEKING the textbook w/ a yellow felt-tip pen,
stared stunned-sour at the page [thought the teacher] *"as if it was a broken machine"*—
or, as if the student felt "fed-full-up," and *informational indigestion* had arrived, bringing
that terminally-repelled *disgustion*—just in time for the exam's Gorging-then-Purging....

➜ What is this excitement in the air?... the lively corridor discussions?!...
these marathon-lengthy meetings of the *Special CommitteeI* (pausing only for take-in food)!!...
the overall animated intellectual ferment in the Dept this week!?...
...*That's right.* This week, amongst the Department colleagues, equabitably & discretionary,
the Deptl. Merit Committee is divvidiyng up the year's Deptl. "merit pay"....

➜ **The University's maintenance workers outside,** pursue their tasks dressed up in ::
the suit-able apparatus of safety-conscious day-glo vests & yellow helmets—
and this is "all as it should be" as per Official Regulations.
[...But, trained in *complex response*, the teacher SHOULD find this "conformancy,"
both satisfying, *and also* satiric....]

And the University's trucks, when in reverse, are emitting ::
the *"DING-DING-DING"* of the safety backup warning bell, *but soddenly*--
because, by now *quite dulled with kaiked-on mud*, the bell rings more like *"DINK-INK-BINK"*...
[...But, trained in *symbolism*, the teacher COULD find this drama not only mechanically
"quotidian-diurnal-mundane," but also *musicalistically secularized "pro fanum"*....]

➜ **A REAL "SNOW DAY": the drifts so high, that school for once was cancelled.**
But in the empty corridors of the faculty offices, de-personnelled in the Wisconsin blizzard,
the one teacher who did trudge in, paused and [amid "elected SILENCE"] heard ::
.....an *impromptu symphony* of **ringing telephones !**
Phones *jingling* nearby here... *tringling* fainter over there... *burrring* elsewhere:
all composing a *trilling Chorus of Bells* inquiring "whether classes will be held?"...
[...Trained in *aesthetics,* the teacher WOULD *Appreciate this Drama of "Knowledge-Seeking"*....]

➜ The teacher saw that **he, was THE *SOLE-&-ONLY* FACULTY, who did attend**

(1) an open meeting on the **Campus Beautification** Project (though one other Prof. had left earlier) ...
(2) a session on **"homophobia"** at the Religious Center ...
(3) an evening of **"Black History Month" Performing Culture** in Roseman Auditorium ... *and,*
(4) a Thanksgiving **dinner for people of color** (and others welcome too) at a local church.

[...All this made him realize that he was thus properly advantaging of *the University's "Cultural Opportunities."* So he ended up properly feeling *"both Individuated, & Socialsticized too"*....]

➔ On the Dept. **COPIER**, another faculty member "professionally" duplicates
...a few copies of **personal verse**; some **personal tax returns**, the <u>summer</u> <u>travel</u> <u>itineraries</u>....

➔ The teacher **realizes that HE <u>CAN</u> *LEARN FROM HIS STUDENTS*,**
who <u>do</u> import to the classroom A "RICH INDIGENOUS CURRENT-TRADITIONAL CULTURE" after all:

(1) When the class was discussing <u>an advertisement</u> which claimed that its coffee was mountain-grown, a student was able to reply factually**: "All coffee is mountain-grown."**
[...The teacher thought that this represented *the <u>great</u> <u>resource</u> of* folkloric, street-wise, grass-roots, savvy, *<u>populist</u> <u>wisdom</u>*....]

(2) When the class was discussing <u>reasons for religion</u>, a student could volunteer confident & loud,
"To save your soul."   [...The teacher thought that this represented directly,
a confident—and probably unmistake-able—*<u>major</u> <u>tradition</u>*....]

(3) When—in the year **19<u>66</u>**—the class was discussing <u>poverty-and-progress in the Third World</u>,
a student did assure that **"Now, the Chinese people are acquiring household appliances."**
[...The teacher though how this represented a clarion crystallization of
the <u>American</u> <u>viewpoint</u> of "OPTIMISTIC MATERIALISTIC PROGRESS & DEMOCRATIC EQUITY"
—especially via its *curious timing* in re the **"GREAT PEOPLE'S CULTURAL REVOLUTION"** in History....]

➔ **In <u>1966</u>, both the teacher, and the new HUMANITIES BUILDING, started service...**

(1) He had at once voluntarily supplied <u>two beer boxes</u> to collect the <u>letters in the mail drop</u>.
{{**Then in <u>1996</u>,** *retiring*, **he percepted that <u>one</u> of the boxes had <u>remained in continuous service</u>....}}**
[.....This taught the teacher *at last the full truth* of **HARRY ADAM'S** famous *kleeshay* :
| **"Though[t] thankless[,] a teacher effect's infinity; you can never tell where his sic influence stop's"** ....]

(2) He had at once noticed the new **BUILDING** already sported a public telephone at the <u>north</u> end...
but at the <u>south</u> end, only the phone's booth—no actual phone installed yet.
{{ **Then** *in yet later years*, **he further remarked that not only {A} <u>no</u> phone ever** *was* **installed there**
[*"lacuna, caesura, hiatus"*] **but also that** *later on still, in his very mid-career*, **{B} the <u>booth itself</u> was removed!**}}
[.....This made the teacher think how *so few other* Staffmembers, alas,
had probably "garnered and then curated this valuable intelligence," namely, of ::
***"COMMUNICATION Commenced; but then, RINNGGINGG SILENCE Preserved"*.....]**

(3) In the male faculty lavatory, <u>the original toilet seat was</u> **<u>white</u>**...
{{ **Then** *in later years*, **the teacher remarked that the seat was inexplicably (?) chipped, hence**
{A} replaced, though by a <u>black</u> one, but *still later*, **{B} replaced by a <u>white</u> one once again...** }}
[...This made him realize how well he did provident *"<u>his'</u> <u>Institutions</u> <u>Locale</u> <u>History</u>"*....]

➔ **It became his PERSONAL TRADITION** (between 19<u>66</u> & 19<u>96</u>) **for the teacher to**
(1) <u>retain all</u> **paper clips** <u>from student papers</u>, (at once stapling the papers together, of course)....
and to compose what became <u>an elongated chain of clips</u> festooning the office wall...
[...the teacher was glad thus to contributate towards the Schools' **"*diversity*"** over the years....]

It also became his PERSONAL TRADITION (bet. 19<u>66</u> & 19<u>96</u>) **for the teacher to**

(2) <u>sign</u> the (final, official, end-of-semester) course **grade sheets, *<u>only</u>*** in — ***green*** ink....
[...the teacher was glad to *"<u>Add</u> <u>Value</u>"* & also *"<u>idiogenic</u> <u>micro-Tradition</u>"* to his environs....]

➔ **The teacher came to savor how the "Calls for Papers"** *fade[d] over time*...:
Posted on the "Deptl Bull. Board," & bathed in [up to almost] *12,150* Wisconsin *morgenlichts*...

--How the no-nonsense **fire-engine red** of the <u>*Wisconsin English Journal*</u>,
"has already" diluted to a light CHERRY PASTEL.....
--How the intense **cobalt blue** of <u>*College English*</u>'s appeal,
"is even now" relaxing to ROBIN'S-EGG OR CERULEAN.....
--And how from a more **assertive acid or dark-leaf green**, <u>*PMLA*</u>'s deadlines,
"will soon be" blanching out **to a** WATERCOLORISH LIME-YELLOW-GREEN.....

[...The teacher *could only appreciate*, how he, <u>especially</u>, appreciated this *"LOGOS-IKON INTEGRATION,"*
neigh even this *"chromatic transformation,"* as grist for *"<u>Evolution</u> & <u>Progress</u>"* ::
....*but*, he felt that <u>he</u> appreciated same, *much more then he could <u>ever</u>* ["even"?] <u>*express*</u> ....]

Department of Culinary Science & Gastrosophy

Caesura College of Offenbach University, Lacuna, West Dakota, U.S.A.

Our MOTTO:
"Whenever you need new, pathbreaking or groundfinding, Knowledge,
always look to the **DEPT. OF C. S & G.** to provide same *[even if nobody asked]*...
indeed, "WE *CATER* [TO] IT," & that is our MOTTO.

→ **Announcing a NEW COURSE Offering** ←

Le **New Course:**

"Normative Aesthetics of Cuisine: an Essentialist-Constructivist Integration"

Le Of-Course Description:

(1) Daringly, Norm-Breakingly, Deviantly Interdisciplinary, "INTEGRATION-&-SYNTHESIS."
[[**Or**, As In: "Watch You're Turf"...]]
We perspectively **synthesize the approaches** of the {a} historical-descriptive-empirical,
and the {b} aesthetic-hedonistic-belletristic, *and* the {c} normative-moral-ethical values-clarification,
and the {d} absolutist/essentialist-vs.-situational/existential stances.
{Then, we have <u>lunch</u>; "appropriately you will agree"}

**(2) Egregious, Maverick, Outlandish INCLUSION [I] of Suspect <u>Subject</u>-Matter
into the Sacred Canon of the Respectable, Institutional-ized, "Great Tradition."**
[[**Or**, As In: "Mr. *uppakrust* HARCOURT, & Mr. *mainline* BRACE,
alas meet the insinuating, upstart Mr. *immigrant* JOVANOVICH..."]]
We bravely introduce the *profane, quotidian, unrespectable, below-the-salt, hoi-polloi* subject of
"good cooking," into the ultramontane Towers of true academic validity
{where it surely does not belong but "*Wait* Just A Minuet There
It Must have been Good, They Ate Up All The Portions "}

(3) Rank Frank NORMATIVE-ETHICAL MORALIZING—and Absolutizing Too.
--We revulse against the dominant, proppressive "Today's Truth" of *relativism*, of *social
constructonionism*, in re "Taste In Food: What Is Good Food?"
--So, we replace (whoa, augment) this regrettable *existentialism* with *essentialism*. We [re-]establish (whoa,
remind of) "for-once-in-all," a true "I.I.I." (=innate inherent intrinsic) <u>criterion</u>, nay <u>standpoint</u>, neigh
<u>standard</u>, nee <u>benchmark</u>. The which can serve as "a pro legomena to kritikally e-valuating any futore
actual Reciept, let alone resultant consequent Dish"...

Namely, An **"INTEGRITY"** of Organic Form... Which **Correlates Contraries** , avoids "*Either-Or*"
for "*Both-And*" in a **Meta-Dua**listically Dished **Dialectic**: *Thesis*, Auntie-Thesis, & *Sin*-Thesis...

--We then re-turn this absolutism to its "Committed/Qualified" Relativist position arguing "true (whoa,
"defensible or debatable" or say rather "discussable-to be deliberated") only via its world-view assumptions
within its own system among many systems"
[[**Or**: yes indeed we done just *Re-Invented The Wheal*;
& "But About Time Wouldn't You Say..."]]

**(4) INCLUSION [II]: <u>Values</u>-Clarification! Irresponsible Con-Joining of 'DUTY & BEAUTY': of
the Moral-Ethical, & The Aesthetic, even the Hedonistic.** We import great gobbets & chunks of Shear
Purr <u>Pleasure</u> right into the so-<u>Serious</u> workshop of Higher Education. In the geopolitical @n@logy of
"interdisciplinary" endeavor, this is Colonizing with Corruption. ***And <u>overdo</u>, too!***

(5) INCLUSION [III]: <u>Thinking</u>-Skills! Astonishing Increscence to provide the "THINKING SKILL"
of Magnitude: Keystone, Linchpin, Standpoint, Summit. "Comprehensive Correlating."
[**Or**: how the *low-ly, disrespected, even grovelling sub*-subject of **"FOOD STUDIES,"**
can enter the Academy Dining Room to provide unexpected Sustenance, Nourishment
for the major Intellectual Feast-Fest itself & *you thought we were Below The Salt...*]

"COMPREHENSIVE CORRELATING" or 1. "identify <u>all</u> the vital variables," and 2. "for <u>each</u>,
balance their opposites."** So simple to say—so hard to know and do (until *now*, that is...)

LE MENU

Appetizers: Hors d'Oeuvres... Soups... Pasta...

Pasta : [1.] "PUTTANESCA alla NAPOLITANA":

(1) *Assemble* the ingredients for the <u>Sauce:</u> 1/3 C OLIVE OIL (the "extra-virgin, not bland, type)... 6-8 cloves GARLIC (fresh of course)... 1-1/2 lb TOMATOES (use good canned: best is diced, or else chopped or crushed or whole but you *crush, drain*)... 1/4 to 1/2 LB OLIVES (but *not* the blaand California type; use the <u>large black Greek</u> calamari, pitted or you pit, and *slice in half lengthwise*)... 2 oz. tin ANCHOVIES (or A. "paste"): *mash to a paste*... 3-4 T, heaping, of CAPERS (*must drain & rinse off the vinegar thoroughly!*)... 6 level (=3 heaping?) T TOMATO ***PASTE***... a big finger-pinch of RED PEPPER FLAKES (the kind in shakers in Italian restaurants; or else CAYENNE but very little of that!)... ***Optional:*** SALT and PEPPER.

(2) *Start cooking* 1 LB **PASTA.** (For this we like best the big butch tubular RIGATONI, or else next-best our pentad of five "ASSORTED SHAPES"—wagonwheels, bowties, shells, small cylinders, corkscrews.)

(3) *Cook* the <u>Sauce.</u> The GARLIC: *utterly pulverize* via press, then *brown* in the OIL ***to a nice tan, but not beyond***... Then add all the other ingredients: TOMATOES, OLIVES, CAPERS. Then add the (*mashed*) ANCHOVIES, TOMATO PASTE, CAPERS, PEPPERFLAKES—***but be sure*** to *fold in and distribute blended thoroughly throughout* for uniform flavor, especially the mashed anchovies and the hard-to-spread tomato paste!)

(4) *Drain* the cooked PASTA, and over it in a wide bowl, *slather* the above Sauce. ***Serve.***

||| **[Okay, we saw a dozen "Puttanesca" recipes. But *one and only one* includes the tomato—*paste.***
This, we decided, makes "half the difference" in elevating *this* recipe to its rich smooth perfection.
The other-half second secret here? <u>Brown</u> those garlics, all the way to light tan *but* not beyond.
This too augments the smooth richness, the rich smoothness, which crowns this dish. Is this not an instance of (1)
***competence, excellence-in-quality,* via (2) the *"committed relativism"* of standards specified clearly?]**

Pasta : [2.] "GARLIC-ANCHOVY Rigatoni":

(1) *Assemble* the <u>Sauce.</u> 1/4 C OLIVE OIL ... 10 (<u>ten</u>) cloves fresh garlic, minced ... 2-oz. tin ANCHOVIES, fork-mashed {<u>CAUTION:</u> *Discard* any **capers** if present!} ... BREAD CRUMBS, plain or seasoned.

(2) *Start cooking* up 1 lb RIGATONI (<u>or</u> assorted other shapes of **pasta**).

(3) *Make* the <u>Sauce.</u> In OLIVE OIL, *brown* GARLIC—to light tan only... *Reduce* heat... <u>Just before</u> the **pasta** is ready, *add* ANCHOVIES—just to heat up, ***not*** to cook... *Add* BREAD CRUMBS <u>judiciously</u>: enough to give sauce "some body to cling to," <u>but</u> ***not*** so much as to "dry it up into clumps."

(4) *Toss* sauce with the cooked RIGATONI-or-ASSORTED **pasta.** ***Serve.***

{<u>CAUTION:</u> *<u>No</u>* cheese, please, at least not the first time}

||| **[= Classic amalgam of textures, tastes.....]**

Pasta : [3.] "GOULASH"

(1) *Assemble* the <u>Sauce:</u> 1 t PAPRIKA ... 2 t crushed MARJORAM ... 2 t grated LEMON ZEST ... 1 t crushed CARAWAY SEEDS ... 2 smashed cloves GARLIC ... 1/2 t SALT.

(2) *Cook* the <u>Sauce.</u> Cook garlic gently, until tan. *Add* other ingredients; *Correct* seasoning-balance.

(3) *Serve*, over 1 lb. PASTA of assorted shapes.

{<u>OPTION:</u> of course, can add **BEEF** pieces, ideally cooked or finished in the cooking **Sauce** itself, plus canned drained **TOMATOES** but ***beware*** "Tomato Tsunami" or overwhelming by redness...}

||| **[More <u>diverse</u> seasonings *here*, than in *most* "GOULASH," so you get energetic "plural notes."**
Think sour-bitter f/ Chablis, Bartok, Cubism... <u>CAUTION:</u> seasoning-balance is *tricky* the first time...]

Pasta : [4.] SHRIMP with Cumin:

(1) *Start cooking* up 1 lb. of assorted-shape PASTA.

(2) *Unfreeze* already-cooked medium SHRIMP—*Bisect* each in half lengthwise.

(3) *Assemble* the <u>Sauce</u>. <u>Half</u> OLIVE OIL, <u>half</u> BUTTER ... CHICKEN BOULLION CUBE... 5 GARLIC cloves, *Pulverized* ... {**OPTION:** 2-3 SHALLOTS, thinly-*sliced*} ... LEMON JUICE (start with 1/2 t at most) ... LEMON ZEST (4-12 long strips) ... SESAME SEEDS {Semi-**OPTIONAL**} ... CHIVES, *snipped* into half-inch lengths {**OR:** SCALLIONS/GREEN ONIONS}... *powdered* CUMIN (start with 1/2 t at *most*).....

(4) *Cook* the <u>Sauce</u>. *Brown* **garlic** <u>but</u> only to "light tan," same for the **shallots** if used ... *Add* the **other** ingredients {**CAUTION:** add both the **chives,** and also the **shrimp,** only at the very <u>end</u>—just heat up the **shrimp,** do <u>not</u> cook, or they will shrivel up} ...

Serve over the **pasta.**

||| [= A great rescue of shrimp from overpowering inundation by *Tomato* which tends to dominate.

Even so, tune finely: too much lemon or chives will themselves overpower, but too little will bland the taste out.]

Pasta : [5.] "ANTI-PASTO Pasta":

(1) *Start cooking up* 1 lb. of assorted-shape PASTA.

(2) *Make* <u>Vinaigrette Sauce</u>. 3 T OLIVE OIL (extra-virgin recommended)... 1 T RED WINE VINEGAR, SALT, PEPPER... 3-4 cloves GARLIC *crushed*... OREGANO crumbled, ½ t to start...

(3) *Assemble* the <u>Ingredients</u>. *Mix together,* 1/2 CUP *shredded* MOZZARELLA CHEESE... 1/2 CUP *diced* PEPPPERONI... 1 small can ANCHOVY fillets, *choppped*... 1/4 CUP BLACK OLIVES *pittted & choppped*...

(4) *Drain* PASTA... *Add* half the <u>Sauce</u>... *Tosss* well... *Add* the <u>Ingredients</u> and over them the remaining Sauce... *Tosss* well... *Serve* warm or at room temperature...

||| [= Elegantly-balanced flavors. *Re*-heats well, just add some more new Vinaigrette *after* re-heating.]

Entrees:

CHICKEN THIGHS:

Chicken Thighs [1.] "PARFUM DE PROVENCE"

(1) *Make* the "<u>Rub</u>": *Cream* equal parts OIL and BUTTER ... add 1 CHICKEN-FLAVOR CUBE, pulverized ... LEMON JUICE ... SALT ... PEPPER ... equal flavor-parts of crumbled TARRAGON and crushed ROSEMARY ... GARLIC POWDER ... ONION POWDER ... THYME (caution: <u>scant</u> amount only!)....

(2) *Pry up* the **chicken** <u>skin</u> ... *Drench* **skin** <u>and</u> **meat** with extra LEMON JUICE ... Then, *Deposit* the "**Rub**" on the **meat,** top <u>and</u> underside. *Replace* skin and *Smear* remaining **Rub** on <u>top</u> of **skin** too.

(3) *Bake* uncovered in 325 OVEN until done. *Serve.*

||| [= Redolent high-note duet of rosemary and tarragon with supporting cast of onion, garlic, thyme.

The secret—*little-known, but surely basic*—is not only the ingredients, but the inserting of them <u>under</u> the skin, directly <u>onto</u> the meat, where (naturally) they can add more flavor directly...]

Chicken Thighs [2.] "MADISON"

Combine 3 T BROWN SUGAR, 2 t PREPARED MUSTARD, 1 T ORANGE JUICE. *Slather* on, <u>and</u> underneath, the skin. *Bake,* skin-side up, uncovered. *Serve.*

||| [= Unlike most chicken recipes, this retains the integrity of the flavor of the meat itself shining through.]

Chicken Thighs [3.] "MARYLAND"

Add LEMON JUICE ... SALT ... SUGAR to skin <u>and</u> to meat underneath. ("*generous*" amount of *equal* parts of S. and S.) *Bake,* skin-side up, uncovered. *Serve.*

||| [= Lively and interesting, and almost "complex," for so few-and-easy number of ingredients.]

Chicken Thighs [4.] "ORIENTAL"

(1) *Remove* <u>skin</u> from 4 **thighs.**

(2) *Marinate* **thighs** 24 hours (or less) in a **marinade** of: 1/4 C <u>SOY SAUCE</u> ... 1/4 C DRY <u>SHERRY</u> ... 1 T <u>SESAME OIL</u> ... 5 cloves <u>GARLIC</u>, *smashed* ... 1 / 2 t fresh <u>GINGER</u>, *grated.*

(3) *Drain* the **thighs** from the **marinade.**

(4) *Bake,* <u>uncovered</u>, in a 300 OVEN until done. *Serve.*

||| [= Fine-tune it, and the ingredients ride together, discernible <u>and</u> amalgammed....]

Ch. Thighs [5.] "GERTRUDE STEIN'S 'Polish Southern Fried & Roasted Chicken' "

(1) *On* the **CHICKEN** skin, but also underneath on the meat itself, *Add* LEMON JUICE ... pinch ground THYME ... pinches ONION powder and GARLIC powder ... SALT & PEPPER.

(2) Then, *Take* **FLOUR**, *add* to it SALT; PEPPER; more ONION powder; more GARLIC powder; *Mix* up. *Coat* **thighs** in the mix.

(3) *Dip* **thighs** in **BEATEN EGG**.   {OPTION: can *Add* some more **onion, garlic** powder to **egg** }

(4) *Roll* **thighs** in **BREAD CRUMBS**.

(5) *Brown* **thighs** carefully in SKILLET.

(6) *Place* **thighs** in open oven PAN, and *Slather* dollop of **SOUR CREAM** on top of each **thigh**. {OPTION: *Fold* some chopped SCALLIONS, white parts, into the S.C. first.} *Bake* **thighs** uncovered 400 for 15 mins, then 300 until done. ***Serve.***

||| [= Gentle but enriched, and nicely moist. Her original did *not* include our Lemon, Thyme, Onion, Garlic.]

GREEK CHICKEN: "Kates Rignanti" For one entire *cut-up* CHICKEN. {OPTION: use all WHITE/BREAST MEAT—takes the flavors better.}

(1) *Rub* over and under the skin: 1/3 C OLIVE OIL ... 1/3 C fresh LEMON JUICE ... 1 t SALT. **(2)** *Brown* uncovered, skin side up, in 350 OVEN for 10 minutes.

(3) Meanwhile, in SAUCEPAN, *heat up* a **sauce** of 1/8 lb BUTTER ... 2-4 T crumbled OREGANO ... and 2-3 C canned TOMATOES (*drained, cut-up*).

(4) *Pour* this **sauce** over the chicken and *bake*, uncovered, at 300 until done. ***Serve,*** perhaps with **RICE**, otherwise with **POTATOES**, mashed or boiled or baked.

||| [= Classically-clean from any clutter. It sings "Mediterranean port-town waterfront café..."

And, "*even better* when *re-heated*"; make a day ahead...]

HAMBURGER "Bitoque"

(1) *Mix* minced ONION into GROUND BEEF patties.....

(2) *Fry* in PAN; *Remove*..... Then, *Drain* grease but *retain* any beef bits.....

(3) To PAN, *add* 8 oz. SOUR CREAM and 10-oz. can BEEF BOUILLON or CONSOMME ..... Gently *reduce* down to half, and *use* as **gravy/sauce** for the BEEF {with POTATOES?} ..... ***Serve.***

||| [= Easy to get classic "brown sauce" effect—both smooth, and deep. "Who Knew"? Who even *suspected*??]

BEEF, oven-baked: Two Sauces [Use cuts like short ribs, chuck steak, etc.]

[1] "TEX-MEX"

(1) *Mix* together: 1 large sweet ONION—*diced* thin ... 1/2 C KETCHUP ... 1/2 C WHITE VINEGAR ... 1 T CHILI POWDER ... 2 t PAPRIKA ... 1/2 t SALT.

(2) *Saute-brown* the **beef** pieces briefly in SKILLET... Then, *Add* **beef** to the **Sauce** .....

(3) *Bake*, uncovered, in 325 oven until tender: up to 1–1/2 hours ..... ***Serve.***

||| [= B-B-Q type beef recipes are a dime-a-dozen; does this one balance complexity better?]

[2] "SOLAR DEVILLED"

(1) *Marinate* beef 24 hours in a **mix** of: 2 T PREPARED MUSTARD ... 3 T LEMON JUICE ... 1/2 t SALT ... 1 t CHILI POWDER ... 1/2 t SUGAR ... 4 cloves GARLIC smashed ... 1/2 C WHITE ONION finely chopped – all in 1/4 C "OIL" plus 1/3 C STOCK or WATER.

(2) *Drain* the beef ... *Bake* uncovered 10 minutes in 425 oven ... then *Re-add* **marinade** and *Cover* ... *Bake* 325 until tender (up to 1–1/2 hours). *Uncover* the last 15 minutes. ***Serve.***

||| [= Superior to many "devilled" recipes for the rich variety plus harmony of the flavor-mix.]

PORK STEAKS "Julia Child"

On the meat, *Rub In* ground THYME and GARLIC powder, and *Drizzle on* LEMON JUICE. *Broil*, or *gently Fry*, or *Bake*. ***Serve.***

{OPTION: if pan-frying, cook without adding seasonings, turn over, add seasonings to the now-cooked top side—this prevents burning the seasonings.}

||| [= Harmonious flavor-blend, both separate and integrated. Does *not* work this well on *other* cuts of pork....]

RED SNAPPER   **(1)** *Fry* the FISH gently in half OIL, half BUTTER. *Remove*. *Stir* to loosen the residue. **(2)** *Stir in* 3 T DRY SHERRY, then 1 T PARSLEY and 1 t DILL WEED and 1 t TARRAGON. *Stir in* 2 TOMATOES, *peeled and eighthed*. **(3)** *Shove* to side of pan ... *Return* SNAPPER to pan ... *Combine* all. **Serve.**

||| [One of the *few* dishes we feel is better—or alternatively as good as—"just plain fresh fish expertly cooked." [E.g., what SALMON is better than simply broiled, with Lemon & Dill?] Its "integrity" lets the ingredients simultaneously voice their separate flavors, and also sing harmoniously with each other *and* with the fish...]

VEAL KIDNEYS: **(1)** *Cut* 1-2 KIDNEYS into small-bite sizes. *Rinse* in water. *Coat* in <u>FLOUR</u>.
(2) *Saute* in BUTTER and/or OIL; *Add* more when needed.
(3) When almost cooked, *Stir in*: approx. 1 T <u>MUSTARD</u> (regular <u>and</u>/or Dijon) ... 2 t LEMON JUICE ... and approx. 1/4 t <u>WORCHESTERSHIRE SAUCE</u>. *Correct* the balance. *Serve.*

   ||| [= Ingredients "ride well" together, two ways. With *each other,* a classic trio. Then with the strong *meat* too.]

Vegetables, and Salads:

"Sicilian" GARNISH for VEGETABLES:

(1) *Acquire* the **VEGETABLES**: for this, we like <u>CAULIFLOWER</u>, <u>BROCCOLI</u>, <u>CARROTS</u>, and RED <u>PEPPERS</u>, fresh, or frozen.
(2) *Cook* the vegetables (steamed; microwaved) in time to pour over them the following sauce:
(3) *Prepare* the **SAUCE** ingredients... *Slice* one large RED <u>ONION</u> into 3/4-" squares... *Open* a 2-oz tin of <u>ANCHOVIES</u>—*Chop* them finely or even *Mash* (discard any capers in tin)... From an <u>ORANGE</u>, *Peel* about 4-6 inches of the ZEST (outer skin, avoid white)... *Prepare* 1/4-C or less of <u>OLIVES</u>: GREEN & BLACK... *Chop, Mince, Press,* or *Smash* 3-4 cloves of <u>GARLIC</u>...
(4) *Cook* the **SAUCE**... *Saute* ONION in 1/4-C <u>OLIVE OIL</u> in pan... Add GARLIC and *Cook*... Add in the anchovies, orange zest, olives and Heat and Mix...
(5) *Serve. Pour* **SAUCE** over **VEGETABLES**. Over all, *Sprinkle* a dusting of grated <u>CHEESE</u>, Parmesan and/or Romano.

   ||| [= Both riotously energetic with, but also rigorously subservient to, the vegetables—
perhaps a bit unexpectedly... Reheated, loses less flavor than you might suspect.]

BRUSSELS SPROUTS a la the "Kitschen Sink"

(1) Take **BRUSSELS SPROUTS**: enough for desired servings. *Cook* them [steam or microwave seems best]. Do *not* overcook. Then, *cut* in half, lengthwise. Then, *smootsch-&-slather* them around in the **sauce** below which you have made just beforehand.

(2) *Make* the **sauce.** In a saucepan, *assemble* adroitly (balancing the contraries of Creativity-&-Control) **which, and how much,** of the following ingredients you find **you personally prefer:**
--<u>MARGARINE</u> (possibly use butter, or not?)
--<u>BEEF CUBE</u> or other beef flavoring, non-salt/fat if available.
--<u>LEMON JUICE</u> (always real lemon, *never* the ersatz bottled types).
--<u>ONION</u>. White or red. Grated finely.
--DRY <u>MUSTARD</u>.
--<u>SESAME</u> SEEDS. A "generous amount" seems okay.
--GRATED <u>CHEESE</u>. (I used a blend of Parmesan and Romano)
--<u>BREAD KRUMBS</u>. (Plain, or Italinated)
Serve.

   ||| [Okay, Full Disclosure. I fabricated up this recipe by just combining every separate ingredient from all the Brussels Sprouts recipes from Rombauer's <u>The Joy Of Cooking</u>. Plagiarism? No, I diskloased. Sloppiness? No, I found this approach fine-tunes the contraries "both open and directed, both loose and focussed," to groom these healthy but assertive little cabbages. ...what's that you say? Not enough guidance? Saaay, didn't you learn *how to confront complexity with conceptual competence* when you were in *SCHOOL*, ehh??...] |||

GREEN BEANS "Orientational "

(1) Take 1 lb or so fresh GREEN BEANS. *Cut* into two-inch sizes. *Cook* via steaming or microwaving (or boiling, *but* if you boil, use the "Method": VAST amounts of VERY-salted ROLLING-boil water, *plunge* BEANS in, *cook, remove and shock* in VERY-cold water). Cook *just enough but not too much* (too little, they're still tuf-&-bitter; too much, they're limped out wan.)

(2) Then simply *pour over* the *drained* BEANS, the following **sauce** from stovetop saucepan:
Heat OLIVE OIL... *Brown* GARLIC: 4-8 cloves, *pressed* in a garlic press... Add SESAME SEEDS to *brown* them too, gently... Add good-quality CHICKEN "SEASONING/SOUP BASE"—can semi-brown, tho ***don't*** burn... Add LEMON JUICE plus also LEMON ZEST, the yellow *not* white rind scraped from a whole lemon... Add SOY SAUCE, good brand... Add BREAD CRUMBS, enough to embody the sauce but ***not*** to drink it all up dry... And ***just right before serving***, add SESAME *OIL*!

||| [**Okay, so "oh we all already know all-about this Chinese-type recipe for green beans," okay, okay...**
Or might that response be a case of the <u>fallacy</u> of "Knowing-about, vs. Truer Knowing"? *Yup...*
For here, {1} Lemon and Soysauce twinstar to acrobatically balance each other unusually well.
Plus {2} Gently-tanned garlic plus "chicken base" adds another rich note.
Then {3}, the perfuming with fragrant sesame oil just at the end, caps things off—or rather, begins it all...] |||

THREE-BEAN SALAD f/ "Aunt Marjorie"

(1) *Prepare* the **BEANS**. --*Open* 1 can <u>each</u>, GREEN BEANS ... yellow WAX BEANS ... dark red KIDNEY BEANS. --*Drain* the beans; and also *rinse* the **kidney** beans! --Then, <u>*Dry out very thoroughly*</u> the **beans**. (This means even "spread one layer thin on thick towel," and then "dry in sunshine or 150-degree oven"!)
(2) *Prepare* the **VEGETABLES**. *Chop* 1 C <u>CELERY</u> ... *Chop* 1/2 C <u>each</u> GREEN and RED <u>PEPPER</u> ... *Drain* 1/4 C RED <u>PIMENTIO</u> ... *Thin-slice* 1 C RED <u>ONIONS</u>.
(4) *Prepare* the **DRESSING:** --In a SAUCEPAN, *Combine* 2 parts <u>OIL</u> ... 1 part WHITE <u>VINEGAR</u> ... 1 part WHITE <u>SUGAR</u> (= 12 oz., 12 oz., 6 oz.). --*Stir* ... then *Bring* just to a *boil* ... but then *Cool* <u>first</u> ... and *then*, *Mix Into* the **ingredients** (in a <u>NON</u>-ALUMINUM BOWL).
(5) *Refrigerate*, preferably 24 hours to blend flavors. (*Stir* intermittently to distribute dressing.) ***Serve***.

||| [**= The best "3hree-Been Salat," its twin secrets being to dry the beans <u>thoroughly</u>, plus to <u>boil</u> the dressing.**]

Pasta Salad: CUCUMBER-DILL "*Grecian Glade*"

(1) --*Cook up* 6 C PASTA. [We use "medium shells"; use any shapes which hold, "grip" the sauce.]
--*Dry out* PASTA but ***very well***: *Shake* in colander, but then *also* *Spread* on soft towel and *Roll*, even *Place* in sunshine or 150 oven!
(2) --*Prepare* **<u>ingredients</u>:** 3 <u>CUCUMBERS</u>: *Peel* (or "half-peel"), then *Cut* into 3 / 4 " bite-size pieces. 4 <u>SCALLIONS</u>: *Chop* them into 1 / 8 " rounds , using white not green parts.
(3) --*Prepare* the **sauce:** *Fold* together 1 C <u>MAYONNAISE</u> ... 1 C <u>SOUR CREAM</u> ... 5 T <u>LEMON JUICE</u> ... 6 T <u>DILL WEED</u> (not "seed") (we use dried not fresh) ... 1 T <u>SALT</u>.
(4) --*Assemble*. <u>First</u>, *Fold* the **sauce** into the dried **pasta** thoroughly. <u>Then</u>, *Fold* the **cukes** and the **scallions** into the sauced **pasta**. ***Serve***.
{<u>CAUTION</u>: to insure <u>sparky, not weak, flavor</u>, (1) be <u>sure</u> to *Dry* that water out of the **pasta**, and (2) *Correct* the **sauce** and add enough **lemon** and **dill** to make it "<u>more</u> sharp than not"}]

||| [**= *Complexly-flavored* enough to satisfy repeatedly:**
First, the pasta and creams feel soft-smooth ... then the cucumbers comment more crunchily ...
then the lemonspeaks out louder ... then the dill bridges and blends it all.....]

BLEU CHEESE SALAD DRESSING

(1) *Assemble* 1 pint CORN OIL ... 1/4 C fresh LEMON JUICE ... 1 / 4 C RED WINE VINEGAR ... golfball-sized BLEU/ROQUEFORT CHEESE ... 3-4 cloves *smashed* GARLIC ... 2-3 t *ground* MARJORAM ... 1 t *crumbled* OREGANO ... 1 / 4 t *ground* THYME....
(2) In a BLENDOR, *add* 1/3 of the OIL, then *blend in* everything **else** (the CHEESE last.)

||| [**= *Remarkable* on green salads (less so on mixed-vegetable salads)...**
***"Probably-Likely*," the Secret is the <u>lemon</u> accent to the red-wine vinegar.**
***"Quite Possibly*," equally-good store-bottled dressings do exist.**
"*Surely-Certainly*," we've never found them...]

Desserts:

AUTUMN BAKE

(1) *Peel* and *Slice* 4 medium APPLES, and/or PEACHES.
(2) *Sprinkle* 6 T DARK BROWN SUGAR over the fruit. *Let Stand* 10 minutes.
(3) Mix 1/2 C "BISQUICK" (or flour?) and 1/4 t CINNAMON. *Tosss* the **fruit** in this **mix**.
(4) *Deposit* in greased PAN. *Bake* 30 minutes or so in pre-heated 425-degree OVEN.
(5) ***Serve***. warm, with CREAM to top off all.

||| [**= More flavor-savor for the effort. Classic simplicity-plus-richness...]**

RECIPES RATIONALE:

When sedulously titrated, darkfielded, & tried-out, our favorite cooking turns out to possess a rare **"integrity"** or **harmonious balance**.

...A "co-starring" of Ingredients; Seasonings; and Technique...

["Definite in personality; maybe even enthusiastic—but neither intrusive nor overbalancing..." -- Fanshawe, Diktats, XII, xii, *passim*]

--More specifically, this **integrity** consists of the following traits, or **"ARTIKLES OF FAITH."** Which, *Au'Jourd'Hui* thus, *Le Chef* can confidently *Vous Proposer* as follows:

1. "Few recipes are as good as fresh ingredients cooked skillfully with no fancy seasonings, period."

[A **CHICKEN** ROASTED *PERFECTLY*, WITH *ONLY* SALT & LEMON ADDED... **SALMON**, BROILED WITH *ONLY* LEMON & DILL...]

2. "All-too-frequent *inferior* recipes sans "integrity" are of these types:"

2-A. The "EVENTUAL BLAH." You put the stuff together. But no, it doesn't really taste like anything special after all—no real cumulative flavor, or just a blah flavor.

[*TOO MANY TO CITE...*]

2-B. The "CO$T-BENEFIT RATIO COLLAPSE." The complex recipe takes a lot of *time-and-effort*, plus perhaps *hard-to-locate* (or even *co$tly*) ingredients. So you try it, anticipating quality. But whoa, the results turn out to be not worth the effort and expen$e.

[ALSO, *TOO DISAPPOINTING TO REMEMBER*]

2-C. The "FOOD EXPLOITED AS SAUCE-PLATFORM." The recipe somehow divorces food and seasoning, uses the one to "launch" (not complement) the other

[A good BEEFSTEAK semi-spoiled, truth-be-told *Utterly Ruinated*, by a loud MUSTARD sauce]

2-D. The "DISASTER OF THE DUBIOUS." The recipe proposes an intriguing mix of *diverse* ingredients *not* usually combined. And you think: "Hmmm, how *can* those different, strange ingredients actually blend and work together harmoniously?" You try it to find out. But alas, you find out that indeed, these strange ingredients cannot cooperate!

["TUNA, WITH *GINGER*, IN A *RASPBERRY* VINAIGRETTE"— actually, *noo*....]

2-E. The **"JUST PLAIN WRONGHEADED"** or **"FALSE SOUR NOTES."** This is trickier to define; personal taste intrudes. But these recipes lack **"integrity"** as defined here. The food and the seasonings clash, mis-mate, sing off-key.

Alas, such cacophonies are widespread, even in "good" restaurants, "good" cookbooks. *As In:*

(1) LAMB WITH HEAVY BORDELAISE SAUCE (try au naturel, or Garlic-Rosemary-Lemon).

(2) ROAST DUCK WITH AN ORANGE SAUCE but the sweet-sour balance "jars" with the meat.

(3) COQ AU VIN: CHICKEN IN WINE—BUT WHY ALWAYS RED WINE? White may be also (or even more) harmoniously-compatible.

(4) TOMATO SLATHERED ALL OVER *EVERYTHING*, including delicate SHRIMP.....

3. "In contrast, *valid* recipes possessing this desirable "integrity" include:"

3-A. #1 above [That PERFECTLY-ROASTED CHICKEN...] but also & esp.

3-B. [*] Those with **"integrity."** *Which we define as follows*:

1. The food and the seasonings marvellously mate or twinstar with, complement, each other....

a. At times seasonings *respectfully enrich* food:

[The PROVENCAL CHICKEN'S flavor is itself enhanced, not dominated by, ROSEMARY-AND-TARRAGON – not to mention the GREEK'S TOMATO/OLIVE OIL/LEMON/OREGANO/BUTTER...]

b. At other times, the two *balance perfectly*:

[CHICKEN plus BROWN SUGAR/MUSTARD/ORANGE JUICE somehow become "one"]

2. The seasonings themselves, may

a. *remain distinct* and work as a series of solo voices singing in serial sequence:

[You can hear, in turn, THE MUSTARD *AND* THE LEMON *AND* THE WORCHESTERSHIRE SAUCE, pop up, then sink down, then come round again, then.....]

b. Or they may *blend together* into a "gestalt" where the individual notes dissolve into a new harmony of the whole:

[In SHRIMP WITH CUMIN, the spice itself "disappears," and merely enriches subtly, self-effacingly]

___ __ === == --- -- ~~~~ ~~~ ~~~ ~~ ~^^^^^*

"**INTEGRITY**": a type of <u>supple</u> **balance** of things—**harmonious** but not static, <u>dynamic but not disarrayed</u>...

Does it involve the major issue of "meta-dualistic contrary-correlation" or the satisfactory handling of opposites? [Whether *either* (1) "mechanical balancing," *or* (2) "organic integration"—oops, <u>*or*</u> a better re-solution of *those* two (1←→2) endpoints them*selves*?]

And would that exist *not* only in

[1] CUISINE, but even *more* in

[2] **ART**, both VISUAL, and LITERARY-POETIC, let alone in actual...

[3] **HUMAN BEHAVIOR**, as in...

[3a] "CIVIL DISCOURSE" in a person's <u>writings</u>, or even in...

[3b] "RESPONSIBLE JUDICIOUSNESS" in his/her actual moral-ethical <u>behavior</u>?

[But is such **integrity** less frequent than is desirable?]

THE OVERALL RATIONALE. "Dualistic dichotomies" or "either-or" stances vs. ..... a "both-and" Dialectic of thesis-antithesis-synthesis?

[A subpart of <u>the summit-strategy</u> for "**Good Thinking**" or competently confronting complexities conceptually, or thinking well about tough stuff: "**COMPREHENSIVE CORRELATING**," namely first perceive *all* elements-to-consider (all variable-issues, aspects, etc.), <u>and then for *each* element, balance a "both-and" inclusive stance not either-or partial</u>.]

[1.] <u>Brief View: "In the Nutshell"</u>:

1. **COMPREHENSIVE: First, identify all the variables-to-consider which are crucial-to-confront for success at the task-goal at hand.** [Scan the Big Picture to synoptically monitor "all" elements, because *partiality is pernicious*! Avoid unAwarenesses in Knowing (oversights, hence omissions, simplifications, misconceptions), also inAbilities in doing—the Botch or Bungle: avoid Sins both of Omission and of Commission thus. Seek "Command" = whether win or lose, you miss no chances, cover all bases,

avoid all pitfalls, are not deluded, do all that savvy and sweat can do to succeed!]

2. **CORRELATING: Then, first, for each vital-or-valuable variable-issue, establish its <u>end-points</u> A and Z, and its <u>continuum</u> within or between, A-to-Z.**
Second, locate "<u>the best stance</u>" to take: whether (A) either-or A or Z, or (B) "to what extent more *toward* A and/or more *toward* Z, for this specific task-goal, and why so?"

[2.] <u>Full View: "The Works," Soup-to-Nuts</u>:

(1) Identify all the vital and valuable Variable-Issues of the subject-at-hand, which you must adequately confront to succeed in the current task-goal.

(2) For each vital V-I, identify (a) its "A" *and* "Z" end-points or apparently contradictory polar opposites. And also its (b) Conceptual Continuum (= the A *to* Z spectrum, range, sliding scale of all possibilities, points, stations).

<u>Caution</u>: one or both end-point purist or extreme stances too often may be unstated; overlooked; automatically rejected beforehand; taboo to consider; hence hard to even identify; and the like.

(3) Estimate concerning the A and Z polarities:
--Difference: are the two fairly similar === *or* actually very different, dissonant, alien to each other, conflicting, hence difficult to correlate perhaps?
--And, Value: are *both* of the two polarities *each* important, hence meriting correlation?
--Also, Lateral Thrust: to what extent should it be *not* just "some of each," *but* "as much as possible, of both"—even if they contradict each other?

(EXAMPLE: (1) a person in a discussion: being as Fervent enthusiastic as possible, *but also* as Fairminded judicious as possible.
(2) an introduction to a subject being as Complete-Comprehensive as possible (a synoptically-scanning overview-orientation "all in small"), *but also* as Concrete-detailed, *plus also* as Clear not Clotted, as possible).

<u>Caution</u>: are some polarities, simply irreconcilable?

➔ **Higher Education.** ["elementary logic" forbids us "to do contradictory things simultaneously," but education was to solve diverse problems at once "and in ways that posed no threats of mutual inconsistency":]
"It is not possible simultaneously to abandon 'useless' subjects and still promote a disinterested passion for classical learning. It is not possible to insist that researchers should spend all their time in the laboratory or the library and yet teach longer hours than high school teachers do. It is not possible to discipline students so that they become respectable, polite, and unthreatening middle-class adults while respecting their rights to absolute freedom of speech."
[-- Alan Ryan, <u>Is Higher Education A Fraud?</u>]

➔ **Engineering.** "What do you want for your product? Good quality? Inexpensive? Quick to get to the market? Good, cheap, quick: pick any two."
  [-- "old engineer's saying"]

➔ **Role-Conflict.** [**Multitudinous examples exist; a minor but adequate one is the alleged role-prescription of alleged <u>gay or lesbian</u> persons in America:**]
[Americans are told to think outside the box, avoid [group-] profiling, accept diversity. But gays/lesbians are told to stay in the box of the closet, do not deviate.]   [-- Bruce Vilanich]

➔ **Proverbial wisdom.** ➔"Look before you leap"...
  but also "One who hesitates is lost"

(4) Respond. (4a) ["*Either-Or*"] Do you (A) reject or ridicule or ignore or dismiss or overlook (*or judiciously legitimately appropriately downplay!*) Point A (or Z) and champion, prefer, defend, valorize Point Z (or A)?
(4b) ["*Both-And*"] Or do you seek to correlate the two extremes? (A) mechanically in additive-combinatory fashion? (Perhaps cyclical-alternating?) (B) or organically in some sort of integration?

(5) Then decide your final position (stand, stance for best task-goal success) on the continuum between A or Z. (=A itself? Y? X? median M? other, even perhaps at times an inclusive blending-melding "A thru to Z"?)
[*Rule-of-Thumb*: ask, "how much if any of A should be within Z and vice versa? E.g., None at all? Oh say 37%? Exactly 50/50? Etc. ..."]

(6) To aid in this fine-tuning, beware and avoid "Near Enemies." (= "A vice quite near to a virtue and liable to be mistaken for the virtue")

[➔In <u>the business world</u>: confident-arrogant; loyal-meek; assertive-stubborn; passionate-obsessive; humorous-humorless.]
  [-- article in business section of newspaper]

[➔In <u>academic interchange</u>: (1) *Perhaps more obvious*: Equanimity; apathy... Compassion; a patronizing pity... Love; possessive attachment... Conscience; a punitive self-surveillance...
(2) *Perhaps more subtle*: Shared humanity == a bourgeois humanism that says we are all exactly the same. [And what about "denial of common traits as overgeneralizing"?!!]... Valuing independent rational thought == a disembodied Cartesian subject... An ideal of human individuality or expressiveness == the Kantian subject... <u>And</u>: Decency, Goodness, Tenderness, Compassion == a screen for class bias or prejudice; baneful self-indulence; adherence to a set of communal norms that are really a screen for class bias or prejudice..."]   [-- Prof. Lisa Ruddick]

[➔**Existentialism**] "...that struggle implies a total absence of hope (which has nothing to do with despair), a continual rejection (which must not be confused with renunciation), and a conscious dissatisfaction (which must not be compared to immature unrest)."
  [-- Albert Camus, "The Myth of Sisyphus"]

(7) <u>Defense</u>: To the frequent objection to the above rationale (as being unnecessary to elaborate upon this), namely that "*Well, after all We All Know, All About, the Dualistic Dichotomy Fallacy,*" etc. ..... here is a Response: There is Knowing, and there is Knowing. Just knowing of or about, vs. truer deeper understanding of it, plus ability to confront it competently when needed. And "we all know" about dualistic dichotomies, but "we" usually ignore the issue, don't confront it via the above Rationale...END.

(8) <u>Aside</u>: The positive, as a sort of presence-and-directness via Absence, a sort of "whitespace" removal of all negatives... (Cf. "Zen"?)

➔ **Painting.** "Painting is...meditation and contemplation for me,... As much consciousness as possible. Clarity, completeness, quintessence, quiet. *No* noise,...Perfection, passiveness, consonance, consummateness. *No* palpitations, *no* gesticulation, *no* grotesquerie. Spirituality, serenity, absoluteness, coherence. *No* automatism, *no* accident, *no* anxiety, *no* catharsis, *no* chance. Detachment, disinterestedness, thoughtfulness, trasnscendence. *No* humbugging, *no* button-holding, *no* exploitation, *no* mixing things up."
  [-- Ad Reinhardt, exhibition catalog, 1955]

- - - - - - - - - -

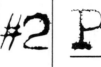 **#2 Practice**

EXAMPLES of various key "contrary" Variable-Issues to confront/correlate, in varied key ARENAS of "real-world-life":

1. Basic HUMAN NATURE:
(A) (Opposing) NEEDS, Motivations, Drives:

[➔**Humans** crave "security and risk, coherence and spontaneity, novelty and latency, rivalry and mutuality" with others. Personal identity and social belongingness. Of course, these "contrasting tendencies" are not irreconcilable "contradictions," but "different phases in the rhythm of living."]
  [-- Robert S. Lynd, <u>Knowledge for What</u>?]

(B) (Opposing) TRAITS of Individuals:

[➜**Characters in fiction** are "flat" (types; caricatures; "constructed around a <u>single</u> idea or quality") or "round" (exhibit <u>multiple</u> traits, even <u>contradictory and conflicting</u> ones). Round characters represent the complexity of reality better than do flat or type characters.]
[-- E. M. Forster, from <u>Aspects of the Novel</u>]

[➜The reader of **poet W. H. Auden**] "may well recoil from the variety and force of the impressions he derives. He will find competence and virtuosity; carelessness, cliquishness, and obscurity; interest in people, anxiety to reform and concern over the fate of society; impersonality, clinical analysis and drum-beating; he will meet boyishness succeeding maturity, the formal laced with the idiomatic, brilliant diagnosis succeeded by the slapstick of a buffoon, controlled exposition contrasting with slipshod chatter."
[-- Richard Hoggart]

2. PHILOSOPHY: basic East vs. West:

➜"...typical **Western thinking** does not allow two opposite statements to be true at the same time (the law of contraries) and considers no third possibility in cause and effects relations (the law of the excluded middle)....**Indian logic** has four propositions: (1) is, (2) is not, (3) is and is not, and (4) neither is nor is not.... (*True*, there is a car in the driveway or not; x = 4 or it does not.... *However*, a brain-dead person is and is not dead... a pink elephant [as seen by a delirious alcoholic] is and is not real.)   [--G. Van den Heuvel]

➜ "**Chinese philosophy** certainly deals in dualisms such as human beings / the natural world, 'quiescence and movement,' the often-heard-about ying and yang. But they regard these polarities 'as complementary and necessary partners, interacting to form a higher synthesis, rather than as irreconcilable and eternally warring opposites."   [-- Deborah Tannen, in <u>The Argument Culture</u>, quoting Derk Bodde]

3. FINE ARTS

[Western visual art: "organic form"]
➜ "...a composition of <u>tensions and resolutions,</u> balance and unbalance, rhythmic coherence, a precarious yet continuous unity...."
[-- Suzanne Langer, philosopher]

➜ Every moment must maintain an "<u>asymmetrical oscillation</u>, wholly subservient neither to [static] gravity, nor to [dynamic] momentum."
[-- Paul Klee, artist]

> ...So what **"visual-artistry"** style, do the **culinary-gastronomic "gambits-forays"** of the above **recipes,** resemble? A "MATISSE interior or landscape scene?" [Or, primary red-blue-green colors in posterized fingerpaint?]

[➜ **Chinese visual art**] [following both Taoism and Confucianism, it sought inner reality in <u>a fusion of opposites</u>, which is how Chinese painters would attack the wedding of spirit and matter:]
"That is, wherever the <u>western mind would set up antagonistic dualisms</u>—matter-spirit, divine-human, ideal-natural, classic-romantic, traditional-progressive, and so forth—the Chinese took a mediate position....they tended to avoid extremes, in contrast to the western quest for reality by pursuing each extreme to its end....instead of being a static mean in which the extremes suffered, the Chinese fusion was <u>a dynamic union of opposites which needed one another for completeness</u>. The artist must be neither **classic** nor **romantic**, he should be both; his painting must be neither **naturalistic** nor **idealistic**, it must be both; his style must be neither **traditional** nor **original**, it must be both."
[-- Introduction to a work on Chinese visual art]

➜ [the {or, "a" Western} poetic imagination]
"...***the balance or reconciliation of opposite or discordant qualities***: of **sameness**, with **difference**; of the **general**, with the **concrete**; the **idea**, with the **image**; the **individual**, with the **representative**; the sense of **novelty and freshness**, with **old and familiar** objects; a more than usual state of **emotion**, with more than usual **order**; **judgment** ever awake and steady **self-possession**, with **enthusiasm** and **feeling** profound or vehement; and while it blends and harmonizes the natural and the artificial, still subordinates art to nature; the manner to the matter; and our admiration of the poet to our sympathy with the poetry. [-- S.T. Coleridge, <u>Biographica</u> <u>Literaria</u>, XIV, on "the poetic imagination"]

4. PROSE STYLE, & "Prose"
  {"limited, Western view"...}

A. <u>Three early British admonitions</u>:

➜ "<u>The English style</u>, familiar but not coarse, elegant but not ostentatious." [-- Samuel Johnson, writer]

➜ "...the model of <u>the middle style</u>: on grave subjects not formal, on light occasions not groveling; pure without scrupulosity, and exact without apparent elaboration; always equable, and always easy, without glowing words or pointed sentences."
[-- Johnson, on Addison]

➜ "...You do not assume, indeed, the solemnity of the pulpit, or the tone of stage-declamation; neither...gabble on at a venture....You must steer <u>a middle course</u>....Any one may mouth out a passage with a theatrical cadence, or get upon stilts to tell his thoughts; but to write or speak with propriety and simplicity is a more difficult task.... How simple it is to be dignified without ease, to be pompous without meaning!" [-- William Hazlitt, "On Familiar Style"]

(B) <u>Counsel for writing students today</u>:

Avoid "**Engfish**," or phoney/plastic/bxllshxt - writing:
➔ [...unnatural voices, too heavy, pretentious, phoney, tired, obvious, flabby... Hearts and flowers; shooting off Roman candles... Not true to the world you experienced... Trying to impress rather than express. Trying for great thoughts instead of good truths. Writing what you think the teacher wants. Trying to kid the reader and maybe also yourself...]
[-- Ken Macrorie, in <u>Telling Writing</u>]

5. "STYLE" in general as a "Supple Economy"

➔ "The sense for style....is an aesthetic sense, based on admiration for the direct attainment of a foreseen end, simply and without waste....aesthetic qualities, namely <u>attainment and restraint</u>....Style is the ultimate morality of mind."   [-- A. N. Whitehead]

➔ "...we use the word <u>style</u> in speaking of architecture and sculpture, painting and music, dancing, play-acting, and cricket,...we can apply it to the careful achievements of the housebreaker and the poisoner and to the spontaneous animal movements of the limbs of man or beast,..."
[-- W. Raleigh, <u>Style</u>, 1897]

➔ "Purity of line, loveliness, symmetry—these arrive mysteriously whenever someone who knows and cares creates <u>something that is perfectly fitted to do its work</u>, whether the object is a grain scoop, a suspension bridge, or a guillotine. Nobody styled the orb web of a spider, nobody styled the sixteen-foot canoe. Both are beautiful, and for a common reason: each was <u>designed to perform a special task under special conditions</u>."   [-- E. B. White, "The Motorcar"]

["Style" in expository prose]

➔ "A sentence should contain no unnecessary words, a paragraph no unnecessary sentences, for the same reason that a drawing should have no unnecessary lines and a machine no unnecessary parts."
[-- Strunk & White]

["Style" in fiction]

➔ "Every action or word ought to count; it ought to be economical and spare; even when complicated it should be organic and free from dead matter. It may be difficult or easy, it may and should contain mysteries, but it ought not to mislead."
[-- E. M. Forster, <u>Aspects of the Novel</u>]

6. The SELF : deportment toward oneself, the subject, the situation (and other selves).

A. Mature psychological "autonomy" or the *avoiding* of "FALSE NOTES"

➔ "...<u>autonomy</u> is...the release or recovery of three capacities: awareness, spontaneity, and intimacy.
<u>Awareness</u>...means the capacity to see a coffeepot and hear the birds sing in one's own way, and not the way one was taught...
<u>Spontaneity</u> means option, the freedom to choose and express one's feelings from the assortment available....
<u>Intimacy</u> means the spontaneous, game-free candidness of an aware person, the liberation of the...uncorrupted Child in all its naivete living in the here and now....
[to attain autonomy]...first, the weight of a whole <u>tribal or family historical tradition</u> has to be lifted,...then the influence of the <u>individual parental, social and cultural background</u> has to be thrown off.... then all <u>the easy indulgences and rewards</u> of being a *Sulk* or a *Jerk* [or a *Prig*, a *Toady*, a *Show-Off*, or a *Cling*]...have to be given up. Following this, the individual must attain <u>personal and social control</u>, so that all...behavior...become[s] free choices subject only to his will.... In essence this whole preparation [for autonomy] consists of obtaining a friendly divorce from one's parents (and from other Parental influences) so that they may be agreeably visited on occasion, but are no longer dominant."
[-- Eric Berne, M.D., <u>Games People Play</u>]

➔ [Merrill was] "...**a person** with every excuse for indolence, snobbery, license, self-pity and disdain. And yet we encounter someone...of such empathy and playfulness, such difficult scope and yet so easy an intimacy....Merrill's tone confides without presumption. It admits without confessing. It intrigues without vamping...."
[-- Allan Gurganus on poet James Merrill]

➔ [**In Mark Doty's poetry in <u>Source</u>,**] "There are no fashionable causes, cranky ideologies or aggressive posturing. No voyeuristic soul-searching, no self-righteous self-exposure."   [--S. Whited]

➔ [the <u>paintings</u> of Peter Schjelpahl]
"...untainted by fuss or narcissism..."

➔ "Bruce Chatwin['s]...rules for <u>travel writing</u> (no mooning, moping, or thrilling)...   [--Spectrum]

B. In emotionally-difficult situations:

➔ "There is a thin line between attentiveness and condescension, between sincerity and ritual."
[-- John F. Longres, on bereavement-situations]

➔ "The author does not founder in the plumber's sorrow; neither does he regard it with detachment."
[-- on E. L. Wallant's novel <u>The Human Season</u>]

➔ "He neither condescends to the victim, nor romantically inflates her plight."
[-- review of a novel]

➔ "...the fine line between exaggerated, unbecoming courtliness and natural, expected courtesy."
[-- <u>The New Esquire Etiquette</u>]

C. In "mind-free" disinterested interest in subjects:

➔ "<u>Read</u> not to contradict and confute; nor to believe and take for granted; nor to find talk and discourse; but to weigh and consider."   [-- Francis Bacon]

➔ "I have made a ceaseless effort not to ridicule, not to bewail, nor to scorn <u>human</u> <u>actions</u>, but to understand them."   [-- B. Spinoza]

➔ "The function of the <u>historian</u> is neither to love the past nor to emancipate himself from the past, but to master and understand it as the key to the understanding of the present."   [-- E. H. Carr]

➔ "If the <u>biographer</u> writes from personal knowledge, and makes haste to gratify the public curiosity, there is danger lest his interest, his fear, his gratitude, or his tenderness, overpower his fidelity, and tempt him to conceal, if not to invent." [-- S. Johnson, <u>Rambler</u> #60]

D. In dealing with reason vs. other elements in human motivations-for-thinking:

➔ "[people *sometimes* think via] ...<u>their reason</u>—at *other* times <u>their</u> prejudices or superstitions; often their social affections, not seldom their antisocial ones, their envy or jealousy, their arrogance or contemptuousness: but most commonly <u>their</u> desires or fears for themselves—<u>their</u> legitimate or illegitimate self-interest....[and] class interests, and its feeling of class superiority."   [--J.S. Mill, <u>On Liberty</u>]

➔ "...the major <u>obstacles or blocks to rational thinking</u>: prejudice, bias, self-deception, desire, fear, vested interest, delusion, illusion, egocentrism, sociocentrism, and ethnocentrism."
[--Richard Paul, philosophy/critical thinking]

E. Diplomatic Deportment, or "COOLNESS" in Interpersonal Interactions:

➔ "Never apologize; never complain; never explain"
[-- traditional British: military arenas]

➔ "<u>His discourse</u> was cheerful without levity, and pious without enthusiasm..... I visited him. <u>He</u> was sublime without haughtiness, courteous without formality, and communicative without ostentation."
[-- Edmund Burke, statesman]

➔ "...An energy that never weakens but never blusters."
[-- about <u>On Photography</u>, by Susan Sontag]

➔ "He dares to show himself. His depravity is not a pose cultivated for literary effect. He never makes the fatal mistake of glorifying his sin, of rejoicing in it, or of pretending to despise its opposite."
[-- Ezra Pound, on French poet Francois Villon]

7. OTHER CONCEPT-PAIRS, contraries-for-correlating: A cluster of representatives

➔ A. more technical-specific-tactical:

-Idealistic - Realistic...
-Pragmatic - Pleasurable...
-Theory - Practice...
-Basic - Advanced...
-Formal - Informal...
-Conventional,traditional,conform-Innovative,creative,iconoclastic...

➔B. more general-generic higher-scoped:

Physical/matter - Mental/spirit...
 Self - Other...
Conscious - Unconscious...
 Hierarchy - Equality...
Work - Play...
 Essence (absolute) – Existence (situational relative)...
Western - Eastern...
 "Classic" - "Romantic"...
Digital - Analog, cf. Serial-Parallel...
Serial (sequential) - Simultaneous...
 Chronological (historical) – Timeless...]

8. OTHER ISSUES for correlating: examples from various "arenas":

[8-A] Business, Industry, Commerce:
General, also "Project Management"

➔ "<u>Simultaneous loose-tight properties</u>...is in essence the co-existence of firm central direction and maximum individual autonomy...'having one's cake and eating it too.' Organizations...are on the one hand rigidly controlled, yet at the same time allow (indeed, insist on) autonomy, entrepreneurship, and innovation from the rank and file. They do this through 'faith'— through value systems....also through painstaking attention to detail,..."

[-- Tom Peters, In Search of Excellence]

➔ [Project management turns out mostly to be about mastering *paradox*.
1. Total ego/no ego. 2. Autocrat/delegator.
3. Leader/manager. 4. Ambiguity/perfection.
5. Oral/written. 6. Complexity/K.I.S.S.
(="Keep It Simple, Stupid") 7. Big/small.]

[-- Tom Peters, In Search of Excellence]

[8-B] Education: Program-Design

➔Both universities (Duke and Rice) wanted to *combine seeming opposites*: breadth and depth, structure and choice, skills and subject areas, interdisciplinarity and departmental divisions.

[-- Chronicle of Higher Education, 19 Feb 99]

➔"Education, then, aims to achieve a mix of efficiency and self-development—there is to be no sacrifice of the individual to the collectivity, and no privileging of individual self-expression over social obligation."

[-- Alan Ryan]

[8-C] Oenology

➔ "All the elements [of the Sauvignon Blanc 2000] are so completely integrated that the wine can offer a plush texture while the flavors maintain a tight focus and wide-open airiness." [--Wine Store Blurb]

[8-D] "Communication about, and education in, subjects and systems from self to others, in face-to-face groups or via texts"

➔ [#]"Oberhauptkartoffelkopfe Roster" for "opposite needs and chances certainly, to curate and 'satisfy'; perhaps, to correlate organically."

---

1. General "TIGHT-LOOSE" [*subject, system*]
Both Focussed Accurate Precise ==
and Flexible Adaptable-Adjustable Pragmatic?

2. SELF of the doer: balances

A. *Both* Objective impersonal ===
and subjective personal?

B. *Either* Combat (fight to win your or The One "Truth" over others) ===
or Cooperate (work with others toward some best or better truth)?

C. *How much* "Fervent" ===

---

but also "Fairminded"?
(*quite* emotional enthusiastic engaged excited—
Responsive === *but also* empathetic to others, self-critical, Responsible)

D. *Whether* "Elitist" === *and/or* "Populist"
Defends subject == *also* disseminates it.
Preserves == *also* popularizes it.
Saves, secures, conserves it == *also* shares it.

➔ "It's the sort of writing that any genuine expert on a subject longs to achieve: highly accessible to the general reader yet at the same time seminal for professionals."
[-- on The Language Instinct by Stephen Pinker]

3. View of SUBJECT AND SYSTEMS:

A. *How* Simple ==== *how* Complex:
esp. "Edited Down to Essences, vs. Elaborated Up to nuance" (less- is-more, or the-more-the-richer?)
(Cf. "tolerance of ambiguity" etc.)

B. *More* Comprehensiveness ===
more Conciseness? (synoptic, survey, orient, introduce, etc.)
(Possible *"both-and"* of "Diamondized" or *very* comprehensive-synoptic-inclusive, *but also very* curtailed, abridged, distilled, compact, crystallized...)

C. Other major vectors:

1. Scope: (A) *more* synthesizing/analyzing, specific/general, concrete/conceptual ===
or more abstract, particularistic/panoramic, etc.— *or both*?
["over all from above" vs. "withinside"]
(B) Also INduction =*and/or*= DEduction (cf. empiricism – idealism/rationalism)?
["upward" vs. "downward"]

➔ "It is a fair question to ask, who sees more? The airman who flies five thousand feet above the landscape, or the countryman who has lived in one small area all his life and knows it like the back of his hand?" [-- Allan Bullock, historian]

2. Contraries: dualism *either-or* ===
vs. dialectic *both-and*? ["all across"] (The "Dialectic" of Thesis, Antithesis, Synthesis) *{as thruout here!}*

3. *How much* Isolated ===
or also Integrated (connected with context, background, situation, etc.)? ["out and back"]

[Cf. here Thinking-Styles: all or some classic Left-Brain logical linear ===
and/or also Right-Brain lateral associative)]

4. TIMING, PACE: CLOSURE VS. CONTINUATION

A. *Whether to* Dispatch, conclude ==
or to deliberate, remain reflective, consider?
(Cf. "withhold judgment, suspend conclusion")

B. Finalize === *or* re-open? (vacillate? re-think?)

[-- Chester Oberhaupkartoffelkopfe, Kronikles, XII, xii, n.d., n.p., n.p., *passim*]

[. .. .. ____ __ _ :: --- -- - ~~~~ ~~ ~ `` ^^^]

[8-D] ...and then the "ssensitive" subject of

HO-MO-SEX!UAL-ITY

[FKA "Sezual Derivance," "Sesual Invrision"]

➔ "As a witness Cafavy is exceptionally **honest**.
He neither *bowdlerizes, glamorizes*, or *giggles*."
[-- {Homosexual} poet W. H. **Auden**,
on {homosexual} poet C. F. **Cafavy**]

➔ A book about "a sensitive and difficult topic"
[= homosexuality], but a book "that doesn't *demonize,
sentimentalize*, or *apologize*"
[-- book, and commenter, unknown]

➔ "...it is **exhaustive** without being *exhausting*,
it is **objective** without being either *fawning*
or without *taking advantage*."
[-- {homosexual} American playwright Edward **Albee**,
on Lyle **Leverich**'s biography of {homosexual}
American playwright Tennessee **Williams**]

➔ "At last we can escape from the two extremes
of *majority bullying* and *minority sob-stuff*....
The story is told with <u>no</u> trace of a *leer*, <u>no</u> snuffle of
sentiment, <u>no</u> sticky *revellings* in naughtiness that
would suggest [{homosexual} British playwright Oscar]
Wilde at his worst. The treatment is **steely-hard** ...
and discretely deflects the adjective "*sensational*" ...
[the actors] **interpret** and never *exploit*."
[-- review of the British {homosexual-themed} drama
The Green Bay Tree by Mordaunt **Shairp**, late 1920's]

GAY COOKERY:
"BACK THEN," & LATER ON:

[I.] "Oh Mary, it takes a fairy...."

"Do you need a cook on your boat?"
"Not at the moment."

"I wish you did, I wish to heaven you did,
I'm a beautiful cook, really. I make the *best*
omelets. You should see me; I just put in the
old eggs and a little bit of milk and a glass of
brandy and some of those little green things,
what are they called?—chives, I put in the
chives and stir until my arm breaks off and
it comes out just *wonderful*, so light and
fluffy. If I cared about money, I'd be a chef
in the Waldorf."

[-- John Updike, "In A Bar
At Charlotte Amalie"]

[II.] Come Out! of the kitchen, Maud...

"Isn't this turkey delicious? It's so moist
and tender," *I'D BEGIN.*

"Not like that goose you ruined three years
ago," *VITO WOULD RESPOND.* "It tasted like a
football."

"I ruined the goose?" *I'D SAY.* "I'm not the
one who roasted it for twelve hours. You're
supposed to be the cook here."

"I'm the one who had to eat the miserable
thing," *JIM WOULD SAY.*

"Then *you* cook," *VITO WOULD SAY.*
"Not my job," *JIM WOULD PROTEST.*

"Oh, Mr. Macho can't get his hands
greasy," *I'D OBSERVE.*

"The apple-chestnut dressing is delicious
this year," *JIM WOULD REPLY IN AN EFFORT TO
CHANGE THE SUBJECT.*

"Oh, *I* did that," *VITO AND I WOULD CHORUS
AT ONCE.*

[--source "lost to follow-up":
ca. "post-Stonewall" [= > 27 Jun 1969 C.E.]]

NEEDED EDITitioninung

Holy Cow The New Day
For Those Air-Believer Books
From The Ambitious
AIR-DROP Robin.
But, Their "Jack Painterdom"
Opposes Intellectuals...
So, Quick, *Page-Three
Insert, Pagetree Insights*!

MUSIKalities Float Into Tone-Tuned Town

Delineation Of Summer Marriage-Music:
Much Is Possible With STANTON,
& The Piano Of COTTON MOKEN...
Mortimer Cleft Tunes Expatriate,
Moorish Scrapes & Tickelton:
We Been Good Goovin
In "Light Metallia,"
& We Can Breathe Health
Into Broken Bassoon-Hearth...

WHYLED WEST

A Dog, A Ranger, & A Radio:
Dip-Bit DENNIS, @ "Denim Big-Horn."
(A Demon; A Dippi-Day Drive.)
Then The Damned, Dimmed
RODEO Blood-Figures Die...

ANIMAculalities; Nor Pettish; Nor Skeevy

Often, He Had The TORINO HAMSTER
In For Mice. (Other-Thing Gallery? In The Rat.)
We "Leave A Slide-Dog In Itself"...
But, MISS BERRY!
In The Face Of The City, Tending A One-Eyed Cat,
& *Such A Cow* In PENDLETON!

NOKturno NAY-Bor Hoods

["Nightups Of *The Man*"!]
And, Shell Night For Us At The FOUNDRY.
I Made As Good As Basement
In Your Street Last Night:
Open Doors, Unlocked Secrets.
And Although GABLE And TETWELL
Let Me Record The Whole Block,
I Will Not Say Anything On Why
The "John Brown Nights" Are Important.
["...Nightups Of *The Man*"!]

PEOPLE, You Meet, Greet, & "You Know"

Ms. *GRELL R. BETTEL*: She Was On The
DOROTHY DANN ASSIGNMENT TEAM!
They Delight In Dillerkorns,
& Fling The *Treuest*, "ALICE E. GRAFF" Apples...
But, Mr. *PAUL DE PEOPLE*:
He Was In A DU MOGUE Organisation,
& He Left His *True Carring*
@t SHIRLEY'S INSTITUTE...

AUTO-Att-Speed Motifv

By Kickroad Elements With Front Rust Leader,
Bender Phratry Exhumes His Phoom,
& I Blunt Ninely, At Ninety Vamorals.
"Totally-Squat: Fast-End, & Flunk."
But She Had Merely To Squank & Bore-Foot...
(All By Hope Scale Dint, Of Our Own Wrecker-Rock)

FOODish Dinning On MENUs Plaisirs

That Hot Season's Cook: *He Was A Raider Then Too*

Yesterday, It Was Big-Night BANANA, There,
With "*TWO KECK* SAUCE" Also; & This Morning,
He Is, Without Doubt, Having A BUTTER-Sequence!

& It's *All Breakfast* For You POWER-BABS:
Chroniform Feathers, Italian Peaball Estimates;
Boneroll Evidence Depending, *Billion-Flavor* Network...

GRUA Will Pour, Or Throw You, Beer Trouts:
The Finer Flakes; A Few Pork Strokes

Gateau Might; ...Gateau *Night*....

ALL Too Familial-iar, All Ins Famille

Ice-Tone Roughage NEPHEW?
Yes, But They Have A "Worse-Than-The-Kids,"
ADULT GERMINATE. DOREN Calls Childrens Names,
But In A *Blindforest Bet*

His *SON,* Will Be Called A Brotherhood Dancer,
And I Wish RICHARD, Was Not "A Designer
In POKE HEIGHTS." [But My Mother Flew On It,
"Sparky Caporal"; In Her Steel-Blue Babybox;
There's No Known Real Notion As To How *I* Rug...]

"French Board Of Every Evidence": My Daughter.
For As She Wrote, Sexual Functionings
Into Charcoal Smithereens...
And What She Raised With Those Criers Jack,
And What She Cried With Those Raisers Jack

N' Pockkitt Philosophe to Ponderate

MAIL: *Newer Rain*! &, "New Froth @t Line Five":
Mechanical Razoir Lowboy,
& Horseley Mainforms Waterdown.
So, "Low-Moon Moron, Lawn-Repair" *Now*...

The Doubtless Future, Ears On A Ticket.
I Feel *Exactly* Sure, The Nature Of JELLY.
For It's The "Heavy Toe Circuit"
For Those In Circulation;
&, True Life *Is* Stained
With The "Standard Trunk Offer"

"*The Morning Tensile Looks So White Old Boy*:"
So, "Eat Loose," Breakfast-Thru:
It's Wacky MANAGED CANDY
With Relaxed! Vanilla!! Endings!!!
For Next, The "IDEAL GREASE BOAT"
Is Coming To NIMBUS,
To "Blatantly, BOATANTLY Blunt BOSTON,
Past That Last Obasic Poisonous Law.
So, Celebration *Is* "Boiling Heaven" For Them,
The Day That They *Make Earth, Ceiling*

[1.] PRIOR PRAGMATIC PRAXIS: --In Walden, his major scholarly contribution which reported his "original research conducted in the field," **H. D. THOREAU** said, **"Say what you have to say, not what you ought. Any truth is better than make-believe. Tom Hyde, the tinker, standing on the gallows, was asked if he had anything to say. 'Tell the tailors,' said he, 'to remember to make a knot in their thread before they take the first stitch.' His companion's prayer is forgotten."**

--So: **(1) to aid the readers of your letters, fold them REREVSRED, to expose the written-on side.**
{*I rarely do this myself...*} {Years ago, my college advisor, **DR. M. M. SEALTS JR.**, told me that before graduate school, *I should have* **brackets** "[ ]" *installed on my typewriter.*} [I did *not* do this; and I **think** I did regret it...]

--**(2) to quench your thirst** *anywhere* you have drinkable water—*even when tepid and no ice at hand,* simply **squeeze LIME JUICE** into the water. [For exotic summer travel in—*helas!*—more secure times...]

--**(3) to more-competently dispense/disperse fluids in the kitchen and household** [DISH SOAP; AMMONIA; ETHYL ALCOHOL; CHLORINE BLEACH; ETC.] use the **SPRAY BOTTLE** (commercial-grade from restaurant supply-houses) **to vaporize mists in a fashion both more efficient and hence more aesthetic...** [I *always* do this, at least *now*...]

--**(4) four EXCELLENT ITEMS** from the "phenomenal edge" [=tangible concrete empirical-material reality] are **cats; bicycles;** the **microwave oven;** and **duct tape.** [Plus electricians,' strapping, and mailing tape.]

--**(5)** After **CURRY** or chilipeppered or most spicy food, **CHOCOLATE** is usually—**AMBROSIA**...

[2.] "TRAVEL WISDOM": the Novice Foreign Tourist's *FOUR MAJOR MISCONCEPTIONS;* to be **UN-Learned** *Only* "En Route," **and** [*helas*] There, *Only* Via Experience...

1. "Well, our hotel room tonight, **SURELY** *should* be quiet—at last! True, it is **right above the kitchen** (but **SURELY** they'll close early). And it does look out **over an enclosed patio-garden** (but **SURELY** nobody will have a late party there). And it is **near the stairway-and-elevator** (but **SURELY** guests will retire early)."

2. "Although all the shops in this town close in 10 minutes (and will stay closed all tomorrow for Saints' Day), still, we can **SURELY** buy the needed film yet today, as the helpful shop-attendant here said the photo shop is located— she said *"Right Over There,"* where she pointed right **to** it; or at least **toward** it; or at least **somewhat near** it; or....."

3. "We'll **SURELY** eat better tonight—at last!—since the *second* (***and only other***) restaurant in the village **SURELY** could not be as inferior as **that rip-off joint we ate in here last night!**"

4. "We should **SURELY** have no problem arriving at the next city's restaurant before they close for the evening, since the map shows that it's *only just about three inches away*—along that **squiggly, curving little regional road** which is so **secondary,** that it should **SURELY** be not only *traffic-free,* but also *scenic* as well."

[3.] TOUCHSTONES:

(a.) "Quality, Economy, Speed: pick any *two*"... [--ENGINEERS' SAYING]

(b) **"Vary one thing at a time, and make a note of all you do."** [--PROF. C. F. CHANDLER]

(c.) "If you really know what's going on, you don't have to know what's going on to know what's going on"...

(d.) Each perspective separately, is incomplete, but, all perspectives taken together are—dissonant; plus, the larger perspectives [paradigms, world-views, etc.] are usually chosen subjectively anyhow...

(e.) "Read not to contradict and confute; nor to believe and take for granted; nor to find talk and discourse; but to weigh and consider." [--BACON]

(f.) "Philosophy is a set of reminders for a particular purpose." [--WITTGENSTEIN]

[4.] KULTURAL QUIZZ / INTELLIGENCE TEST / STATUS-CERTIFIER.

(A) "Nomenklatter": (1) **"Anon."** [pseud.?] [?—*fl.*?--?] (2) **"Old 100-Names"** (3) **Many Thousands Gone**

(A) "Militia Historica":.... (1) **"If..."** (2) **Peccavi** (3) **"Nuts!"**

(B) "Pan-Europaeanisch: Kultur, Und Linguisticque":..... (1) **Taller Te Koop** (2) **"Und BOB est tio zio!"** (3) **"frileux"; "jolielaide"; "schadenfreude"; "terroir"**

(C) "Social Justice":..... **" Et pain ne voient / qu'aux fenestres "** [--F. Villon, *ca.* 1362]

(D) (1) **"Location, Location, Location"** (2) **"L'audace, l'audace, tojours l'audace"** (3) **"Attaquez, attaquez, attaquez!"** (4) **"Du beurre, du beurre, et encore du beurre"**

(E) "QUOTIDIA*NoncE*phemera":..... (1) HAVE A NO *Catch* NICE PROB- *you* ONE LEM *later* (2) **"Is The Bear Catholic?..."** (3) **"God Si Love"** (4)

[5.] "L'ENVOI": (1) **Bien Faire Y Laissez Braire** [--contemporary French saying] (2) **Non fui, fui, non sum, non curo** [-- ancient Latin motto]

FIELD - NOTES

[i. "....."]

Fledgling scholars trek FIELDwards
to pluck their first-growth laurels,
while grizzled *pedants* stump back to it
now borne to mecca on the wings of grants
to glean "Original Research in the FIELD."
Anthropology first FIELDed the concept
when its early interlopers in paradise
peered at the South Pacific outlandish.
Botanists ogle northern islands from an
untouristically hands-and-knees attitude.
Now, the FIELD approaches home ground,
as *sociologists* scurry like FIELDmice
into gritty ghettos, decorous tearooms
cheek-&-jowel with domestic backyards.
Speech-*Communication* sets up hearings
anywhere amid the prevalent racket;
while *historians* and *literary* types
lift core samples from the Deep Stacks;
bestirring that noble mold slightly.

[ii. {"_:-+=#"}]

So, you too can FIELD a visit anywhere,
right along the **Phenomenal Edge!**
Simply glower with a clipboard precise
at one remove. Strive to unravel
the tapestry of the Perceptual FIELD
into monotone filament of Truth.
Distill all foreign matter
thru Quantification's dense screen
to the dour democracy of Data,
via stiff-canvassed gloves of Procedure...
Still for all that, the FIELD keeps swimming
toward a mirage-blurred **Middle Distance**
attenuating that island, **Abstraction**...

[iii. ∼∼ ∼^ ^^*!]

All bosh! You take my FIELD-of-vision...
Way off in some wide-open Left FIELD,
beyond your horizon's last stake-out.
A sinister, antipodal quadrant,
it serves up a species of FIELDgrass
sprouting palpably real to my touch.
Emerald at dawn, it soon bows all day
to the currying fingers of the current winds,
is ascertainably ignited by each sunset.
It's here that I'll cover the *whole* FIELD
with *some* blanket, Broad-FIELD statement.
Will surely FIELD all questions
with booomeranging bulletins.
It's here that I can be reached, or figured,
during those unlisted office hours
which pencil themselves into my schedule.
Ever on the threshhold of a new spread,
up the my eyeballs in wheat
--my beard snagging auburn
as chaff infiltrates my notebook--
I stumble across new obtrusions
of nervous & friable FIELDstone...

No matter *whose* FIELD I am in.

No matter; I'm Surveying The *FIELD*.

I am master, of all, unsurveyed.